THE
RELUCTANT
BRIDE

Also by Lucy Mangan

Hopscotch and Handbags
My Family and Other Disasters

THE RELUCTANT BRIDE

ONE WOMAN'S JOURNEY (KICKING AND SCREAMING) DOWN THE AISLE

LUCY MANGAN

JOHN MURRAY

First published in Great Britain in 2010 by John Murray (Publishers)
An Hachette UK Company

1

A CIP catalogue record for this title is available from
the British Library

ISBN 978-1-84854-069-9

Typeset in Sabon by Servis Filmsetting Ltd, Stockport, Cheshire

Printed and bound by Clays Ltd, St Ives plc

John Murray policy is to use papers that are natural, renewable and
recyclable products and made from wood grown in sustainable forests.
The logging and manufacturing processes are expected to conform to
the environmental regulations of the country of origin.

John Murray (Publishers)
338 Euston Road
London NW1 3BH

www.johnmurray.co.uk

For Toryboy

This is the story of my wedding. It all passed in a blur, so I cannot swear to the literal truth of everything that follows (plus some identities and names have been changed to protect the innocent). But although some things have been left out, some things have been put in and others have been completely mixed up, I hope that anyone who has ever been a party to the organisation of a wedding – whether as bride, best friend, parent or appalled bystander – can recognise that the essence of the nightmare is true.

PROLOGUE

'Freak. Weirdo. Why? Why am I here? Why are we doing this? This is girlfriend abuse. That's a capital crime in America, you know.'

It is the last and most utterly freezing day of our three-week holiday in New York and my boyfriend Christopher has insisted that we leave the cosy warmth of the Italian restaurant in which we had been lingering over a meal and take in what he claims is the best view in Manhattan of its famous skyline – from the far end of the Central Park reservoir, at twilight.

I do not like the cold. I am never particularly enamoured of views. I would have thought that someone who has shared my home and my life for the past three years might have picked up on these two, currently very salient, facts. Much of this I mutter under my breath as I trot ahead of him, eager to get it over with and then get back to our centrally heated hotel and order a gallon of coffee and a toasted, salmon-stuffed bagel the size of my head. In my keenness to make this dream a reality, I am starting to outpace the joggers who, swathed in thermal sports kit, are still gamely circling the park.

'When you reach the end of the reservoir, STOP!' he

orders, as I pull another few yards ahead. I sigh and reluctantly obey. He has, after all, been banging on about doing this ever since we first arrived.

'There!' says Christopher triumphantly when he has caught up and we are both at last standing at the reservoir's furthest edge. 'The most beautiful view in New York!'

I look. He's right. Across the water, around whose reeded edges globules of perfectly translucent ice are beginning to form, the sun is gradually sinking behind the skyscrapers. As we watch, they become stark silhouettes, dotted with yellow shining squares, backlit by the deepening orange glow – one of the world's greatest man-made sights suddenly, graciously illuminated by nature. It is amazing.

'Actually,' says Christopher, 'it's the second most beautiful view in New York. Because you're here.'

I turn round, expecting to see him pulling any one of the variety of revolting faces he keeps to accompany his delivery of ridiculous lines, but there is no one next to me. Then I realise that he is down on one knee and holding up a ring.

'Will you, you midget, hypothermic fool of a woman, whom I love so much, marry me?'

What? Who? Me? How did this happen? To me, someone who has never thought she could, would or should get married. Who has never understood why other people felt the need to proclaim their love in public, let alone organise a giant frock and party to go with it.

And yet here I am, standing in the middle of Central Park, grinning. Grinning like an idiot, never mind a fool.

Christopher pushes back the sleeves of the three giant jumpers I'm wearing and peels off the left-hand set of my multiple pairs of gloves. Just before he puts the ring on my finger, he stops.

'You haven't actually said "yes" yet,' he points out.

'Haven't I?' I say. I honestly can't remember. 'Well, then – yes. Yes, please.'

He slips it on. It sparkles like the ice that limns the reservoir.

'And now,' he says, 'we can go home.'

CHAPTER ONE

We met three years ago. I was working as a waitress in a cocktail bar . . . No, not really. I was working six days a week at the bookshop in my local high street. The pay was shite but the job was great. I had previously been working at a supermarket, which is a bit like a war zone. Everyone is keen to get out of there as quickly as possible and on the till you always feel as if you are ducking for cover – from flint-eyed stares of contempt from middle-class women who cannot belieeeve their day is being held up by people in polyester uniforms daring to charge them for their goods, from tuts of exasperation flicked at you from harried mothers, and – occasionally – from outbursts of verbal abuse from the seriously stressed, with expletives raining down like bullets. It was a nice change of pace to be selling people things they wanted to buy rather than simply be the hated entity parting people from their money in return for a trolleyful of boring but necessary groceries, toothpaste and Vim.

My best friend in the bookshop was Val, who had been there for ever and knew everything. And I mean everything. I once had a customer who came in and said anxiously, 'I'm looking for a book.'

'Well,' I said brightly, 'you've come to the right place! If you'd picked the café next door it would have been a disaster.'

'I don't know the title . . . ' he said.

'That's OK.'

'Or the author . . . '

'Hmm. Less OK.'

'But I know it's got a blue cover.'

'Well, why didn't you say so! It'll be right over there on our blue covers table!' I didn't say, but only because Val at this point swooped in and said, 'It's *The Lovely Bones* – Alice Sebold. Let me just go and get it for you.'

She came back ten seconds later with the book in her hand. 'Is that the one?' she asked.

'Yes,' said the man delightedly. As he paid, I gaped.

'How did you do that?' I said to her after the man had left.

She shrugged. 'Man comes in looking worried, doesn't browse – he's here looking for a present for his wife or girlfriend. If he doesn't hand over a scrap of paper with the title scrawled on it, then he's looking for the one he's seen in the papers or on a tube advert. This week, that's *The Lovely Bones*. 'S easy.'

I mimed doffing my cap. 'I wonder how many birthdays and anniversaries you've salvaged?' I said admiringly. 'I wonder how many relationships you've saved over the years?'

'I don't know,' she said, modestly. 'Dozens, certainly. Maybe hundreds. I should probably be given some kind of award.'

Yes, the bookshop was definitely better. But it was also definitely harder on the feet. Standing for seven hours behind a counter is murder on them, no matter what kind of shoes you wear. As we suffered one Friday afternoon, late in May, Val and I were both breaking managerial protocol by leaning heavily on the counter so that we could stand one-legged, taking the weight off each of our feet in turn, like a couple of fatigued storks.

'Left!' said Val, and we switched legs with a small sigh of relief.

'Ahhh! Count to ten and . . . right!'

We sighed anew.

'What are you up to tonight?' I said.

'The usual,' said Val. 'Home, hot bath, and a night in with the cat, raging at the cruel fate that led Elvis to die before I could turn eighteen, fly to Vegas and marry him as planned. What about you?'

'I'm going to a friend's book launch,' I said.

'Ooh, get you!'

'I know. Cambridge University Press are publishing his PhD.'

'What's that about?'

'The enclosure of Irish peasant fields in the fifteenth century.'

'And are the film rights still available? Someone should snap them up.'

'I know,' I groaned, leaning further forward and lifting both my feet up for one brief and glorious moment before one elbow slipped and I crashed to the ground, taking a load of memo slips, pens, rolls of special-offer stickers and assorted other desk detritus with me.

'Are you all right?' said Val, scanning the shop for signs of concerned and/or annoyed management brought down from their eyrie by the noise.

'I'm fine,' I said, levering myself to a sitting position amidst the wreckage, detaching a few stickers from my clothes and brushing dust off my jeans. 'In fact, I'm actually a lot more comfortable now than—'

'Erk!' said Val suddenly. 'Erk! Erk!'

'Oh no!' I exclaimed softly and started batting more frantically at the dust and stickers.

For 'Erk!' is the sound Val makes when our one and only handsome male customer comes into the shop. His name – a swift but thorough perusal of his credit card as he buys his weekly selection of tasteful, middle-brow paperbacks and occasional best-selling hardback has revealed – is Michael Beechwood. He does justice to the name – tall and broad-shouldered, with nut-brown hair and skin and a general air of dependability and solidity.

'He's like a walking wardrobe,' said a disgruntled male colleague, after witnessing Val and me clutching each other and panting after Michael the first time he came in, but our colleague is both jealous and wrong – Michael is every young girl's, and grown shop assistant's, dream. And lately, we have noticed that he hangs back after he has chosen his books until he can be sure that he will be served by me, and then lingers, chatting over the purchase until a queue forms behind him and he is forced to move away. Even I – who usually find myself halfway through having sex with someone before I realise there's a chance he might be interested in me – can tell that he is trying to get up the courage to ask me out on a date.

In many ways, it's a worry. For a start, he's far too good-looking for me. This isn't false modesty, this is simple fact. I'm not bad-looking, but I'm not great either (or, as my mother once put it, 'You'll not stop clocks, or traffic') and he is rather lovely. I suspect that his interest betokens one of three things:

a) he's recently had a small, undiagnosed stroke
b) he's got a tiresome sexual fetish and has confused my professionally helpful and approachable air with a willingness to slather him in liquid latex, lard, or whatever other goddamn thing it is that gets him off and makes a mess of my sheets
c) he's after my discount.

Then there was the fact that after nearly two years with my last boyfriend, followed by two more of being single, I suspected I had lost whatever rudimentary dating skills I once had. The idea of shaving my legs, painting a smile on my face and finding the energy to sally forth and engage in flirtatious repartee over a dinner table for an entire evening filled me with something that was neither entirely panic nor dread nor fatigue but some unholy mixture of the three.

I was now at peace with the situation. Yes, the first six months had been spent recovering from the break-up with David. And yes, the next six months were filled by a rising panic – as I watched all my happily married/partnered friends drop sprogs and move out to the back of beyond to give their offspring more space and less lead poisoning – that I was now doomed to spinsterhood, that I would never find someone who would fancy me ever again, and that I had better start mastering a variety of art and craft skills with which to fill the long, lonely years ahead. But after that uncharacteristic burst of neuroticism, sanity reasserted itself and I settled happily – not resignedly, not sadly-but-smiling-bravely, but truly happily into single life.

For the last year, I had been living in my own flat, without a boyfriend, without a flatmate, without even a cat, and I had never been more content. I began to realise why people – by which I mean our mothers – have always been so eager to see their daughters settled before thirty. They know that once you've sat out your twenties, once you have experienced the deep, deep peace of a home and disposable income of your own, you have a clearer-eyed view of the world that is not conducive to mating for life. You know the joy of returning to a place that is exactly as you left it. No flatmate has plundered your fridge. No one has finished the toilet paper and not told you about it. Once you have shut the door behind you, the place, the time, the television remote is yours to do with as you wish. You know what you are? You're flat 'n' happy.

By the time Michael started frequenting the shop, the idea of interrupting this routine by welcoming another person into my life seemed absurd. As Karen once put it in *Will & Grace*, whose 8 p.m. repeats on Living TV I was so enjoying with my dinner every evening, what's so great about another person anyway? They just manhandle your boobs and eat all the ham.

Still, even the most hardily self-sufficient, I reasoned, could make an exception now and again. How else could we maintain an appreciation of our splendid isolation if we didn't occasionally experience the hell that is other people?

So I peeled the last sticker off my T-shirt and myself off the floor and greeted Mr Beechwood with my nearest approximation of a dazzling smile. Both he and Val took a startled step back, but he recovered admirably quickly.

'I was wondering,' he said in his low rumble, which Val once described dreamily and almost indecipherably as 'very tree-y', 'what time you finished work today?'

'We close at five-thirty,' I said. 'Then we usually have to spend about half an hour tidying up, because although the shop might look fine, I can assure you the stockroom is another story!' I laughed mirthlessly because I could not control what I was doing from the neck up. Val was kicking me on the ankle to try to bring me to my senses. In between, my body was numb.

Forget everything I said before. *This* is why I liked being single. Because in any other situation I am a moron.

I fell silent. 'So,' said Michael cautiously, 'we could meet in the pub on the corner at about half six for a drink – if you wanted to?'

'No,' I said. Michael nodded his head quickly and started to turn away. 'No – I mean, yes – but I mean – I've got to go out tonight to a friend's thing – very boring do, but I've got to go and support him – and we can't really bring guests otherwise I'd say, you know, "Come along!" but—'

'Bring it home,' muttered Val under her breath as she pretended to reorganise the paperback display behind the counter. 'Bring it on home, gel.'

I took a deep breath. Blimey, that was better. What a difference oxygen can make to stressful situations.

'But – we could go for a drink tomorrow night. If you wanted to.'

I thought about risking the dazzling smile again, but it hadn't gone down too well the first time and I was now too drained of all feeling to muster anything more successful, so I just stared at him, unsmiling, haggard, nauseous and probably pale green, across the desk.

'Great,' he said beaming back at the shell of a woman before him, 'half six tomorrow. See you then. Bye!' He bounded off and I slid back down to the floor.

Val observed me from above. 'That was . . . ' She paused, searching for the word that best summed up the scene she had just witnessed. 'Appalling.'

'I know,' I groaned.

'I've known acne-spattered seventeen-year-old boys handle first encounters with the opposite sex with more grace and style. Religious hermits could have coped better. Medieval religious hermits. Medieval religious retarded hermits.'

'I get,' I said, pushing myself painfully upright once more, 'your point.'

'But,' she said, suddenly grinning, 'you have a date!'

'I do, don't I?' I said. 'Oh, fuck-a-doodle-do. What am I going to wear? What are we going to talk about? And what am I going to wear? Can you lend me a cleavage?'

'I don't know,' said Val. 'But you should take comfort from the fact that you have never looked worse than at this moment, so it can only be an improvement and a delightful surprise to him tomorrow. And you can talk about books. He paid for these,' she said, lifting up the handful of volumes Michael had left by the till, 'but your witty repartee clearly thrilled him so much that he forgot to take them with him. So, I shall bag these up – like this – and give them to you – like this – and you can hand them over tomorrow – like this, or like this –' she twisted her body this way and that to mime the suggested action and its alternatives – 'thus at least getting you over the initial meet-and-greet horrors.'

'Thank you,' I said faintly.

'You're very welcome.'

After we closed up the shop, I changed quickly into a skirt, shoved my jeans into my bag and ran through the drizzling rain, as quickly as someone could who was limping with both feet, to the train station in order to get to the book launch more or less on time. On the train, I slumped wearily down in my seat, rousing myself only in the last five minutes of the journey when I remembered that I really should put some make-up on.

By the time the train got into Victoria, it was pouring down and the only thing blacker and more unforgiving than the sky was my mood, particularly when I couldn't get a taxi and had to present myself at a gathering of suited, booted and perfectly coiffured fellow guests looking like something to which a drowned rat would offer a towel and a pitying stare. I pushed my glasses up on to my head, partly to keep my straggling hair out of my face, partly because they were covered in water and I didn't have a spare inch of unsoaked clothing on which to dry them and restore visibility, but mostly because it is, albeit counter-intuitively, always better to reduce a roomful of strangers to a vague haze of formless faces before you venture forth. They look friendlier that way, and you feel already slightly drunk and pleasingly confident. I strode determinedly forth and into a wine waiter.

At least it was white wine and at least I was already too wet to care. As we disentangled ourselves, the host-and-author Ed came over to see if he could help. 'And if I can't help, can I at least point you to the corner in which you can do least damage?' he said politely.

'No, but could you grab me a napkin or something.' He produced a clean handkerchief from his pocket – I had forgotten he was posh. 'Thanks. If I can just dry these things . . . ' – I waved my glasses – 'future risk promises to be minimised.'

Once I was back in full possession of my faculties, Ed took me round the room and introduced me to some of the strangers, who even close up seemed friendly.

As I was chatting to a group of them, I noticed a man standing by the window. He caught my eye for many reasons. First, there were the clothes. Working from the feet up, an ancient pair of brown suede boots were lapped by an equally ancient pair of blue needlecord trousers, into which a red gingham shirt – frayed at collar and cuffs – had almost been tucked. This vibrant ensemble was completed by what in its heyday would have been readily identifiable as a green velvet jacket, but which had clearly been found – perhaps under a forgotten set of back stairs in the rambling country house in which the wearer almost certainly had grown up – by him long after that.

Second, there was the posture – although he was clearly only around my age, he had the stoop of a much older man. A much older man who had really worked hard on – possibly won awards for – his stoop. And finally there was the hair. At last I knew what a shock of hair looked like. Very thick, very straight, and very prematurely very silvery-grey, it stuck vertically up from his forehead and went off in a variety of directions thereafter. This natural tendency, I discovered on further observation, was aggravated by his habit of clutching it at moments of high tension, which were obviously many, as he engaged in a variety of heated debates with different guests who slewed round to talk to him.

I was entranced. He couldn't have looked more perfectly The Eccentric Academic if you had built him yourself from a kit off the internet. I almost wanted to go up and congratulate him on putting it all together so well. 'The hair! The clothes! The curvature of the spine! Don't tell me you did it all by yourself?'

When he at last took a break from his heated debating, he turned round and I saw his face properly for the first time – long, hawk-nosed, beetle-browed and furious but again, the mere consistency of it all was very attractive. He scanned the room and caught me looking at him. He raised his glass so unsmilingly at me that my first thought was to wonder whether you could be hit in the face by a face. My second thought, which was the one I acted upon, was to raise my glass in turn, go cross-eyed and stick my tongue out so far to the right that I almost licked my shoulder. A moment later he was by my side.

'I've been looking for a woman who would realise that I can't help my terrible face all my life,' he said. 'I hoped I was beaming at you over there,' he said, frowning ferociously. 'But I wasn't, was I?'

'No,' I said.

'What about now?' he said, still frowning in a manner that would have killed any small child in the vicinity.

'Not really.'

'I give up,' he said. 'I'm just going to tell you about myself to convince you that there is no art to find the mind's construction in the face.' He looked – furiously – at me.

I was impressed. I've never had a man make literary references at me before. Or maybe they have and I have just never noticed. I only recognised this one – from *Macbeth* – because this was the point at which Samantha Sullivan in our English GCSE class – after we had spent a billion years staggering, line by agonising, incomprehensible line, through the sodding play – cracked and ran out of the room screaming that she wasn't going to do any more Shakespeare even if Miss put a dagger through her own adolescent neck. I think she got an extra coursework mark for Making Appropriate Contemporary Reference to an Important Plot Point, but we all felt her pain.

So I let him tell me about himself. It was much as the clothes had predicted. His was a world full since birth of oak-panelled walls, tweed suits and Tradition with a capital T. He was impregnably self-confident, difficult, argumentative to an almost pathological degree, and potentially infuriating. If I had been scanning a description on a dating website, I would have run screaming for the hills. But I didn't. He was so different from anyone I had ever met before that I was intrigued and I stayed.

We talked for a while before being joined by other guests and gradually drifted apart as enforced mingling took place, but I kept half an eye on him and when it came time to leave I made a big deal about finding my coat and saying my farewells so that he would know, if he was paying any kind of attention at all, that I was going. He met me at the door.

'Where are you heading?' he scowled.

'I was going to get a cab to Charing Cross.'

'But we're only in Piccadilly.'

'I know, but I always get lost.'

'But it's only a four-minute walk away.'

'Not the way I do it. Last time I tried, I ended up in Marble Arch.'

'It is clearly not safe to leave you unattended. I will walk you to Charing Cross.'

He tells me now that he was impressed at the time by my willingness to pretend to a sub-imbecilic sense of direction to force him to escort me. 'Now, of course, after years of losing you in familiar and unfamiliar shops, streets, beaches, and – on one memorable occasion – our own house, I know that you spoke merely the truth and that in fact I was lucky you had made it to the correct door at which I was planning to waylay you.'

A four-minute walk took us two and a half hours because we stopped first for something to drink, then for a meal and then for another drink. Thus by the end of the evening I had also learned that he had appalling table manners, a spectacularly hard-working liver, a history degree, a job in a right-wing political think-tank and a festering rage against most of humanity. In almost every way except the last, we were ideally unsuited.

But I also discovered that he was funny. Thanks to the wine and my own relatively inefficient liver, I can't remember a single word either of us said, but I remember nearly laughing my leg off all evening. And he was clever. And he didn't mind that I wasn't. As time wore on and he started to gauge the depths of my ignorance in the two areas with which he was most concerned – history and politics – he started to add little explanations in parentheses as he went along. It was like having my own personal Google and John Craven's *Newsround* rolled into one. And even these miniature lectures and sidebars made me laugh. Now that's a good trick.

When we eventually got to the station, the last train was two minutes away from departure. Christopher kissed me quickly on the cheek and asked for my email address. I scrawled it on a scrap of paper I found in my handbag and ran for my train.

The next evening, I was staring into my wardrobe looking for a suitable – or failing that, simply clean – outfit for my date with Michael when I realised that something was wrong. Where, I wondered, was the roiling bellyful of nausea that we try to call delicious anticipation? Where was the embryonic stress headache building behind the eyes that usually precedes a night out with a stranger? Why was I not cursing myself for not having a peachy bottom, a recent manicure and selection of clean, unladdered tights to hand like any normal adult woman with a modicum of pride and decency?

I didn't have time to think about it as, naturally, I

was already running late. I threw on a skirt whose stains wouldn't show if I took off my jacket after I'd sat down, a top whose creases from being folded up so long would at least, I reasoned as I dashed downstairs and along the road to the bus stop and back again when I realised I had forgotten his books, prove that it was clean. On the bus, I put on my make-up. It's not that I want to live like this, you understand, it's just that that's always the way it works out. Sometimes I dream of taking three months off work to learn how to be grown-up. I would spend it decluttering my flat, putting all my old bank statements and paperwork into some kind of impressive concertina file, 'edit' – as the magazines say – my wardrobe, which would probably translate to 'binning everything but my jeans and pyjamas' but at least would be quick, finding a hairdresser who does not ask me what I want but simply tells me what I need, setting up all necessary direct debits, programming the speed dials on all my phones, defrosting the freezer and generally getting my shit together. I would emerge at the end of the three months a new, well-organised, serene woman who sat at a dressing table with a well-lit mirror before her to do her make-up instead of risking blindness by applying her mascara between stops on the overcrowded 225.

When I got to the pub, Michael was already there. As I approached the table, he jumped up, grinning, to greet me.

'I'm so sorry I'm late,' I said.

'No problem,' he said affably. 'What can I get you to drink?'

'Gin and tonic, please,' I said, taking my jacket off, sitting down and remembering too late about the variety of unlovely marks festooning my lower half. He brought the drinks back and sat down. I gave him his books and he thanked me.

'So,' he said, looking taller, slimmer and better-looking than ever in the kindly mellow lighting of the All Bar Slug and Piano or wherever we were, 'how long have you been working in the bookshop?'

We made small talk while we looked at the menus. We ordered our food. He was charming. He had lovely table manners. He asked if we could go out again. It was – damn, blow, blast and bloody fucking hell – no good.

'I'm so sorry,' I said, and I really, really was. 'This isn't going to work out. You see, I've fallen in love with a grey-haired, Tory-voting Quasimodo and he's ruined me for normal men.'

CHAPTER TWO

This was, of course, an exaggeration. I did not fall in love with Christopher at first sight. But he had – at least for the moment – ruined me for other men. I couldn't stop thinking about him. I had had such a good time that no one else could compete. I couldn't wait to see him again.

So it was even more galling than usual when the days ticked past with no word from him.

'But you're normally quite philosophical about this kind of thing,' said Gillian a week later as she drained her glass of Chateau de Second Cheapest on the Menu as we sat at our usual Friday-night table in the local. 'We both are. We have to be. You chat to someone at a party, you swap numbers, maybe a few of the more minor bodily fluids and then you never hear from him again. That's OK. He's too shy/ lazy/rude/secretly married to call. You're too dull/ ugly/frigid for him to want to call. The wine, the atmosphere, the planets aligned momentarily to make him think you were an attractive prospect – in the cold light of day, he forgets all about you or realises he could do better. There is not much you can do about any of those things, and if you take it personally you will go off your tiny rocker before you're twenty.'

I nodded agreement and drained my glass too. Gillian poured two refills, slopping wine over the top of each glass as her gaze roamed the bar. To the uneducated observer it might have seemed that she was trawling for talent. I – having known her for the better part of twenty years, ever since we were seated next to each other on our first day of secondary school – knew better. It is simply that Gillian has the attention span of a gnat.

Ever since that first day of school, Gillian has treated boredom as her own personal enemy. The soundtrack of our years together at the Generic Comprehensive for South-East London Girls comprises not Rick Astley telling us that he's never going to give us up or let us down, or Belinda Carlisle asserting that Ooh, Heaven is a Place on Earth, but the restless shiftings of my impossibly tall, thin friend next to me, sighing and rustling like a reed in a high breeze, followed by a small thump near my elbow. This was the sound of Gillian banging her head on to her exercise book, which she would have opened to an empty double-page spread preparatory to issuing an instruction to draw round her head. After I had discreetly complied, she would lift her head, gather up the book and rock with laughter at the sight of her silhouette. Most people had to sniff entire bottles of Tippex to get the kind of high Gillian could wring from a simple act of idiocy.

'My head!' she would crow hysterically. 'My tiny pinhead!'

When she was ordered out of the room, she would stop abruptly, nod soberly, and tuck the book under her arm as she walked out, looking as if she was going to do some quiet compensatory work in the corridor. For the rest of the lesson, though, you could hear occasional hoots of laughter drifting in from outside.

It was she who let Karen Oliver dangle her out of the classroom window to alleviate the boredom of a particularly dull geography lesson when we were in our second year. When the teacher paused in his monotonous real-time recital of how glaciers are formed and realised what was going on, he had to leap over thirty giggling girls and reel her in like a fish.

Gillian's attitude was a perfect contrast to my essentially passive and fearful character, and I became all the more grateful for it in later years when, to assuage the even more crushing boredoms of teenagerdom, she did all the experimenting with sex and drugs so that I didn't have to. Happy – and, in my case, non-health-endangering – days.

Finding nothing of interest in the bar, Gillian's attention returned to our table. I asked her how her date had gone the night before.

'Rubbish,' she says. 'He turned out to be on anti-depressants. That's my fourth one in a row. Are there no real men left? You know, ones who just drink to blot out the pain? But it doesn't matter because I've come up with a plan to earn me enough money to go part time even without getting married and splitting the rent.'

This is big news. Ever since one of Gillian's pupils – she's an English teacher – appeared on YouTube taking a dump in the corner of her classroom while one of his mates distracted her with an intelligent question that he had found on the internet about *Wuthering Heights*, she has been trying to find ways out of teaching. And also of bringing down the internet, but as she only rarely manages to send email successfully, she has had reluctantly to acknowledge that this is a longer-term project.

'So what's the plan?' I say, intrigued.

'I've thought of a new slogan for Lidl.'

There is a pause. 'Go on,' I say cautiously.

'It came to me when I was in Lidl.'

That makes sense. All the best artists need to immerse themselves in their material before they begin work. 'And what is it?'

'It's – are you ready? – "We like Lidl a lodl"! Isn't that brilliant! I'm going to send it to them and they will pay me enough cash to let me give up my job and decide what I want to do next. They may even put me in the new advertising campaign. Or at least make me a copywriter. And I can do that at home!'

Over the years, as I say, Gillian's optimism has frequently been a valuable and necessary corrective to my own profoundly pessimistic outlook – the kind of outlook that sees the glass not only as half empty but also suspects that the liquid in the remaining half is likely to be somebody's warm spit rather than a refreshing beverage – although sometimes you do have to tug her gently back down to earth. I explain, with some sadness, how unlikely it is that events would unfold to her satisfaction. Corporate behemoths being what they are, I tell her, it is a racing certainty that her brilliant idea will be stolen by some low-ranking employee and the next time she hears it, it will be on the television. For the rest of her life she will be dogged by the knowledge that some unworthy little scrote got rich off the back of her inspiration.

'Oh well,' she says, knocking back another glass. 'Back to the drawing board.'

Despite Gillian's semi-sage counsel, for the next fortnight, the question of how I could have misinterpreted the evening so badly gnawed at me. I stomped around the bookshop, snarling at customers (though not at Michael, who had made this easier by not visiting the shop at all since our date) and cursing my own stupidity.

Then one day I returned home, flipped open my laptop to check my email and found a message in my inbox from an address I didn't recognise. I had given up all hope at least a week before, so my stomach didn't flip until I opened it and saw his name at the bottom of an email that ran:

Dear Lucy,

The pleasure of your company had filled me with what I now know to have been unfounded confidence in the integrity of your handwriting. Ms look like Ns, As like Os and vice versa (both times) and you also appear to think that yahoo.com is synonymous with yahoo.co.uk. It has been the work of several weeks to decipher your scrawl in the absence of our mutual and currently holidaying friend Ed.

Never mind. I found a friend of a friend who remembered a tiny, blonde, half-blind, geographically challenged friend of Ed's from university and was able to determine for me not only that your name comprises one M and a brace each of A and N, but also the order in which, in this, the best of all possible worlds, they should appear. Let us put these orthographical difficulties behind us now and move forward.

Would you consider letting me take you out for a meal? If you indicate that you are amenable to this nascent plan, I will send you an *A to Z*, compass, gyroscope or long length of string and we can arrange things from there. If you are not, I will sow the desert air with grief and shame and return to my original life goal of drinking myself to death before I'm forty.

Sincerely yours

Christopher

No one, upon receipt of that email, could possibly argue that they didn't know what they were letting themselves in for. And I never have.

So, after a full three days of panic, nausea, drycleaning etc., I went. And it was good.

Six months later, he – along with seventeen tweed jackets, four threadbare gingham shirts, three pairs of disastrous shoes and two thousand books – moved in. Thus it was that I finally lost my cohabitation virginity. And like sex it was at first painful and only gradually did we learn to rub along together in a manner designed to produce deeper harmony rather than agonising friction.

And when I say 'only gradually', I mean 'Over the next twelve months I nearly went off my goddamn head.'

A NOTE ON COHABITATION

I thought there was something wrong with me at first. I am, after all, someone who had to have a long, explanatory lecture from my parents after watching *Papillon* one evening because I hadn't understood that solitary confinement was supposed to be a punishment. I thought Steve McQueen was a favoured prisoner in receipt of special privileges. That was my mum and dad's first inkling that they were the proprietors of a congenitally antisocial child. They did their best to mitigate the damage their combined DNA had wrought (which, it occurs to me, is as handy a definition of parenthood as any) but we all knew that it was a lost battle.

So for six months after Christopher moved in, I blamed misanthropy for my misery and fought against its rising tide. I choked down minor resentments and criticisms. I made concessions. I recognised, for example, that while most – perhaps all – men are a bit hapless domestically, Christopher was basically institutionalised. He needed to be led gently out of his oak-panelled existence and into the garish light of the real world. It wasn't his fault.

I put up with the extra noise (and noises – truly you do not know even a tenth of the extraordinary sounds the human body can make until you have lived in close proximity to its male incarnation for an extended period) and tried to embrace the new experience. Yes, I hadn't had a good night's sleep for half a year because of the stertorous breathing next to me. Yes, more mugs, plates, small household ornaments and appliances had been broken since he moved in than in my previous thirty years of ownership, but such is life. It wasn't worth getting upset over. Who needs more than two unchipped pieces of crockery in life anyway?

As time moved on, I started trying to view my situation as a valuable socio-psychological experiment.

Do men see dirty underpants on the floor but are blind to laundry baskets, or does nothing that is not currently covering the body register? I would muse as I picked up said items from the bathroom, the bedroom and, on one memorable and still-unexplained occasion, the balcony. Why is it that when two people of the opposite sex share a bed, a woman – even when barely conscious, even if she has to rouse herself to do so – instinctively turns over in such a way that the duvet is not disturbed, while the man simply turns, taking everything with him? Do They simply sleep more deeply than Us? Or are We truly so programmed for empathy that we, dimly but sufficiently, perceive the consequences for others of our tiniest actions even when we are unconscious? I would ponder at two, three, five and seven o'clock in the morning. Every morning.

I recruited other research subjects – friends who were years into their various partnerships – to see if they had suffered as I did. When I broached the subject, each one would take a furtive look around, lean across the table, sofa, toddler or empty wine bottles between us and snarl through gritted teeth:

'He dries himself on the bathmat.'

'If I see another skidmark on his pants, I'm going to start putting him in nappies.'

'To all appearances he is a normal, productive, civilised member of society. But every morning he wakes up, picks his nose and eats it.'

'When he spits out his toothpaste, he redecorates the bathroom in Colgate.'

One of them spoke of spending her first year of married life shaking with fury and dragging her cowering husband over to the site of the latest sin and begging him to explain the 'thinking' behind his decision.

'Did you actually put "thinking" in quotes?' I said.

'God help me, yes, I did,' she replied.

'So what happened after that first year?' I said.

'I had twins and lost my mind,' she said. 'We've all been a lot happier since.'

It seemed a drastic step so, now that this well of comfort had run dry, I moved on to tequila and the constant inward reminder that one day I would be granted the sweet release of death. Either mine or his.

When the effectiveness of that charm wore off, I started to weigh up the pros and cons of splicing the tequila with toilet cleaner. I could call it the Cohabitation Cocktail.

I rose every morning in a fog of despair, spent the day maddened with anger and sank into bed every night under a crushing weight of frustration. At one point, I remember, while he was out I carried out a small experiment to satisfy my curiosity – yes, the sitting room door *could* be opened quietly. In fact, it seemed to me to be a virtual impossibility to open it any other way without disapplying the laws of physics. In this, as in so much else, I muttered to myself as I took the top off the Harpic, it wasn't Me, it was Him. I remember reading a story in the newspaper one morning about how it was estimated that 35 per cent of the population would be living alone by 2021 and crumpling the paper in my fist as I offered up a heartfelt silent prayer that I would be one of them.

Christopher, of course, never noticed a thing. 'Why would I?' he says now. 'I was in love. And one of the things I have always loved most about you is your unwillingness, even though your heart may be blistering with rage, to admit anything is wrong. It makes life very peaceful. Until it doesn't.'

Ah, yes. Until it doesn't. One day, of course, I cracked.

It was at the end of a particularly bad week, in which I had found myself for the 8,000,006th time cleaning the remnants of his post-breakfast crap off the toilet bowl, engaged in a detailed discussion of why we couldn't move the fridge in front of the kitchen window, even if it did mean the milk would be three feet closer to the kettle, and watched him 'helpfully' put the apples I had just bought into the fruit bowl by dropping them in from chest height.

So my reserves of tolerance and patient explanation had been severely depleted by the time I came home to find that he had put leftover sausages in the fridge. Not on a plate. Just in the fridge. I stood, jaw agape, looking for about forty seconds at those porky fingers resting on the wire shelf, until Christopher broke their spell by coming into the kitchen to admire his domestic handiwork. 'You see?' he said proudly. 'I remembered not to leave them out this time.'

So I flipped. I had never truly lost my temper before. This is not because I am patient but because I am lazy. It takes a lot to stir me to any kind of action. It soon became clear, however, that I had saved up all my energy for this. I went absolutely mental. I screamed. I shouted. I cried. I screamed and shouted while I cried. As my fury swelled, I turned red and purple and advanced towards Christopher.

'You looked like an enraged summer fruit,' he says today, but then he was pale with fear as I backed him up against a wall, and still I raged and raged.

I listed my broken possessions, my broken nights, the sodding sausages, the 800 billion calculations, compromises and concessions I was making in having him here while he sailed, oblivious, through the days – and more. Much more. I don't remember half of it, and I only hope I didn't get carried away and start vilifying him for the bogey- and bathmat-based sins of others. Eventually, I finished and sank in a little, boneless, whimpering heap to the floor.

'Why didn't you say anything?' he asked, bewildered.

'I thought it would get better.'

'I think we need a new strategy,' he said, moving me on to the sofa and handing me a fistful of tissues with which to wipe the congealing mass of tears and snot from my face, 'don't you?'

I nodded and from the ashes of my despair rose a new framework for our home-sharing life. I would tell him what he was doing 'wrong' – the word to cover everything from objectively provable misdemeanours, like shoving things into cupboards until they break rather than engage in a little light rearrangement, to things that I would merely prefer he did differently – and he would attempt to do them right thereafter. And not to insist too strongly on defining into which category each one fell before doing so.

Gradually, things improved. A tally of our successes would include:

1. His proficiency at supermarket shopping.

   At first, Christopher simply gazed in awe at the source of all the foodstuffs that had hitherto magically appeared on his plate in cooked form, occasionally taking a packet down to examine it more closely.

   'What are these?'

   'Those are Sharwoods egg noodles.'

   'Like the ones I get from the Chinese?'

   'Basically, yes. If we took those home, boiled them, then stir-fried them, they would taste like the ones you buy from the takeaway.'

   'Then, my good woman, let us buy hundreds and execute this splendid scheme!'

   Slowly he learned the theory of shopping – a list, a trolley, a trundle round with an eye peeled for red stickers and freezable special offers with which a list may usefully be supplemented – and eventually the practice. Now he can take himself off to Waitrose with the week's needs in hand and return with an easy 80+ per cent success rate.

2. We discovered that he is much better at remembering to put the landline phone handset back on the charger and at keeping track of the TV remote control in the evenings. We also discovered that we both love *Malcolm in the Middle* but loathe the theme tune, and that we always agree on the ideal volume for whichever programme or CD we are listening to. Upon such details do I truly believe a strong and lasting happiness can be built.

3. The establishment of Quiet Time.

As I suspect is clear by now, I like solitude. I like peace and quiet. I like silence. And this goes double for when I'm working. It is my great misfortune to have fallen in love with a man who likes none of these things. Christopher talks. It is as natural to him as breathing and occurs almost as incessantly.

Eighteen months into our new living arrangement, I gave up my job in the bookshop and began working from home, freelancing for newspapers and magazines. Christopher too changed jobs and began spending more time at home, ceaselessly roaming the house in search of conversation. You can imagine how thrilled I was at this development.

So we brought in a new rule that he is not allowed to talk – at least, not to me – when my study door is closed. He can knock, in an emergency, but he must remember that not being able to find one of the cats (see below) or a clean pair of trousers is not an emergency. If he goes and looks in a second or even a third place, he is almost certain to find them both.

4. We got cats. Patrick and Henry, two ginger kittens from a shelter who took up residence, grew rapidly into giant marmalade monstrosities and have defused by their exits, entrances and antics at least three-quarters of all rows that have brewed since. It is a great myth that it is single

women who need cats for company. They are far more use after you have paired up.

5. And finally, I have learned to silence that inner voice that was doing so much to destroy my equilibrium. I have stopped listening constantly with half an ear for the opening of Christopher's study door and the sound of breaking glass and china as he makes his lunch. These things can be replaced. And the ones that can't are safely locked away now in cupboards. I do not keep semiconscious track of his movements round the house and automatically work out what he's doing, anticipate his next move and nip downstairs to avert imminent mess, inefficiency or disaster. Only the last of these matters, and it happens relatively rarely.

I knew that we had turned a corner when he went away on a three-day work trip and I realised I missed him. Only for the last ten hours or so, but still I missed him. Whether this indeed amounted to progress, personal growth and maturity, or to a breaking of my spirit, is for others to judge. I just get through the days the best way I know how.

I look back over all these trials, tribulations and occasional celebrations as I lie awake on the overnight flight home from New York. I have taken a Valium (I hate flying) but it hasn't worked. Every time I start to drop off I am jerked awake by the realisation that there is nothing between me and a 50,000-foot drop but a thin skin of metal and the pilot's brain, either of which could rupture at any moment if I am not here to keep an eye on things.

I look at the ring which (Christopher told me once we were back at the hotel) is not the real thing but a £15 interim job he spotted in a local fleamarket – 'I judged from remembered howls of protest at an episode of *Sex and the City* that you believe the bride-to-be should make the choice rather than be presented with a fait accompli' – and then over at Christopher. He, secure in the knowledge that no plane he is on would ever dare crash, is snoring lightly next to me, the perennially furious expression on his long, Easter Island face only slightly softened in sleep. I try to absorb the fact that we are engaged. To be married. To each other. Though a quick glance out of the window tells me that my mighty will continues to keep us steady at 40,000 feet, I still have a distinct sensation of falling.

Just then, Christopher stirs, flails briefly, knocking his books, my magazine and an empty water bottle to the floor, and wakes.

'Did we land?' he says.

'Not yet.'

'Oh. Are you all right, proto-wife?'

'I'm fine. I was just watching you and, you know, thinking back to how we met, and you moving in and everything.'

'You were?' he says warily. 'And you still say you're feeling all right?'

'Yes.'

'That Valium's a wonderful thing,' he says, rearranging the blanket over his knees. 'I wonder if we can ask for a forty-year supply of it as a wedding present?'

'I've got one tablet left,' I say. 'But I'm saving that for when we get to Mum's and tell her the news.'

'I'd forgotten about that,' says Christopher, paling slightly.

The pilot's voice comes over the speakers, asking us to prepare for landing. I lean over to Christopher.

'Buckle up,' I say, with a malevolent grin. 'It's going to be a bumpy ride.'

CHAPTER THREE

Three hours after we've landed, our cab pulls up outside my parents' house. Christopher rang his parents as soon as we got back to the hotel from Central Park, but we decided to wait and tell mine face to face. This is because I come from a pathologically parsimonious family – primarily Northern, with good gobbets of Irish and Scottish ancestry, each generation bred with a slightly tighter first – and I knew that if my mother received a transatlantic phone call her mind would be too full of the fears of crippling expense and/or injury to let my actual news be heard.

On the way to my parents', I have tried to call my sister (who lives in Bristol) from my mobile but she is out and I don't want to leave a message. I get out of the cab and ring the doorbell as Christopher unloads our luggage from the boot.

My dad opens the door. 'Hello, love,' he says with mild surprise. 'Were we expecting you?'

'No,' I say, giving him a kiss as Christopher staggers up the path with the first pair of suitcases, leaves them by the doorstep and returns for the next. 'We just thought we'd call in and see you on our way home.'

'Oh, grand,' he says, picking up one of the cases – all

of which are part-filled with Christopher's books – and heaving it inside. 'Have you been away?'

I have a theory that it is not that Dad does not listen to my mother, who will have told him at least thirteen times a day where we are, speculated on what we might be doing, visiting, seeing and when she will call in to see us when we get back. It's that because she never has an unexpressed thought – if it crosses her mind, it comes out of her mouth – his memory banks daily fill to overflowing. So if she mentions something important and/or genuinely interesting after the things have been filled up by her opinions on which bra she should wear for gardening, or whether she should phone her sister Eileen now or wait till she's bumphled the cushions, or risk putting the handwash-only blouse she accidentally bought into the machine, then I'm afraid it just runs over the top and gets sluiced away.

As we drag in the rest of the luggage, Mum comes bounding downstairs to see what all the noise is about.

'What are you doing here?' she demands when she sees me leaning against the wall and gasping with exhaustion.

'It's lovely to see you too, Mum. How I've missed nestling in the warm bosom of my ever-lovin' family.'

'You know what I mean,' she says, giving me a big kiss, picking up five suitcases with one hand and flinging them into the utility room where they fall in neatly aligned rows, filling and switching on the kettle with the other and sweeping us all through to the sitting room. 'I thought you were going straight home.'

'We were,' I say. 'But we've got a bit of news.'

'Are you stopping for your tea?' says Dad.

'What is it?' I ask.

'Chicken casserole.'

'With mash?'

'Aye, if you want.'

'Brilliant, yes please.'

Dad wanders off, I presume to peel some extra potatoes. Christopher coughs meaningfully.

'Oh, yes, sorry. Dad, come back a second. We've got a bit of news. We're engaged.'

There is a pause.

'Do you mean – engaged to be married?' says Mum.

'No, I mean engaged as a children's governess in a turn-of-the-century classic novel. Of course I mean engaged to be married.'

'I don't believe it!' she cries, turning to Christopher. 'Is this true?'

'Not if you don't want it to be,' he says.

'You daft—' she says, swatting at him with the *Radio Times*. 'I don't believe it!' she cries again. 'Well . . . congratulations, the pair of you. Oh, I wish I could tell your grandma!'

As Grandma died six years ago, this is unfortunately not possible.

'I know,' I say. 'Me too. But, you know,' I add as I look at my father who has a faraway look in his eyes and has yet to say a word, 'you can always tell Dad instead.'

'What?' he says, coming out of his reverie. 'Nay, lass,

41

I heard. Well done, that's grand. I were just thinking this calls for pudding but I've no custard. Shall I do extra mash instead?'

'That would be fine,' I say, and, his explosion of joy now complete, he putters off to the kitchen.

'Now,' says Mum, 'let's call your Auntie Eileen and tell her the news.'

She dials the number. As Eileen answers, Christopher reaches his hand out to take the phone. I shake my head. 'It's nothing to do with us any more,' I explain.

'Hello,' says Mum. 'You'll never guess what? Our daft daughter's only gone and got herself engaged!'

The voice on the other end chitters.

'To Christopher,' Mum says. 'I know. I know! I know. I don't know. I know! . . . ' She wanders off into another room with the phone and from then on all we can hear is the occasional phrase about getting the house ready, looking for dresses, deciding on menus and finding a florist.

I call my sister. She is still out.

An hour later, Mum gets off the phone and we sit down to eat. I make her promise not to tell my sister Emily before I do. She reluctantly agrees.

'There's such a lot to sort out!' she says as we dig in. 'But Eileen says she'll have to find out if your Great-Uncle Arthur can still travel with his colostomy bag, so that's one thing off the list. Do you know when you're planning to have the wedding?'

'Not really,' I say. 'I thought, maybe, three months from now?'

Christopher and my mother both look at me in dis-belief. 'You can't organise a wedding in three months,' they say in unison. This, their first-ever moment of agreement, is the most disconcerting thing that has ever happened to me. And, I suspect, them.

'Why not?' I say.

The unavailability of churches, apparently. The dif-ficulty of locating suitable reception venues and menus. The elusive nature of the perfect frock, shoes and flowers. I should be thinking in terms of a minimum of six months' preparation time, I learn, for a September wedding. An avalanche of advice, unconsidered factors and undreamed-of details rushes towards me, meets the jet lag and buries me.

'Just keep your head down and eat, love,' whispers my dad. It's good advice and I follow it willingly.

After our meal, we wedge our potato-stuffed bodies into another cab and head home. My oldest friend, Rosie, has been house- and cat-sitting for us. I call her a friend, but really she is more like family. When I was three, we moved house and came to live next door to Rosie and her parents Annie and Paul, but our two families did not meet until the day my mother's friend Sylvia forgot to pick me up from playschool. My teacher, Mrs Holman, walked me the three miles home but, of course, Mum was out at work (hence the Sylvian arrangement). So Mrs Holman knocked at our unknown neighbour's door and when Annie opened it, I appar-ently took one look at her, announced, 'I think I'll stay here until my mummy comes,' and marched in. It was one of my better snap judgments. Annie's house was filled with squashy sofas, the smell of baking and that intangible but infinitely pleasing sense that it was a place where children could do no wrong.

On one of the squashy sofas was Rosie, Annie's two-year-old daughter.

'Look!' I exclaimed with all the untrammelled egotism of the pre-school child. 'A little me!'

Rosie beamed back. She had dead-straight, dark-brown hair cut in a pudding-bowl style, but it was the late seventies and I forgave her. I climbed up next to her and patted her captivatingly round, red cheeks. All the children I had known so far had had such boring, pallid faces. I put it down to the stress of playgroup, the horrors of which had evidently yet to impinge upon Rosie's world of cosy perches and delicious odours.

It was the beginning of a beautiful friendship, cemented shortly thereafter by the addition of an enormous slice of cake topped with blue icing brought by Annie from her ever-fruitful kitchen and shared between us on the sofa. After my sister was born we all, in effect, grew up together. Annie looked after us while Mum eased herself back into the working world. As we got older, we would all trot off to school and back together, playing in Annie's garden, which was twice the length of ours, in the summer evenings and turning Rosie's bedroom into a giant den or teddy bears' hospital in the winter.

Now we have all grown up and left home, but Rosie still lives round the corner from me, and my sister still rings us up when she knows I am round there so that she can wail that we are ignoring her just like we did when she was little. When we introduce ourselves en masse to strangers, we quite often just tell them that we are sisters, because it seems closer to the truth than anything else.

'Welcome back!' Rosie says as we emerge, by now bleary-eyed and longing for bed, from the cab. 'Did you have a good time?'

'Sort of,' I groan, as I head through the front door. 'We got engaged.'

'I know,' she says. 'Your mum called. She said she had to tell someone and you'd made her promise not to call Emily. I told her she could call all your cousins instead. I thought it would save you a job and keep her busy.'

'Thanks, Rosie-bum.'

'"Save you a job and keep her busy"?' says Christopher as he huffs past. 'We should make that our wedding motto.'

After going to bed without unpacking, I wake up six refreshing hours later with Patrick the cat pawing at my head. He settles on my chest and I scratch his ears as I lie there and wonder – how exactly does one begin to construct a wedding?

Having lived through the Great Late Twenties Marital Bulge, you would think I would know more. The Bulge, for those of you who are too young yet to have experienced the pleasure, is the period during which everyone in your immediate social circle realises they are now within hailing distance of their fourth decade and decides to get married within one hellish summer. By the end of August, I had stayed in what felt like 802 overpriced hotels, peeled the marzipan off thirty-eight yards of fruit cake and sung 'Dear Lord and Father of Mankind' in all known and unknown keys. I was on autopilot. I couldn't walk past a church without going in, baring my teeth in a bright, false smile and saying, 'And how do you know the happy couple?' to whoever I found there. On a weekday, in London, this is usually a meths drinker with poor impulse control, so I went to a number of later weddings with a black eye, which at least gave other guests a conversational opener.

But to the actual details – flowers, candles, centrepieces, ushers, bridesmaids' sash colour, the presence or absence thereof – I had paid little attention. Because, after sitting (and standing. And then sitting again, sometimes neatly in sync with the rest of the congregation, but, at least once a ceremony, humiliatingly not) through all these weddings, I realised a great truth about myself. I was not ready to get married. Not nearly. Not even close. No way, nohow. And I couldn't envision myself ever becoming so.

That's not because I thought it was a ridiculous undertaking – quite the opposite. While, as I am sure anyone who has gone through such a summer will understand, I would occasionally gripe at spending yet another expensive weekend away, watching another two friends get hitched and making small talk with strangers over chicken supreme, I never came to see it as a mechanical or soulless experience. At some point during the service itself I would, every time, become overwhelmed by the magnitude of the thing. Not just assembling unboned chicken breasts for ninety, but promising yourself to someone else for life. For life. For *life*. It always seemed to me the most grown-up thing you could possibly do. I know having children should have taken that pole position but a lot of my friends got pregnant at school (well, not at school – at the nightclub round the corner) so in my mind childbearing has always been more firmly linked with adolescent idiocy and haphazard condom application than maturity and measured decision-making.

Marriage, on the other hand – that's different. Amongst my friends, it is only those who take the matter seriously who have bothered. I've never been to a wedding where people are sitting in the back pews muttering, 'Of course, it'll never last,' because the couple at the front are seventeen, met three days ago in Faliraki and haven't sobered up yet. They have all been solid, significant affairs, by solid, significant couples, and everyone has made me feel more like a seven-year-old child than anyone who might one day feel old enough to do likewise.

It is just another manifestation of my usual backwardness. I was the perennial late-starter. Couldn't catch a ball or tie my shoelaces till I was twelve. Socially, I was a moron – never noticed a fad until it was nearly over. Didn't get a best friend until the beginning of secondary school. Never liked the right pop groups. Never fancied the right one in said pop groups. Useless. And biologically, I was a disaster. The grease and spots arrived on time, but my boobs and periods apparently got lost in the post, and when they arrived I quickly discovered neither had been worth waiting for. I was mistaken alternately for a boy and an oil slick until I was twenty. Difficult times.

'I do know the main building blocks, of course,' I murmur to Patrick, in an effort to justify myself.

You need somewhere to get married, somewhere to convene afterwards, an outfit, some guests, some invitations, some food, some drink and some more drink, and a date on which they can all converge, but where do you begin? Everything is linked to everything else. You can't decide on the date before you have a church. You can't decide on the church before you know your guest list. You can't decide your guest list before you know your budget. You can't decide on the reception venue before you know which church, how many guests and how much money you have. The whole thing is a catch-22 situation in about fifty dimensions.

'It's a nightmare,' I tell Patrick.

A nightmare to people like me, at least. My whole life has been a flight from responsibility. Although I was in most respects a model pupil, I always met requests to take on extracurricular responsibilities with a polite but firm refusal. When teachers were looking for volunteers to help them organise sports days or school fêtes, or for some poor sap to draw up the milk monitor rota, they would fix me with a beady eye and wait for my arm to join the forest of others suddenly flung up, but it never did. I never understood my fellow pupils' eagerness for these jobs. Didn't they know these were unpaid posts? Were they trying to ingratiate themselves with the teachers? I doubted it – that kind of child hasn't existed outside the pages of girls' school stories since about 1963 – so I could only put it down to boredom for some of them and a ravening lust for power amongst the rest.

But I was neither bored (or, at least, not more than the average suburban child in the mid-eighties) nor an embryonic tyrant, so I kept my hands firmly at my sides. So I never milk-monitored, never stopped people running in the corridors, and later never became a student union rep, nor organised an office party, a group holiday or a college reunion.

Allied to this – though whether as a cause or effect I do not know – is the fact that I have always been hopelessly disorganised. My model-pupil status – the clean uniform, the punctual homework, the non-pregnancy before GCSE year – was a result of ceaseless maternal supervision, not personal virtue. I forced Christopher to master and live by my house rules because I have built them up painfully over time and know for a fact that without them life will become a maelstrom of chaos from which we may never emerge.

I have always been consumed with jealousy of anyone who leads a well-ordered life. And yes, I murmur to Patrick, yes this does mean that part of me admires Anthea Turner. I can't help it.

Are you one of the organised? Let's see – how many of the following could you, if required, lay hands on right now?

1. Your dog
2. Your cat
3. Your most recent child
4. Your passport
5. Your TV licence
6. Your cashcard
7. Your handbag
8. Your nail scissors
9. Your best bra
10. Your sanity

I know where my cat is, because he's lying on my chest. And I know I don't have a dog. After that, it's anyone's guess.

I have always been jealous of my mother and my sister, who are both natural-born time-and-motion experts. Their households run like well-oiled machines, though my sister occasionally tries to embrace the bohemian within by not emptying the dishwasher until two and sometimes nearly three minutes have elapsed. They live for projects. As soon as I saw Christopher down on one knee, I had a vision of mother and sister – one in London, one in Bristol – lifting their heads simultaneously and sniffing the first delicious whiff of another one in the offing, like wild beasts on the Serengeti, scenting prey.

'That reminds me,' I say to Patrick, as he pushes his head harder into my hand, demanding more active rubbing, 'I must phone Emily.' I reach for the phone by the bed.

'Hello?' says Emily through a yawn.

'Oh, sorry – did I wake you up?'

'No, I just saw your number and was overcome with boredom before I even picked up the phone,' she says. 'It's six o'-friggin-clock on a Sunday morning, fool, of course you woke me up.'

'Ah. My mistake. Jet lag appears to be fuckin' wit' ma mind . . . '

'What do you want?'

'I just wanted to tell you that Christopher and I are engaged. To be married.'

'Oh,' she says through another yawn. 'Congratu-lations.'

Even allowing for the early hour, she seems markedly unexcited.

'Did Mum already tell you?' I ask suspiciously.

'No,' she says, with a large dollop from the jars of pity and contempt she bulk-buys from the Annoying Little Sister Store every week. 'But I *reasoned*, with my enormous *brain*, that a couple your age, that have been *together* for three *years*, going on a holiday-of-a-lifetime-type-*thing*, might, you know, end up – *duh* – engaged.'

'Well, it took me by surprise,' I say.

'*Really?*' she says, adding another dollop from the jar as it's a special occasion.

'Anyway, I was wondering if you had any thoughts about where I should begin? Or begin to begin? It's like a whole knotted mass and I can't even find an end to pull on to start to unravel it.'

'Don't even try,' she advises. 'You're too stupid. I'll come down next weekend – no, wait, can't next weekend, I've got a life – the weekend after, and we can all talk about it. And if you could try to have some ideas about what kind of thing you want by then, that would be helpful, but not essential.'

I thank her and ring off. As soon as I put the phone down, Mum rings.

'Hello, I've just had a thought.'

'Mum, it's six o'clock on a Sunday morning.'

'Well, never mind that, you're awake now. And your father and I – well, I, but your father doesn't mind – have decided that we'd better throw you an engagement party.'

'Blimey. Now I know it's serious.'

My parents are not really party people. They have one gathering for all their friends in the summer, which involves a (clean) dustbinful of ice and wine bottles, a giant cold salmon and eighty-six chocolate roulades, which annual event is known as 'Getting It Over With'. This is not a title bestowed by people with a natural yen for socialising.

'So when are you two free?' she says.

We're always free. Unlike my sister, we have no life.

But I tell her when Emily is planning to come down and she agrees that it would be sensible to have the party the same weekend. I replace the handset once more and fall asleep again.

By the time I wake up, Christopher is downstairs. I find him lying on the floor of the sitting room, engaged in a staring contest with Henry, our other cat. When I tell him about the planned party he does not reply.

'Did you hear me?' I ask.

'Shh,' he says. 'I am trying to bend him to my will with the sheer force of my personality. Then I'm going to break Patrick. Then you, and then your mother. After that, I will officially be a superhero and be able to make you wear a skirt all the time.'

'We'll need to have a ring by party time,' I say.

Henry rolls slowly over without breaking eye contact with his opponent. My fiancé does likewise. I suddenly wonder what I am getting myself into.

'It shall be so,' he says. 'When Henry and I have finished here, I'll get on the internet and plot our way round the jewellery shops of London.'

'Don't,' I beg as their two heads lower further towards the ground, battle clearly intensifying rather than, as one might hope, dissipating and allowing normal life to restart, 'be too long, will you?'

'It's up to him,' says Christopher.

I head towards the kitchen and coffee and hope for the best. I've done that a lot over the past few years, and I suspect I'll be doing it even more in the months to come.

A few days later, however, he emerges from his own study with a full itinerary. 'Somewhere within these shops,' he says, brandishing his painstakingly compiled document, 'is the perfect ring for your stunted, yet to my eyes, still-perfect finger.'

Six shops later, I plead for coffee and a sit-down. We have been taken through every possible permutation of cut, clarity, colour and carat. We have seen every kind of ring there is. Diamond, emerald, ruby and sapphire. Modern and antique. Four-claw, six-claw, flush-set, shoulder-set, channel-set, bezel-set, banquette-set. Square-cut, pear-cut, princess-cut, oval-cut, marquise-, banquette- and emerald-cut. It was the revelation that any stone, not just emeralds, can be emerald-cut that finally caused me to call a temporary halt to proceedings.

'It's too much,' I say, gulping down black coffee with two standard and one emergency sugar in it.

'I must say, this may go down in history as the first time I ever saw a drawback to modern capitalism,' says Christopher. 'There can be such a thing as too much choice.' He takes a long drink of tea before adding hopefully, 'Can you at least say now what KIND of digital ornamentation you would like to sport for the eternity of marital bliss that lies before us?'

I am so tired it takes a moment for me to run this one through my internal translator and work out that he is asking if I have narrowed down my preferences yet. 'Yes,' I say with certainty. 'I would like a round-cut diamond solitaire, on the grounds that they are nice to look at, easy to pronounce, and anything else is just too complicated.'

'It is the essential, irreducible slothfulness at the core of my beloved that is her most compelling feature,' Christopher tells his cardboard cup of tea.

'And I'll tell you another thing – we are buying the ring in the very next shop we come across, OK? Whatever it is. I'm not wasting any more time. This is ridiculous. A diamond solitaire is a diamond solitaire is a diamond solitaire. It must be.'

'All right,' says Christopher, draining his cup. 'Let's go.'

We step out of the café and find ourselves standing exactly, inescapably, opposite De Beers. There is a moment's silence.

'I didn't know, I promise,' I say.

'I know,' says Christopher. 'If only because the last four years have taught me that your laziness is exceeded only by your lack of observational powers. You are, after all, a woman who has walked into thirteen lamp-posts in just the time I have known you. It may, of course, have been a long-term confidence trick in preparation for this very moment, but I doubt it. Well, come on then.'

We walk into De Beers. Well, we try. We walk through the glass front door into the glass-walled foyer. We can see the shop but we can't get at it.

'Which one's the door?' says Christopher, starting to push on all four walls in turn.

'Stop it,' I say. 'You look like Marcel Marceau.'

We are trapped like flies in a bottle. Very poor, unworthy flies in a very clean, spotlit bottle. Eventually, a buzzer sounds and one of the walls slides noiselessly open. An immaculately suited man glides forward and smiles as if nothing could give him greater pleasure than the tumbling arrival of two idiots who can't work a security door into his beautiful shop full of artfully lit display cases full of sparkling riches.

'Good afternoon,' he says. 'I'm Sebastian Von Poshface. How may I help?'

We explain that we are an Engaged Couple looking for a diamond solitaire ring.

'Of course,' says Mr Von P, guiding us towards a cavernous, impossibly soft, leather sofa, made, I presume, from poor people's skin. Christopher remains standing but I, stupidly, sit down and too far back so that my legs stick straight out in front of me. I sigh. It is very difficult to have poise when you are only five feet two.

Mr Von P glides away and returns with a tall, slim girl who puts out a perfectly manicured hand – she has fingers longer than my legs – and shakes Christopher's hand as I struggle up from the depths of the sofa. No one not born on a country estate should ever try to go anywhere smart without crampons and an alpenstock. I mentally christen her Serena de Snotbum but she actually turns out to be very nice.

She leads us over to the diamond solitaires. Christopher has snapped into public mode and is questioning her charmingly and intelligently about her job and her background. While I try to rid myself of the feeling that at any minute an alarm is going to go off and I am going to be bundled out on to the street by burly security men for being too short and scruffy in a shiny area ('Excuse me, officer – we apprehended this young lady for Lowering the Tone under Section 421(b) (iii) of the British Class Stratification Act, 1802'), Christopher discovers that she qualified as a diamond merchant in 2001, having previously worked for someone who turns out to have been a friend of a friend of a friend of Christopher when he worked in Westminster, and that she was born and bred on Jersey. This is catnip to Christopher.

'Ah!' he cries. 'The last relic of the Angevin empire!'

She looks both startled and pleased. 'Why, yes!' she replies.

I look startled – mostly at the realisation that there are still people in the world who say 'Why, yes!' – and apprehensive.

Christopher turns to me. 'The Angevin empire was basically a collection of states ruled by a Plantagenet offshoot during the twelfth and thirteenth centuries,' he says. 'Although, of course, I'm using the word "empire" ahistorically – they wouldn't have known it as such. But it ran from the Pyrenees to Ireland and included' – he gestures expansively towards S de S – 'Jersey. But they lost Normandy and Anjou to Philip of Spain and that's when the rot set in for the Angevins, I'm afraid, because . . . '

He stops because I have started to go cross-eyed. It is a little signal that I have evolved over the years. It is handy because it is silent and you only have to angle your head ever so slightly away from any nearby third party to disguise what you are doing, and it roughly translates as:

'Darling, I love you, not even in spite of the behaviour you are currently exhibiting but because of it. I know that you are not attempting to show off your knowledge but to share it with me. I know that it is enthusiasm not arrogance that motivates you. But I also know that if I do not interrupt you, you will still be telling me about the rise and fall of the Angevins/ the Portuguese journeys of discovery/the collapse of the Latin currency unit until the rivers and the oceans have dried up, the sun has turned black and the buildings and people around us have crumbled into dust and been blown away on the wind. Recall and return now, please, to the task in hand.'

I see my signal break the spell. His eyes clear. He returns from the bocages of medieval France and turns his attention back to the rings being put out before us. We look. We exclaim. We wonder how to broach the matter of pricing. But smoothly, smoothly, Serena divides them into categories. These categories are never named out loud, but somehow we all come to understand that they are 'Embarrassingly cheap', 'Reassuringly expensive' and 'Out of your price range, but a jeweller does not get to sit in 8,000 square feet of prime international real estate without knowing a thing or two about activating passing customers' latent greed and aspirations'.

The top end of our budget would bring us just to the bottom of the 'Reassuringly expensive' range. I point at one that seems to be winking coquettishly at me. It looks lovely. She slips it on my finger. It deserves a better backdrop – perhaps I could hire Serena to wear it for me at the party so that people could truly appreciate its beauty – but it still looks lovely. The band is far too big, of course, but the stone is perfectly in proportion to my hand. Not too big, not too small, but just right.

'That is a stunning ring,' says Serena, and I can only nod agreement. 'But,' she adds, 'let me just try this.'

She slips it off and another one on. A bigger one. Not hugely bigger, just . . . noticeably bigger. I am entranced. When I eventually look up, the dazzle of the diamond still dancing in my eyes, Christopher asks me what I am thinking.

What am I thinking? Hmm, what am I thinking? On the one hand, I am thinking – this is ridiculous. I do not need this ring. I barely need a ring at all. I have made it almost thirty years without succumbing to the lure of proper jewellery. If I buy a necklace from Accessorize rather than Sainsbury's, folk memories of generations of poverty-wracked lives on windswept Celtic farms and in squalid Victorian slums rise up to greet me. I am a product of my upbringing. My mother hasn't replaced a sofa, kitchen appliance or carpet since 1978. In our house, people, machines and soft furnishings are all required to work until they drop. My own kettle cost £6. My uncle Alan switches off his car engine and coasts down hills in order to save petrol. If I buy this ring, there is every chance that the shock will ripple outwards and kill any blood relative within a 200-mile radius.

On the other hand: I do not *need* this ring, I *want* this ring. I have gone almost thirty years without acquiring any proper jewellery. My dressing table is covered with rapidly discolouring tat from Sainsbury's. I come from a family that would rather sit hoarding its savings against some unspecified and unlikely disaster than in comfort on a springy sofa and soft carpets. I have an uncle who switches off his car engine and coasts down hills in order to save petrol. If I buy this ring, there is every chance that the shock will ripple outwards and kill any blood relative within a 200-mile radius.

I tell him.

'We'll take it,' he says. And we do.

CHAPTER FOUR

The next fortnight passes in a blur of going back to work by day and showing off the ring to all the people kind enough to be both genuinely and pretend-interested in my engagement, and spending the evenings ringing round godmothers, great-aunts and friends to tell them the news.

When I call Gillian, I have barely got the words 'I'm engaged' out of my mouth before she is at my front door demanding to see the ring.

'Excellent, excellent,' she says, bending over my hand and all but whipping out a jeweller's loupe to examine its new decoration. 'Let's go to the pub, because I've been teaching thirty-five teenage morons about *Romeo and Juliet* all day and a cup of tea will not cut it.'

We settle down at our usual table. 'Now,' she says, 'tell me everything.'

I tell her about the proposal ('Not bad,' she pronounces. 'Romantic yet not too sickening. Continue'), the jewellers and the forthcoming engagement party.

'Who's coming?' she says.

I tell her it will be a combination of the Mangans' longest-serving family friends, a scattering of mine and

Christopher's, and anyone – regardless of emotional closeness – who lives near enough to be hauled in for a glass of champagne or non-alcoholic beverage of their choice.

'And you, of course, Gill.'

'Of course,' she agrees. 'Otherwise, Luce – it ain't a party.'

We spend the rest of the night drinking toasts to the happy couple – that's me and the ring – before stumbling home.

As we weave gently down the pavement, Gillian throws a spindly arm about my shoulders and says – or rather shaysh:

'Tell me something, Luce . . . '

'Yes? What?'

'Why do you – What do you love about Christopher? I mean – what do I mean? – I mean, enough to, you know, marry him? I love my cats. You love your cats. We both love gin and *Desperate Housewives*. But we wouldn't marry any of them. Would we?'

I would, as it happens, marry Bree Van Der Kamp. She is so beautiful. She's like a piece of art in twinsets. But I take Gillian's point. Why do I – what do I – love about Christopher?

'What, you want, like – excuse me, just a little burp – a list?'

'Yes,' she says, waving her hands in the air excitedly. 'That's a very good idea. I'll have a list.'

'OK, OK . . . Just give me a second. OK, number one – when there isn't enough cat food left in the tin for both cats, so he has to open a new one as well as using the old stuff, he shares the two lots equally between the cats' two plates, so that each one gets a fair share of the opened and the fresh. I love the cats – even though, as you point out, I don't want to marry them – but I don't bother doing that.'

'It speaks to a deep and great sense of justice in the man,' says Gillian, nodding.

'Number two – because he takes books from the shelves by their sides, not by hooking his fingers over the top of the spine. Number three – he always thanks me when I put a meal down in front of him. And he genuinely thinks I am some kind of genius for knowing how to make fish pie from scratch.'

'That is very useful,' says Gillian. 'Having a boyfriend who thinks you are a genius, I mean, not being able to cook fish pie. I don't like fish.'

'Four – because he is kind. He hides it well, but he is kind. And five – how many things have to be on this list, by the way?'

'Ten,' she says decidedly. 'You have to have ten things on such a list if you are going to – ooh, excuse me too – marry the . . . the subject of the list.'

'OK – five . . . Because this morning, when I was downstairs in the kitchen beating eggs for scrambling at lunchtime, he came into the room and started spinning around, with his arms outstretched until I stopped and asked what he was doing. At which point, this prematurely silver-haired, tweed-jacketed man of thirty-five summers grinned delightedly and said, "I was pretending your whisking was controlling me!"

'Six – because I'll never, ever be bored.'

'Very good. You're over halfway through. I thought we'd be on "He has nice hair" by now.'

'Six – he has nice hair.'

'Ah.'

'No, I'm kidding. Seven . . . I love him because . . . Because he's never given me any shit.'

'Elaborate.'

'Well, you know – we've both had our share of crap boyfriends, haven't we?'

There is a moment's silence while we both look back down the relationship telescope, revisiting past horrors.

'Urrgh!' says Gillian, shaking herself out of the distasteful reverie. 'And ours haven't even been evil. Look at what happened to Aisling!'

Aisling is a fellow teacher at Gillian's school, who recently discovered after four blissful months with a sweet, unprepossessing fiftyish-year-old vet that he was married. He then left his wife – for a woman he had been having an affair with for six years.

'Or Helen,' I say.

She's a friend of ours from school who accepted an invitation – extended without prompting and of his own free will – from her boyfriend of six months to move in with him. She arrived on the appointed day with a carful of boxes and suitcases to find a note on the door – a note on the door! – saying the invitation was withdrawn and the neighbour would let her in to collect the stuff she had already left there.

'Exactly!' says Gillian. 'But would you rather be her or Emma?'

Another schoolfriend, she had enjoyed a light-hearted three-month liaison with a man – a forty-five-year-old, professional, ostensibly full-grown adult man – before calling it a day, amicably she thought, over a meal and a bottle of wine in a restaurant, the bill split at the end with a rueful smile from each party in recognition of the change from coupledom to friendship, and toddling off home. Every day since has begun with her opening her inbox when she gets to work and finding a series of emails, detailing first where she can find her belongings (he is parcelling them out gradually amongst different town dumps) and then all her perceived personal, physical and sexual failings. Terrible.

''S terrible,' I say, shaking my head.

'Or look at my sister and Dom,' says Gillian.

'That's not still going on is it?' I say incredulously.

Because Dom – her on-off and now apparently on-again boyfriend – is a shitbag of the first order. The way he – it, they – work is that they go out for a few weeks and then, just when she is starting to relax into the 'relationship', just when she begins to think that this time, this time, things might be different, he speedily and smilingly retreats, reminding her that she knows he doesn't like to be tied down, that 'we just like to have fun together, don't we?' and carefully ensures that she sees him in the next week or two, hand in hand with someone else. And then, just as she has started to get over this, he comes running once more. 'We're so good together, aren't we?' – and the whole thing grinds into gear again. You could set your clock by it – or, if not your clock, then at least your diary.

In fact, the last time Dom did his disappearing act, Gillian did actually pull out her diary and flick through the pages until she reached six weeks hence. Around that point, as her sister watched in confusion, she shaded in a period of five days. 'There,' she said, flinging down her pencil because there are laws against seeking out a serial cretin and stabbing him through the heart with it. 'I predict – no, I guarantee that within this time, this time here that I have marked out, this period to which I have attempted to give actual physical form to help you believe the truth of what I say, he will call you and want to meet up and start this crap all over again.'

Sure enough, on the fourth of those five days, he called. Couldn't they just meet for a drink? She went, of course, but Gillian clings to the hope that one day, albeit distressingly far from now, she may be able to look back on her intervention as the beginning of the end.

So I love Christopher for being one of the good guys. For always being straightforward – for saying that he loves me and for planning our life together from the beginning. For never messing me about, for never hedging his bets. For looking puzzled by the question, 'Do you want kids?', so obvious did the answer ('Of course') seem to him. For having no more manipulative cunning in him than a puppy does, although he resembles a cute, limpid-eyed squirming bundle of fun in no other conceivable way. For not being, in short, a twat.

'Number eight?' says Gillian, interrupting my internal rant.

'Oh yes, sorry, eight – I love him because every year on my birthday he presents me with a giant box containing my age in second-hand books.'

'Ah, that is nice.'

'*And* they are always books I want to read. Greater love hath no man than that he can pick out a suitable book for his girlfriend, let alone thirty of the buggers. And counting.

'Number nine – because he loves me. And because when I ask him how much, he always stands on tiptoe, stretches his arms out as wide as they go and says, "Nine hundred".'

'And number ten?' says Gillian.

When we were in our first year at school, we went on what I believe turned out to be our one and only class trip. It was to a bird sanctuary, where they crammed us all into a couple of hides, handed out binoculars and got us to match up all the birds we saw with the pictures on our worksheets. Our host told us that real birdwatchers identified birds by their 'giss'. Strictly speaking, he explained, this stands for General Impression, Size and Shape but in practice birdwatchers most often use it to refer to the moment when they 'just know' that the fleeting glimpse – too short to see its size or shape properly, too obscured by rain, leaves or branches even to glean the most general of general impressions – they just caught was, nevertheless, of a hawk, or a pigeon, or a fantail, or a phoenix.

And that, really, is as close as you can get to describing why you love the person you love. Giss. And so number ten is –

'Just because.'

'I'm sorry to interrupt your quality time with both Will and Grace, tiny fiancée,' says Christopher, coming with furrowed brow into the sitting room. 'But is the engagement party tomorrow?'

'Yes. That's why it's marked on the kitchen calendar on that very date.'

'There's a calendar in the kitchen?'

'Why are you asking about the party?'

'I was just thinking we should probably have a discussion between ourselves about The Wedding, before we have to answer questions lobbed at us by friendly guests tomorrow.'

'You know, when you're right, you're right.'

'So, do you have any ideas?'

I know three things about my wedding. I know I should have more, I know. I should have a whole host of tenderly accumulated dreams, schemes and themes and carefully nurtured details, but as we have already established, I am almost entirely useless in that department. Christopher says it's OK. He says that it was my stunted emotional development that drew him to me in the first place. This does not make me feel as good as he expects.

Still, three things is three better than nothing. They are:

1. There will be cupcakes instead of wedding cake. And why? Because I don't like fruit cake. I've never met anyone who likes fruit cake. Anyone, I mean, who if presented with an array of options and granted free choice in the matter, would hesitate amongst the fun-loving iced buns, classic Victoria sponge, creamily oozing chocolate gateau and insouciant gingerbread men, and say, 'I'm sorry – I don't suppose you have a finger of complicated, claggy, oddly bitter and disconcertingly brown cake, made yet more impossibly indigestible by the addition of a layer of ground almond paste and icing like a plaster cast that together comprise three years' worth of calorific intake?' If these people exist, they are in a minute minority who have exercised disproportionate control over wedding confectionery for quite long enough.

'It's time to take a stand,' I explain to Christopher. 'A cake stand.'

I am becoming impassioned, but the subject is one dear to my heart. Most of my happiest memories are cake-based. There was Annie's blue-iced delight, the foundation of a lifelong friendship. Then there was my late grandma who demonstrated her love via many things – poker, pontoon and three-card brag foremost amongst them – but most readily through the medium of late-night Battenberg slices. And when, in the early eighties Dad changed to a job that meant he didn't have to work every weekend, he used to take me and my sister into London every Sunday. He refers to them now as cultural excursions because we used to go to museums, galleries and theatres, or walk the streets and find statues of famous men, and he would tell us stories about what they had done to earn their monuments. Emily and I referred to them then and now as Happy Cakey days, a name that came about when Emily had her fourth birthday, and got confused between the song and the confectionery she knew to be coming her way.

We would set out after a puddingless lunch and, after an hour or two's enforced culture-vulturing, we would go into a café and share a cake as belated dessert. I don't remember much about the statues – except to be able to tell you that a mounted rider whose horse has one foot off the ground died in battle – but I can recall the happy glow that surrounded us in cafés across London, we three united by the division of an outsize Bakewell tart. Emily always got the glacé cherry because she was the youngest. At first, Dad assumed that I was being noble and generous and for a while I basked in his approval. But as the weeks passed (or maybe it was months – I don't know. Time runs so differently when you are a child, and then again in recollection, that it seems a miracle to me that anyone can locate past events in the correct decade, never mind anything more specific), I felt my conscience begin to prick. I confessed that in fact it was an easy sacrifice because I did not like glacé cherries. Always a man to recognise a struggle in the childish breast and treat our tiny feelings with respect, he gave the matter his earnest consideration and said that he was glad I had told him because now he could be proud of my honesty, which was real, instead of my generosity, which had not been, although he was sure that I would be generous from time to time in the future. I left the café full of coconut swirl and joy that he had understood.

Like I say, cake matters.

2. My dress will not be white. To wear white you need to be a fresh-faced, bright-eyed, clean-livered young virgin. I am none of these things. In fact, I believe I have only ever been one of those things, although I remained it for an extremely long time, thanks to the insidious and virtually ineradicable effects of a Catholic upbringing. Which brings us relatively neatly to the third and final thing I know about my wedding:

3. It will be in a church.

Some friends have already expressed surprise at this because I am not religious. In the unlikely event that someone came up to me and required that I plump for one or other of the following statements: *There is a*

God; or *There is no God*, I would have to side with the latter. But I feel scared saying so. Because you never know. Except, you do.

I think I can pinpoint the beginning of my religious disillusionment. I had just turned six (I remember because I was wearing with pride the orange acrylic jumper my beloved grandma had bought for me, so beautifully soft on my skin after the scratchy wool polo necks my mother made me wear every day, to go with my scratchy kilt and even scratchier tights. You could have planed a doorframe with me throughout the late seventies) and a discussion about the naughty boys at school had gradually induced my mother to state that by 'our' – i.e. Catholic – lights (and although my parents have not been to Mass for years now, they were much hotter on the whole religion thing when I was younger and at my most spiritually vulnerable), thinking about committing a sin was as bad as actually committing it.

There is not much that a six-year-old can understand immediately, instinctively and correctly. But the profound, monstrous unfairness of this concept struck me deep in my vitals and lodged there. 'How . . . ? Why . . . ? What the . . . ?' I gibbered, and have been gibbering, I think, at some level ever since.

So if I had the courage of my convictions – or semiconvictions – I would get hitched almost anywhere but in a church. Somehow, though, I can't imagine feeling right about it.

It just seems that the centuries of human history in

the ancient carvings and curlicues around you is the right setting for plighting your troth to someone for ever. More than that, I think it's the kind of setting I need. I have a terrible fear that if I get married in a register office, I simply won't take it seriously. Won't it feel just like going to get a passport stamped or something? No, I need some solemn ritualising and a spot of daunting architecture to help me. And if I get a sense of God watching, then so much the better.

Then there's the small matter of what the rest of the family will expect. Although my parents are no longer regulars at Mass, the beating of auntly breasts that will ensue if we don't get married in a house of God doesn't bear thinking about. Easier all round just to bow to tradition and avoid the weeping and wailing of aged relatives.

'But,' I finish up, 'I don't know which church we would be able to get. You have to have attended your parish church, don't you, if you want to be married there? And we, you know, haven't.'

'Enter the All-Problem-Solving Proto-Husband,' says Christopher. 'Who, as luck would have it, is friends with the vicar of the perfect eighteenth-century guild church that he attends occasionally, which has different requirements from the parish version. He would be glad to join us in holy matrimony.'

'That's brilliant!' I say. 'Is it Catholic?'

'It is not.'

'Is it near us?'

'It is not.'

'Is it near Mum and Dad's?'

'It is not. It is in central London.'

I feel the first faint stirrings of unease. His plan, of course, makes perfect sense. The family can cope with a non-Catholic church. In a curious way, I know a lot of them will get a perverse satisfaction out of it, imagining the serried ranks of left-footers fighting it out on some ethereal plane against the 'nonsense' emanating from the other side of the church and knowing that their collective indomitable will, plus – given the family birthrate – sheer weight of numbers, will give them the edge.

I know the church he means, and it is lovely. London is easy for all guests to get to. It will give us a wide choice of reception venues nearby to suit whatever budget and size of guest list we end up with.

I also know that this is not the way my mother will see things at all. She will be expecting me to get married locally and to have the reception at the house. I explain this with careful neutrality to Christopher. It's not that he and Mum don't get on, it's just that watching them together is a bit like watching lions wrestle. Armed lions. With extra ammo hidden in strategically placed hidden silos just in case. You're never quite sure when it might suddenly turn into brutal carnage and reduce the immediate surroundings to a bloody wasteland.

His brow furrows further. I worry that it might start to crush his brain.

'London is local,' he says. 'We live in London. She lives in London.'

'No, by "locally" I mean – she means – walking, or maybe five minutes' driving distance from here. Or from her.'

'There is nothing within five minutes' driving distance of either of you except dismal post-war housing and the occasional drug den.'

'I know, but—'

'I'll tell her, if you like.'

'Oh yes, that'll be ideal. The irresistible force meeting the immovable object always ends well, I believe.'

If I have learned anything over the last twenty-odd years, it's that opening my mother's mind to new ideas is like turning a supertanker. It takes a long, long time, a steady hand on the tiller and constant small corrections. It is a process that cannot be rushed. It is not a job for a man who has to pause Channel 4 News at thirty-second intervals so that he can shout abuse at Jon Snow every night.

'No,' I say reluctantly. 'You'll just have to leave it to me.'

The day of the party arrives. As we pull up outside my parents' house, I have one last futile attempt at making Christopher look presentable. I have been trying gently to update his wardrobe ever since we met, but have stumbled over the fact that he will not throw out – or indeed stop wearing – anything until it is literally so ragged that it won't stay on his body any more (he once asked me to patch a pair of cords at the crotch. I almost did it, just to see how long he would be allowed to walk the streets without getting arrested or sectioned) and also the undeniable truth that you could put him in the finest Savile Row ensemble and he would still reduce it within seconds to something Worzel Gummidge would hesitate to step outdoors in.

He has, in deference to parental taste, worn his best cufflinks, a fifteen-year-old red-and-white-checked shirt that is frayed only at the collar and one cuff (it's the arm he uses for gesturing furiously at *Newsnight*), beige cords, and a green tweed jacket. I straighten his brown knitted tie – wondering whether I should be pleased or perturbed that I am marrying a man who could share clothes with Alan Bennett – pick some cat hairs off his leather-patched (before my time) sleeve and comfort myself with the thought that at least everyone has met him before.

My parents live in a three-bedroomed Victorian ter-raced house in south-east London. At the moment it is covered in scaffolding because, after thirty years of professing her hatred of it every time she arrives home, my mother has decided to get the pebbledash – you know, that stuff that looks as if the gravel god came down and threw up all over a once perfectly acceptable house sometime in the early seventies – painted over. Not only that, but my father recently agreed to buy a new pair of shoes, even though the decade is not yet over. It is as if my getting engaged has galvanised everyone into contemplating leaps they had once thought impossible. Although, as I look at it now, it also occurs to me that this is the most tangible sign yet that my mother believes the reception will be happening here and that the house will need to be in a fit state for all our guests to come back to.

Maybe it is the thought of all the discussions-stroke-battles to come, maybe it is the thought of having to act as go-between for the next six months between my fiancé and my family, maybe it is the suddenly aisle-ish nature of the garden path we are walking up to the front door, between the garden shrubs that suddenly seem to be rustling like interested guests, but whatever the reason, the notion of an engagement party . . . an engagement . . . a husband . . . a marriage . . . makes me feel slightly faint. There is a buzzing in my ears, and a warm prickly feeling creeps along my arms and up my neck. I slip my hand into Christopher's for reassurance.

'What's wrong?' he says, spontaneous gestures of affection on my part being sufficiently rare occurrences to engender concern rather than contentment.

'Nothing. I've just – I don't know. I think I've just realised that we're engaged. To be married.'

'This is true.'

'I'll be your wife.'

'This is true too.'

'You'll be my husband.'

'Also, true.'

'Will it be all right?'

'Well, I always thought I'd be marrying someone taller, but I think it will be fine.'

'OK then.'

'OK then,' he says, squeezing my hand, and in we go.

'They're here, they're here!' squeals Annie, dancing up to us delightedly. 'Congratulations, darlings! Oh!' She grabs and kisses each of us in turn, and leads us into the sitting room where Mum, Dad, my sister Emily and the rest of the guests are waiting.

Corks pop, glasses fill, the ring is displayed, hugs are given, hands are shaken and Annie – an undying romantic whose entire being since Rosie, Emily and I hit our twenties has been strung to the desire that one of us get married and start popping out the next generation of tiny, cake-guzzling charges for her to look after – heads rapidly towards tears. Behind her, Rosie rolls her eyes.

'Don't start crying now, Mum,' she says, handing two glasses of fizz to Christopher – 'One for you, one for your fiancée!' – before taking Annie by the shoulders and steering her firmly towards the food. 'You'll have nothing left for the wedding. You've got to learn to pace yourself.'

As she is ushered away, Mum comes up and joins us. 'Remind me to bring extra tissues to the wedding,' she says, nodding her head in Annie's direction.

'I think it'll be lovely to have at least one person there displaying emotion on the day,' says Christopher.

'Get on with you, you cheeky bugger,' says Mum, swatting at his head playfully. Playfully-ish.

'So, is Gillian here yet?' I ask quickly.

'She called to say—' Mum begins.

'She was running late,' I finish. 'Of course.'

As I have said, I met Gillian on our first day of secondary school. Her prompt attendance on that first day of term remains the only recorded instance of her appearing punctually for anything. And I believe that was only because her mother dressed her and locked her in the car the night before and, knowing that Gillian can find more distractions and disasters during an unsupervised ten-yard walk than most normal people can manage in a lifetime, actually drove into the playground to drop her off.

We are still well within approximate arrival time according to the Gillian-clock. Only if she is over an hour late should you start to feel any concern. This was established about ten years ago when Gillian got her first car. I thought – briefly – that things would improve now that at least she was no longer reliant on the vagaries of public transport, but as I waited for her to come and pick me up from work in her new pride and joy as promised, this seemed an increasingly foolish hope. An hour and a half ticked past. Eventually the phone rang.

'Hi, Luce,' said a muffled voice.

'Hi, Gill. Are you on your way?'

'Not really. I'm in hospital.'

'What the fu—'

'No, I'm fine, it was just a little crash, just bruised my jaw and got some cuts on my face. And my knee, although I don't know how – maybe it went into my face . . . Anyway, it was my own fault.'

'How come?'

'I'd just moisturised my hands before I set off, and when I tried to change gear my hand slipped off, hit the thing that starts the windscreen wipers going and I got so confused I drove into a tree.'

She wears driving gloves now. I choose not to think much further than that when I am in the car with her.

Next to me, I feel Christopher suddenly relax and brighten. And by 'brighten' I mean 'fractionally ease up on the glowering'. This can mean only one thing, and so it turns out – he has spotted David.

David is one of the main reasons Christopher is marrying me. He is, at eighty-six, our oldest family friend in every sense. He flew Catalinas in the war and uses his RAF leather gauntlets now as gardening gloves. He is a mine of first-hand stories of the Battle of This, That and the Other that Christopher has been ransacking ever since they first met. He hares off to say hello to his hero, taking both glasses of champagne with him, just as the doorbell rings. I know they don't need me, so I go to let in the next clutch of visitors. These include our new next-door neighbours, whose names I have completely forgotten, so I just beam at them and tell them to go straight on through to the booze, and Ed, Christopher's friend, with his girlfriend Kate.

They both offer their congratulations. 'Never thought I'd see the day,' says Ed, shaking his head. 'I never thought he'd ever succeed in charming any woman into giving him the time of day, never mind her hand in marriage. Are you sure you're right in the head?'

'A question for another time,' I tell him. 'But in the meantime, on you go through and enjoy.'

Just as I am about to close the door, a minicab pulls up and out gets my Auntie Eileen. She lives, like 80 per cent of my living relatives and most of the nearly-dead ones, in Preston (thirty-five miles from Manchester) but, as family foreign correspondent, is periodically dispatched to far-flung places like London in order to report back on major events.

She thunders up the path. 'How do, kid?' she says, flinging her arms around me and crushing me to her bosom. She releases me and grabs my hand instead to inspect the ring. 'Nice,' she says. 'And about time. We all had you down as a lesbian.'

'No,' I say, pointing her in the direction of Mum. 'Just backward.' She thunders off.

As I try to close the door again, I realise a pipe-cleaner has somehow got wedged in there and won't let it shut. When the pipe-cleaner speaks, I realise it is Gillian, who has finally made it to her destination.

'Sorry I'm late, Luce,' she pants. 'Just open it a bit more and let me in, that's it – I was accidentally imprisoned in the Little Shop of Horrors. They put the head back up before I'd left.'

This might need a moment's explanation. Gillian has a phobia – not an intense dislike, not even a hatred, but a full-blown, no-talking-her-down-from-it, eyes-rolling-back-in-the-head-type phobia of stuffed animals. Whenever a school trip to a museum was announced, the teachers wouldn't see her for dust. Once, when we were fifteen-turning-sixteen and almost dying of sophistication, a group of us decided we would go for a collective birthday meal at Lewisham's premier and only proper restaurant. We got about six feet into the place when Gillian's eyes widened and – witnesses will still attest – she leaped those six feet backwards, from a standing start, and landed safely outside on the pavement again. Knowing her little problem as we did, we shouted at her to point out where It was. Her shaking finger directed us to a tiny stuffed sparrow perched on a mahogany-mounted twig in the smallest, furthest, dimmest corner of the restaurant. It was the most innocuous example of the taxidermist's art you could imagine. It was barely visible to the naked eye.

'Really?' Claire mouthed at our trembling friend through the window.

Gillian nodded. 'It wants me dead, Luce,' she promised.

'OK,' I said with a sigh. We fanned out. Claire and Donna created a distraction while I took the thing down off its plinth, stuck it up my jumper and walked across the floor to the toilets. Outside the men's loos, I let the evil bird slip down to my feet, opened the door a crack and booted it through. Gillian re-entered, nobody came out of the gents' holding up a wee-stained sparrow and the evening proceeded as planned.

Nowadays, of course, we are genuinely sophisticated and if we see these things somewhere that we want to visit, Gillian or I just ask the owner or the manager if they could remove them for the duration because she is a freaking weirdo, and they graciously do. The Little Shop of Horrors is Gillian's favourite clothes shop but it has a stag's head over the door. She stands and signals to the nearest familiar shop assistant, who comes and takes it down and allows her to pass. Evidently someone not au fait with the arrangement had replaced the head too soon.

'And I noticed it when I was right at the back of the shop, so it was ages before someone I knew came past and I could grab them and get them to take it down again. Sorry, Luce.'

'That's OK, Gill. I'm sorry you've had such an ordeal.'

'Thanks, Luce. And hey – congratulations! Don't have your wedding in a church with any stag's heads.'

'I won't.'

For the rest of the afternoon, Christopher and I work our way round all the guests, fudging any answers about our plans that don't centre on cake, dress colour or church v. register office, and pretending not to hear any talk from any member of my family about how they are going to fit everyone into the house afterwards, whether I will be able to walk to the nearest church in my heels and whether it's really worth hiring a car just to take me to and fro if not. I also pretend not to hear Christopher explaining why he will be in charge of any and all wedding music.

'We were talking about whether there was any piece that had a deep significance for her and she asked if she could come down the aisle to the *Friends* theme tune,' he explains to David. 'So I have excised her from the process.'

These small considerations aside, it is a lovely, lovely afternoon. Everyone is so pleased and happy for us that we are, although we don't admit it to each other, really rather moved. It feels odd, in a way, to be making the private public. The ring suddenly seems to be flashing like a sign, a sign that says that, after all these years of 'just going out' or even 'just living together', actually, this is it. He's the one. I have chosen him and he has chosen me. We love each other. We really think it will last. We really love each other that much.

And I'm glad that people know. I never knew how to tell them myself. But now I can let the ring speak for me, and collect gratefully the benedictions that fall like confetti around us, until it is time to go home.

CHAPTER FIVE

It comes as no real surprise that I am woken the next morning at nine o'clock by the energetic ringing of the doorbell. I pull on my dressing gown, stagger downstairs and find Mum and Emily, bright-eyed and bushy-tailed, on the front step.

'We thought you were probably feeling a bit – you know – adrift in a sea of unmade decisions,' says my sister, manoeuvring herself, eighteen bags of paper, Europe's entire stock of ringbinders and a picnic lunch through the door.

'And you know how much we like making decisions,' says Mum, sailing over the threshold with a stack of wedding magazines under her arm. She strides into the kitchen and glances sternly around the room. Dirty dishes seem to leap into the dishwasher of their own accord, while yesterday's groceries hurl themselves from carrier bag to shelf and shut the doors neatly behind them. She nods with satisfaction, while Emily sets her bags down in the living room and starts lifting out sheaves of paper.

'What is this?' I ask, leafing through them. 'Have you printed out the internet?'

'It's just a few helpful ideas from a couple of wedding

sites,' she says airily, as the stacks grow higher round me. 'You'll see.' Invisible behind her paper walls, I roll my eyes.

'Stop that,' she says.

'Where's Christopher?' says Mum, coming through to join us.

'At the library,' I lie, quickly. 'He suddenly realised there was a book in the world he hadn't read, so he's gone to find it.'

'Good,' she says. 'We don't want any interruptions.'

'Can I go upstairs and have a shower?' I ask as they lay out their folders, Post-It notes, lead soldiers and maps of the Rhineland. 'Maybe get dressed?'

'Please do,' says Emily.

I dash upstairs and warn Christopher not to come down until I give the all-clear signal. 'It'll sound like a huge sigh of relief mixed with a sort of gasping, sobbing noise,' I say. I have a quick shower, pull on a pair of jeans, a T-shirt and a Kevlar jacket, and head back downstairs.

'I've cleaned the kettle and put it on,' says Mum. 'You can make the coffee while we get to work.'

It is a long day. By the end of it, every piece of paper has been annotated, colour-coded and neatly filed or scored through and neatly discarded. Subtle hints from me about the suitability of central London as a wedding location have been wholly ignored. Ditto less subtle hints. We have located every church between my house and Manchester, and I have cravenly agreed to examine them all and cross-reference them in the blue folder according to size, grandeur, price and accessibility. We have discussed the issue of bridesmaids. I would like some company down the aisle, so I ask Em if she would fulfil the role.

'The thing is, Luce,' she says kindly, 'you don't want someone like me to be walking behind you down the aisle. I mean, think about it – I'm tall, I look fabulous in anything and I've got a bosom that makes even gay men weak with admiration. And there you'll be – just a pallid little mushroom-type thing walking in front of me. People would wonder what you were doing there.'

'That is so true,' I agree.

'Also,' she says, 'I just want to be able to sit at the front and laugh at you as you come down the aisle. So I decline gracefully. And before you ask, Rosie says to tell you the same goes for her too. Ta, though.'

We return to our administrative tasks.

I have the names of 14,000 wedding-dress shops within driving distance of me, Mum and Emily, and am to fill in a timetable so that we may coordinate our availabilities. The names and addresses of my 658 aunts and uncles and 34,789 cousins are in the red folder, along with their rankings according to genuine fondness and likely fallout if not invited. I have made mental notes to curse Google maps, God and the many previous generations of evidently indefatigable ancestral wombs.

Eventually, I pluck up the courage to speak. 'This is all . . . great,' I say, gesturing towards the piles of sub-divided folders, bespoke spreadsheets and plans to

annex every spare bedroom on our street to accommodate guests, wishing my voice wouldn't quaver quite so
much. 'Really kind. Really helpful. It's just . . . Well, it's
just that . . . Well, take the churches, for instance. The
thing is – Christopher's got this friend . . . '

I explain about the vicar-friend. I explain about the
church. I explain, thereafter, about the reception. I fall
silent. I have, I know, gone too far and too fast. I might
just as well have let Christopher tell her and let him take
all the flak. The supertanker gazes back at me, stricken.
Emily looks delighted. I expect she has already leaped
forward to my disownment and in her head is spending
my share of the inheritance. I want to tell her it's not that
easy to liquidate three sets of antimacassars and a bread
bin, but realise that now is probably not the time.

'But,' Mum eventually says in strangulated tones,
'how will people get there?'

'Most of our friends live in or around London,' I
say.

'I don't mean your friends,' says Mum waving her
hands angrily as if at some particularly irritating fly. 'I
mean people. The family.'

'They'll be coming from Manchester,' I say.

'Exactly!'

I shoot a furious glance at Emily, who has just settled
back in her chair as if to enjoy the scene in comfort.
'Help me!' says my look. 'Or die painfully.' Eventually,
reluctantly, she leans forward and pats Mum on the
knee.

'It's OK,' she says soothingly. 'It's OK. Wondrous

things have happened since they last left t' mills. Roads have been built. Many of our relatives own cars and can drive on these tarmacadamed miracles. Those that can't can share the cars of those who can and experience the miracle second-hand.'

The great thing about my mum is that although the bursts of horror, fear and fury are terrifying while they last, but they never last long. If you keep your head and don't let fear become your master you can coax her out of them pretty readily. As Emily talks on, maternal shoulders begin to relax and the brow to clear. She doesn't smile, but she no longer looks as though she is poised to tear out the throat of a passing pet.

'It's true,' I continue, entering into the spirit of the thing. 'And for those who cannot secure a spot in one of these horseless carriages, there is yet another wonder – a great iron beast that runs along tracks between the two great cities, transporting the inhabitants of one to the other.'

'Oh, 'tis a rare sight!' says Emily, nodding. 'But they do say that it takes only two and a half of your English hours to cover the vast stretch of land between them.'

'What times we live in,' I say, reverently.

'What times indeed.'

'All right, all right,' says Mum. 'I take your point, you horrible pair.' She sighs, and begins to gather up her papers and magazines. 'But I still don't know how your Great-Auntie Betty's going to get here. There'll be nobody driving from Dundee and she's too fat for a train.'

There is one very easy way to solve that problem, I think to myself, but again – this isn't the time. Fights over the guest list can come later.

'I'm sure we'll find a way,' I say.

Eventually they leave and a blessed silence reigns. Christopher creeps cautiously downstairs. 'I heard the door slam and a car drive off,' he says. 'I came down to check they hadn't bundled you into the boot and were heading for a lock-up by the Thames in which they could beat their definition of sense into you in peace.'

'Actually,' I say, lying on the sofa and signalling for a cold compress to be brought as the tension drains out of me, leaving only a pounding headache in its wake, 'it went quite well.'

'Hmm,' says Christopher. 'We'll see. By the way, I checked my email while I was Anne Franking upstairs, and the vicar's sent us some dates for our marriage preparation classes.'

'Our marriage prepar-whatnow classes?' I say, sitting up sharply.

'The series of classes we have to have with him to prepare us for marriage. The clue is in the title, really. Did I not tell you about this?'

'No. No, you did not.'

'Ah. Sorry. Still, that's the basic MO. We have to fill in a questionnaire before the first one. He's sent it through as an attachment. I personally don't think vicars should know how to do that, but I suppose I must reluctantly accept that times change and we must change with them.'

'Get me another cold cloth,' I say, falling back on to the sofa. 'And wrap it round an open bottle of vodka. I plan to be drunk until September.'

The next day after breakfast we settle down in front of the computer and Christopher starts to read out the vicar's email.

'OK. "Dear Christopher and Lucy – attached is the preparation class questionnaire. Please complete it honestly or you will go to hell."'

'Does it really say that?'

'No. It says: "Please complete this questionnaire honestly. It is designed to identify areas of potential agreement and conflict in a relationship." We've got to fill it in online and send it back to him.'

We click and open with trepidation. The multiple-choice questions fill page after page, like a *Cosmo* quiz on steroids. Unlike *Cosmopolitan*, however, it has sections with headings like 'Values Attached to Beliefs and Practice', 'Expectations about Parenting Roles' and 'Teaching Children Values'.

'So,' says Christopher, reading through further instructions, 'I have to read each statement and then say whether I agree or disagree or whether I am uncertain. I have never been uncertain in my life. What an odd concept. Anyway, then you have to do the same thing and if our answers don't tally, we will discuss our different opinions with William. It is like the homework from hell.'

'Oh, my God,' I say, as Christopher scrolls through the hundreds of questions covering every possible aspect of existence. 'We're going to have to lie so much. Otherwise he's never going to let us get married.'

'We're not lying to a vicar. Unless,' says Christopher, bending forward to read the section on 'Attitudes Towards Sex or Marital Sexuality', 'we really, really have to.'

I take a deep breath. 'Let's get started,' I say bravely. 'Number one. "Having a set of values to live by is very important in my life." I agree.'

'You know that "values" doesn't mean "Creme Eggs", don't you?'

'Just answer the question.'

'I agree too,' he says.

'Good.'

'But which set of values are we going to live by, yours or mine? I believe in the Royal Navy, capitalism and corduroy trousers. You believe in *Coronation Street*, semi-skimmed milk and buying yet more little notebooks that you're never going to use.'

'Let's just get through the questions that are actually there, shall we? I'm supposed to be meeting Gillian this afternoon.'

'Onward, then. "We have discussed and agreed on how we will teach our values and beliefs to our children."'

'Disagree,' I say. 'We haven't, have we?'

'No. But that's going to look bad. Let's do it now. I say, you raise the first one according to your Vs and Bs, I'll take the second one and we'll see which one wins.'

'Agreed. "Question two – I accept that our marriage relationship will come ahead of other responsibilities to my family (parents, etc)."'

'That's an interesting one,' said Christopher. 'How are you going to explain to the man that is going to join us in holy matrimony that I come somewhere below your second cousin eight times removed in your internal pecking order?'

My friend Liz, when she was very small – four, perhaps five years old – once asked her father whom he loved more, her mother or Liz herself. After a thoughtful pause, he replied, 'Your mother – I've known her longer.'

He didn't mean it, of course. He was just trying, in a way that managed to be both primitive and exquisitely clever, to cut a child's otherwise monstrous ego down to size. But at the same time, he had hit on a truth – about loyalty rather than love, but the two march so firmly in lockstep that they are for all practical purposes indistinguishable. It is why we all suffer, at one time or another, but almost always at wedding times, from divided loyalties. I love my mother and my fiancé, but I've known her longer. And yes, she did refuse to let us, as children, have a drink with soup ('soup is a drink and a meal!'). OK, we do have to lay the breakfast table with all the napkins facing the right way, and yes, we're not allowed to use the lavatories until 2 p.m. on Saturdays, so that she 'gets the wear' out of them being clean. Yes, she is, in many ways, a nutjob. But, you know, she's my nutjob. And she's been good to me over the years. Not free with the rehydrating liquids, of course, but that's really a side issue.

We sit in silence for a few minutes, while the ghosts of rows past, almost present and doubtless future rise around us. Christopher chases them all back to the shadows by suggesting that we both put 'Uncertain' and let the vicar sort it out.

'Good idea.'

'Right. Question three . . . '

By the time we get to the last page it is lunchtime and I am starving but Christopher insists that we finish.

'Question eight billion and six—' says Christopher.

'I agree. I want my dinner. Whatever it is, I agree.'

'"I could not under any condition remain married to my partner if he/she were ever to call the midday meal dinner instead of lunch."'

'It doesn't say that – just read me the real one, you turd.'

'"I could not under any condition remain married to my partner if he/she were ever unfaithful to me,"' he says.

'Hey, I do agree!'

'Really? I wouldn't automatically divorce you if you were unfaithful to me.'

'That's *brilliant* news.'

'No, I'm not saying it wouldn't be terrible, it would be the worst thing ever, I'm just saying I can envisage circumstances where it wouldn't be – unsurvivable.'

'Hmm. Well, let me make this very clear now because it's probably not something I should say in front of the vicar. If you were ever unfaithful to me, the question of divorce would actually not arise because I would cut your balls off with a Stanley knife and let you bleed to death where you fell.'

'That's terribly specific.'

'I think about these things.'

'You don't.'

'I do. I plan for every eventuality. Before I go to sleep every night, I run through everything, from what happens if the boiler packs up overnight and there's no hot water in the morning, to how I would kill you if you ever slept with somebody else. We can stripwash at the big sink and I can slice your scrotum off with a single swipe.'

Eventually we finish the thing and send it back to the vicar. That night, Christopher and I lie in bed staring mutely up at the ceiling.

'I didn't know there were so many areas to be incompatible in,' I say.

'We may go down in ecclesiastical history as the first couple ever advised by a cleric never to marry,' agrees Christopher. We lie there in silence a while longer.

'Oh well,' I say, leaning over to kiss him. 'Goodnight, person with whom I have nothing in common.'

'Goodnight, virtual stranger in my bed, goodnight.'

The next morning I am woken, two hours before my alarm is due to go off, by my mother calling for answers to all the points her ever-questing has thrown up during the night. This marks the beginning of a tradition that lasts all week. Although she has accepted the London idea in principle, she is struggling with some of the executive aspects of the plan.

MONDAY

'Hello, it's me.'

'Mum. It's half six in the morning. What's wrong?'

'Nothing. I just have to know – how will the family get there in time?'

'What?'

'How will they all get to the church on time?'

'As Emily noted, it will take most of them around two and a half hours to get to the church. As we are not planning to have the wedding at daybreak but some-time in the mid-afternoon, there is every chance that even the drivers will be able to set off at a reasonable hour and still be able to get there before the vicar starts doing his funky thang.'

She departs to cogitate.

TUESDAY

She rings to enquire how people will find out informa-tion about train times, lodging houses and the precise location of the church.

'I haven't given the matter a great deal of thought,' I say. 'But off the top of my head – how about: the internet, the letter I will enclose with their invitations and – oh, what's the other thing? Oh, yes, *their own brains*.'

WEDNESDAY

'If the wedding is in the afternoon, how will people get fed?'

I should have seen this one coming. My family does not like being too far from food at any point in time or space. It's not that we're a clan of ceaselessly gluttonous fatties – we have a few, naturally, a couple of whom are truly spectacular and possibly coming soon to a Dundee train near you – it's just that the older generation in particular does like to know when and where the next meal is coming from. I think it's something to do with the war.

'Well, with a modicum of forethought, they can travel with sandwiches and buns. The trains will have buffet cars. If they ensure that they arrive in London an hour or so before the wedding, whenever that is ultimately determined to be, they will be able to pop into one of the eateries with which the city – the country's capital city, home to 10 million people – is lavishly supplied. Then, yes, there will be an hour or so inside the church when it will be difficult to obtain food, but if they can just last that out, they will be fed at the reception.'

'Your Uncle Alan likes baked beans.'

'I am not building a wedding breakfast around baked beans. I draw the line.'

THURSDAY

Could he bring some baked beans with him?

No, he could not.

FRIDAY

Have I looked at the caterer brochures she popped through the letterbox at ten o'clock last night, and where was I at ten o'clock last night?

I was in but didn't – ahem – hear the doorbell. I am about to ring round a selection of likely-looking caterers and will call her back with the results.

Would I like her to come round and mend the doorbell at the weekend?

No, thank you, I think it was probably just a glitch.

She rings off. I lie back down and wonder, if I cleared out the understairs cupboard, whether I could sleep there instead? It may be the only way I can get any peace.

An hour later, when my alarm goes off, I roll out of bed, gather up the brochures and start calling round. We know that in an ideal world we would like to invite about a hundred people. We know the church fees. We know the cost of booze, having bought a few bottles of the stuff in our time. Christopher knows, thanks to his experience in booking conferences and corporate do's, roughly the price of a big enough reception venue. The only real unknown is the cost of feeding everyone and once we have all the big financial questions answered, we can start adjusting guest numbers etc. accordingly. Nothing simpler.

So I start calling caterers for ballpark costs of providing a sit-down meal at an as-yet-unspecified-but-central-London location. After the first call, I put the phone down and stare at it for a moment. This must, I reason, be an anomaly. I don't know where my mother sourced these brochures from, but evidently one has crept in intended for people who eat rubies for breakfast and crap gold.

I discard it and call another. This is worse.

I call another. The voice on the other end of the line actually hesitates before naming the price. This can't be good, I think, and so it turns out.

After the fourth call, when it is revealed to me that the prices so far have been just for the food and that the hire of tables, tablecloths, cutlery, napkins, chairs, glasses and, for all I know, the air that people need to breathe while sitting down and availing themselves of all these accoutrements, is extra. I summon Christopher to my study with a yelp.

'You called-stroke-barked, beloved?' he says, bashing his way up the stairs and coming to a halt by my desk.

'Yes. I'm sorry, but I couldn't come to you. I've been

temporarily paralysed with shock at the price of cooked food.'

He picks up a few of the brochures and I tell him what I have been up to.

'Then we won't have a sit-down meal,' he says. 'They're boring and everyone hates them anyway.'

'Hungry people don't,' I point out.

'They won't be that hungry. Apart from your collection of gannets, most people will have had lunch, caught the train in and sat through an hour's holy hush-gush. They won't need a three-course dinner.'

'So what do we give them?'

'Champagne and canapés. And by champagne, I mean any fizzy wine we can lay our hands on that is more or less distinguishable from rat wee.'

Again, this is a brilliant idea. It means people can wander round and mingle instead of being stuck with a functioning alcoholic on one side and a priapic divorcee on the other, as I have been on too many occasions to count. It means we do not have to search for a reception venue that can house tables for a hundred or so. And it means neither of us has to sell all our organs to pay for it all.

But behind all of this I hear the muttering, swelling into cacophony, of a million outraged relatives.

'Champagne!?'

'Canapés?!'

'In London, don't forget!'

'Who does she think she is, Lady Muck?'

Anything more sophisticated than burying your face

in a bowlful of Lancashire hotpot is greeted with suspicion. I dread to think what my uncle Joseph would do if presented with a spear of asparagus wrapped in Parma ham. Try to clear his sinuses with it, I suspect.

But there is no way we can afford anything else, so I keep my reservations to myself and simply prepare myself for tomorrow's phone call.

SATURDAY

'Did you call the caterers?'

'It's 7.08 – never mind. Hi, Mum.'

'Hello, pet. Did you call the caterers?'

'I didn't. Because – no, wait – because . . . Christopher and I have decided to serve champagne and canapés instead of a meal. Well, yes, yes, you can give wedding guests canapés. There's no written constitution in this country. We can all do a lot more things than we actually think . . . But they'll be substantial canapés. I'm not talking about potted meat sandwiches and little cubes of cheese and pineapple on sticks . . . No, I do not think I'm Lady Muck . . . '

The conversation continues long and loudly enough for Christopher to get up, have breakfast and go out for the paper and some peace. By the time he returns, I have good news.

'Mum and I have reached a compromise,' I say.

'Oh yes? By whose definition?'

'If we're not having a meal, she says she and Dad will

take everyone – well, all the family, yours and mine –
for dinner afterwards.'

'No.'

'What do you mean, no?'

'It's my wedding too.'

'I know it's your wedding too,' I say, backtracking
slightly. 'This is just a suggestion.'

'No, I can tell – it's already been decided. Like when
the two of you threw my jumper out just because it had
a hole in it.'

'It was missing a sleeve. And we haven't decided
anything. She's just giving us that option.'

'It's the wrong option.'

'Well, if you really don't want to do it, I'll say so. But
you could say – oh, I don't know – *thank you*, maybe?
She's offering to pay and she's only trying to help.'

'She's trying to muscle in.'

'No, she's *not*. This is what families do. They get
involved. They make suggestions, fling ideas about.'

'It's our day.'

'It's not just our day, actually. It's a little bit for
everyone and I am trying to make sure everyone has
something they want. Unlike you, I don't go through
life actively trying to offend everyone.'

'At least I don't go through life tied to my mother's
apron strings.'

'Oh, I'm *so* sorry!' I say, with quite the best sarcastic tone I have mustered in many a week. 'I didn't
realise that not telling my mother to fuck off when she
offers to take a billion people out for a meal was

being tied to her apron strings. Perhaps I should take a leaf out of your book and start shouting at her the moment she dares to open her mouth and mention the wedding.'

The row continues until eventually we work out a compromise of our own. We agree that we will both continue to be absolutely right and we will both slam the door on our way out.

'Never let the sun go down on your anger.' That's what the wisdom of ages says, isn't it? Rubbish. Just go to sleep and let the worst of it die a death overnight.

The next day I sit at my desk and rehash the argument in my mind. Just as I am about to go downstairs and try my revised version on him, Christopher comes into my study to apologise for overreacting. I forgot – that's number eleven on my list of reasons for loving him. He may get angry, he may appear not to be listening, he may storm out of the house looking as if he's on the hunt for small animals to maim and kill, but he always goes away, turns things over in his mind and if – it doesn't always happen, but if – he agrees with anything his opponent has said, he will march grimly forward and say so. It is deeply, deeply endearing, especially when you know, as I do, that you have been equally if not more in the wrong than he.

'I will tell Mum – and Dad – that we are declining their kind – their very kind – offer and sticking with the canapé plan,' I say.

'Thank you,' says Christopher, and adds after a

pause, 'I'm almost glad to have got our first wedding row over with, aren't you?'

'Oh yes, it was a joy,' I agree. 'Now, if you will excuse me, I have to call my mother and have another one.'

It doesn't, in fact, go too badly. I float the idea of baked bean vol-au-vents and this happy notion, this canapé-based compromise, unites us all once more.

Even better than that, an SOS I put out on Facebook puts me in touch with a caterer that a friend of a friend of a friend used for her wedding and who is, I am assured, both affordable and lovely. Her name is Jo Elwin and both these assertions turn out to be true. I speak to her on the phone. She has a calm and soothing manner. She is free in September. We will let her know the exact date as soon as we can. She will sort out tables and everything else for a sum so reasonable that I make her repeat it three times. She says she is willing to have a bash at baked bean vol-au-vents but if people could be persuaded to live without them, that wouldn't be the worst thing that had ever happened in the history of mass entertaining. She assures me that everything will be fine. I make her repeat the prices once more. I could cry with relief, but I think, like Annie, I had better learn to pace myself.

So instead, I curl up on the sofa with a good book and a soothing cup of tea. Christopher, evidently sensing that a fragile peace has stolen over the place, comes downstairs to destroy it.

'How are you feeling?' he says, throwing himself

down beside me. My drink splashes on the book as it jumps out of my hand and I lose my place.

'I was fine,' I say.

'I've had a thought that will cheer you up,' he says.

'Do tell.'

'At our wedding, we are the bosses, yes?'

'Sort of. Yes.'

'If we are the bosses, we make the rules, yes?'

'Yes.'

'I make this rule: There Will Be No Dancing at Our Wedding.'

My lack of dancing skills has been a potent source of amusement to my friends and family for years, but I at least am within the bounds of normal British arrhythmia. Music does not call to me. It does not move through my soul, wakening primal instincts and unleashing its wordless and transcendent power upon me. I know I can't reliably keep to the beat, and so as soon as the lights go down and the volume goes up, I slink quickly off to the side.

Christopher, however, is appalling. He dances as if he has never heard music before. He dances as if he has never met his own body before. But he does it. Like a soldier going over the top, he steels himself and goes out on to the dance floor as if this time he will wrestle his contrary and recalcitrant limbs into submission and release at last the John Travolta within. It is a sight to harrow the soul. The first time my friends ever witnessed this phenomenon was at a wedding. The sight of my then-boyfriend, red-faced, sweating and throwing his tortured shapes with a look of suffering concentration that most of us reserve for the exam hall or driving tests, gradually drew a crowd of concerned onlookers, wondering if they should step in to help or try and find out which medications he had missed.

On the way home, I made him promise that he would never do it again. 'You have many great talents,' I said. 'You can read and distil in under an hour the mightiest, most complex tome into a handful of basic tenets that even I can understand. You can identify any politician, historian, monarch or pundit from this or any other age from a hundred paces. You have the thickest head of hair of any man I've ever met. But the dance – the dance is not in you. Let it go. For your own sake, as much as that of anyone who ever has the misfortune to witness you, let it go.'

'I can't do it, can I?' he said.

'You truly cannot. And you never will be able to.'

'It's over, isn't it?'

'It is.'

He looked like a man who had just been given his freedom after a lifetime of wrongful imprisonment.

And now here we find ourselves inadvertently putting together a wedding that will preclude all possibility of the nightmare unfolding once again.

'You see,' he says, putting an arm round me and sighing with satisfaction, 'it's all beginning to tie in.'

So it is, I think. Perhaps, I think, as I watch the tea soaking into the crumpled pages of my book, it will all come right in the end.

CHAPTER SIX

'Look at this!' Gillian says, waving a sheaf of paper at me. 'Rhiannon thinks that Romeo's cousin Tybalt – she calls him Table – was a good cousin because he "probably did all the shopping". Is it any wonder I drink?'

It is the beginning of the Easter holidays – or, to put it into the new calendrical terms in which I now think of everything, five-months-before-the-wedding. I have gone round to Gillian's at her insistence to stand vigil over her, make her lunch and ensure she does all her essay marking before she goes off for a week to Marrakesh.

'You can put Rhiannon down and come and sit at the Tybalt,' I say. 'Lunch is ready.'

As we eat, she asks me how the wedding planning is going.

As I have done almost nothing since finding the caterer three weeks ago, I parry. Christopher is drawing up a shortlist of reception venues, I say. My sister is coming home for Easter Sunday and, after dinner *en famille*, she, Mum and I are going to draft a guest list. I can see Gillian is unimpressed with the level of industry. I decide to deflect her.

'And, of course,' I say, gazing neutrally into the

middle distance, 'I asked my sister to be bridesmaid but she refused. So . . . '

Gillian looks up from her lasagne, the shadow of suspicion already darkening her eyes. I press on.

' . . . will you do it instead?'

The shadows deepen to pure horror.

'You couldn't . . . You wouldn't . . . You won't make me do it, will you, Luce?' Gillian begs. 'I mean, thanks for the offer and everything, I'm deeply honoured blah blah but – you won't make me do it, will you?'

I torture her for a few more seconds, carefully pitching my expression somewhere between tears and anger, but I can never endure her suffering for long. For we both know how much I am asking of her.

Agreeing to be someone's bridesmaid is a truly perilous undertaking. First there is the risk that the bride will take this opportunity to revenge herself for all the real and imagined slights that have festered between you over the years and put you into the kind of dress that amounts to assault. I saw a great deal of this in my twenties, when the love-hate relationship between female friends tends to be at its most potent, barring, of course, the early days of primary school. You are falling out over men rather than ownership of Victoria Plum lipgloss, but the feelings run no less deep. I once went to a wedding where the twenty-four-year-old bridesmaids – perfectly nice-looking girls, all four of them – had like all of us long lost, as hostages to the years, the waiflike figures and air of innocence required to pull off the orange satin frocks, overlaid with eighteen yards of lace, that the bride had decreed they were to wear. They looked like giant throat lozenges. Furious, depressed throat lozenges.

Even if the affianced is not malicious, there is the extreme likelihood that she will turn into Bridezilla and irrevocably crush the spirits of everyone around her. I went to another wedding in which the tyranny of the bride was everywhere apparent: in the fiercely enforced colour scheme (the ushers were chosen by hair and eye-hue), in the creased, frightened face of the MOTB, in the vicious hissing sound that punctuated the day as Bridezilla doled out further instructions to various exhausted lackeys who had apparently misinterpreted subsection (b) of clause 128 of their thirty-four-page briefing notes sent round by courier three weeks before. She made her sextet of bridesmaids lose half a stone each before the big day, a command she ensured would be followed by informing them that she would be having their dresses made in the 'correct' size and if they couldn't fit into them on the day they, and they alone, would be responsible for Ruining the Most Important Day of Her Life. She booked them all in for a full body wax at the local beauty salon (I am almost impressed by a woman so committed to matrimonial perfection that she even annexes her friends' pubic regions), forced them to design and decorate their own headgear (out of pre-approved materials), get their hair cut and highlighted in harmonising shades the day before at the same hair-dresser (none of which, incidentally, she paid for) and stay over at her house for THREE DAYS before the wedding 'to centre her'.

I went over to say hello to one of them at the wedding and she was a broken, whimpering shell of a woman. Why did they all go along with it, I asked, as she related her experiences in tremulous tones?

'It began with just little things, like agreeing to wear the same nail varnish,' she whispered. 'You'd wear a specific nail varnish if your oldest friend asked you to for her wedding, wouldn't you? And then it was "Would you like to make your own headbands and fascinators? I've brought you the stuff!" We all sat round the table and did it together and it was quite fun. We were like frogs in cold water. She kept turning the heat up very gradually and before we knew it, we were being boiled to death.'

I am pleased to relate, however, that my informant did have sex with three of the ushers before the night was out, though, so at least the full body wax was worth it.

On top of these dangers common to all, Gillian also has a specific bridesmaid-related psychodrama.

For when Gillian was a fourteen-year-old Smiths and Consulate fan, spending most of her time in Camden market wondering what she could pierce next, her cousin got married and appointed her favourite young cousin chief bridesmaid. Before Gillian could assemble fake papers and leave for Cuba, she was fastened into a peach satin and net confection, her hair teased into a bouffant that threatened to develop its own gravitational field and sent down the aisle in high-heeled satin shoes. Even today, Gillian can barely walk upright in heels. Then, she had to stagger her way down like a newborn foal.

A few weeks later, her mother was presented with a picture of Gillian in all her finery – her face, just visible amidst the peachy frills and tangerine flounces, a mask of bitter resignation and weary acknowledgement that this day, this vision, this horror has been captured for eternity. Sure enough, her mother put it in pride of place on the mantelpiece, and many is the time since that her mother and I have gathered before it to laugh ourselves sick. Once, about ten years ago, when Gillian was well set on her chosen path of dating only the lost, the medically unsound and/or the irretrievably insane, she finished with her latest social misfit and he immediately began stalking her instead. Soon afterwards, he burgled her mum's house, stripping the shelves, drawers and photo albums of everything that contained an image of his beloved Gillian. The only one he left was the bridesmaid photo.

On top of that, she points out, if I am an old bride – and statistics as well as a variety of friends and relatives have made clear that I am – then she would be a positively geriatric bridesmaid. After the age of about twenty-five, following the bride down the aisle is tantamount to walking the streets with a sandwich board saying 'Ovaries starting to rattle like marbles – free to a good home' and drawing to you every fat old perve, functioning alcoholic and forty-year-old virgin within eight postcodes like iron filings to a magnet.

We both know the truth of all of this. So I give in, and tell her that of course I won't make her be my bridesmaid.

'Oh,' she says fervently, 'thank you, Luce. I won't forget this, honest I won't.'

'But,' I add warningly, 'I am calling in all my chits. For all the times I've ever covered for you at school, at home, at work – for all the times I've held your hair back while you vomited over my shoes, for the time you made me tell Miss Beynon that I ate your homework, for making me test with your lunchtime Diet Coke Mr Maskell's claim in biology that the human swallowing reflex is so strong that you could stand on your head, drink and it would still go down your throat, and finally and most especially for the time you almost persuaded me to try a tampon up my back bottom – you have to be around to help me. From now until the wedding, you have to consider yourself on call 24/7. My mother has mastered email and I need to have somewhere to run. You are to be at my side throughout the preparations on the day. You are to fend off with one hand all those who would seek to distress me while the other supplies me with all the booze, fags and drugs I need to get through the day.'

'You don't smoke.'

'I will almost certainly start.'

'OK'

'You understand? This is not a tyrannical bride talking, this is your friend in her darkest hour of need.

And in return, I will not make you my bridesmaid. That's the deal. OK?'

'OK,' promises Gillian, wiping up the last of the tomato sauce with a piece of bread and popping it into her treacherous mouth. 'Let's start now.'

'Now?' I say, startled. 'What with?'

'Well, let's see . . . ' says Gillian as she gathers our coats and bags, sweeps us out of the flat and on to the high street. 'What have you done about your dress?'

I cringe. We are standing in the middle of the pavement and I have nowhere to hide. 'Nothing.'

I am scared of the very idea of The Dress and want to avoid having anything to do with it for as long as possible. I am aware that this approach is flawed, but honestly – is there any part of a wedding more fraught than choosing the right frock? It is, after all, the equivalent of wearing a banner that says: 'Please pass judgment on my body and my taste as I parade slowly in front of you all and record whatever appalling misjudgments I have made on a hundred different digital cameras and then post them in various public arenas online so that they may haunt me in perpetuity. Thank you.'

Of all the component wedding parts, this is the one I have been furthest from picturing over the years, the one I am least prepared to decide upon. I mean, I have seen dresses in shop windows and magazines occasionally and thought, That's nice, or more often, That's disgusting, but I have never made the mental leap and envisioned myself in one. When girls in the playground played Brides (which used to merge seamlessly into Princesses every lunchtime if the smell of spam fritters, always a severe depressant to even the most lively childish imagination, had dissipated enough. Brides to Princesses – if the boys had spent a little more time taking note of such potent elisions instead of tearing each other's guts out on the tarmac, perhaps there would not have been so many terror-struck grooms to be sighted in later years), I always volunteered to be in the congregation. Or audience, as they called it (again, boys, the clues were there).

Everyone was happy with this arrangement. After all, there is nothing more reactionary than a pre-pubescent child and it was tacitly understood that Princess Brides could only have long, preferably blonde hair. Mine was short, and kept so by a monthly session of Mum wielding the kitchen scissors and telling me not to move in case she missed again and Mr Spocked my other ear. Add to that the fact that she made me wear school uniform – dark-green tunic, white blouse, black shoes – to a school that didn't have one and, looking back, I realise I was lucky that I even made it to audience status.

'Nothing?' says Gillian, recalling me to the present.

'Nothing,' I answer.

This is not entirely true. When the engagement was first announced, my friend Charlotte, knowing how much I hate, hate, hate shopping for anything except food and books, if not quite the depths of my terror at the prospect of having to make a personal statement in satin, rang me up and offered to lend me her wedding dress. Charlotte being a woman of both impeccable taste and suitably short stature, I leaped at the chance and raced round to her flat. She drew her beautiful raw silk dress out of the wardrobe and we managed to get it almost all the way up to my knees before it jammed.

'Oh yes,' she said. 'I forgot. I lost two stone before my wedding. Sorry.'

I don't tell Gillian for the same reason I didn't tell my mother, sister or Christopher about it. It makes me want to kill myself. And then have another doughnut.

Gillian rolls her eyes in predictable dissatisfaction. 'Right,' she says, 'come with me.'

It turns out that there are 82,000 dress shops in the high street, all of which have been utterly invisible to me until now. As Gillian drags me unwillingly towards a clutch of shops I have known all my life, a branch of Pronuptia suddenly pops up between them where no branch, I could swear, ever existed before. It's like something out of Harry Potter.

'How do you know about these?' I ask Gillian as we barrel into Previously Invisible Outlet No. 2,134.

'I like to be prepared for every eventuality,' Gillian replies. 'What if I meet my soulmate on a Friday night and we decide to get married the next day? I'll need to be able to put everything together quickly, won't I?'

As ever with Gillian, her logic is unassailable. If it wasn't, I wouldn't be able to assail it anyway, because she has darted away to examine the racks of dresses at the back and disappeared amidst the frothing folds.

'Where are you, Gill? Are you OK?' I say, padding softly forward and trying to catch a glimpse of her skinny frame. Thankfully, Gillian has enormous feet – throughout her adolescence she resembled nothing so much as a golf club with spots – and I spy one of them poking out from under the rack.

'What are you doing back there? Come out!'

'No, you come through! They've got rows and rows of stuff back here – it's like the Himalayas in tulle!'

By the time I fight my way through, she has divested herself of her clothes and is wearing about six of the dresses at once.

'I couldn't decide which one to try first,' she beams. 'I thought this would save time. But—' she adds thoughtfully as she begins to list dangerously to the left, 'they are unexpectedly heavy and I think I'm about to fall over.'

She is right and she does. I take most of the dresses off her and she regains the perpendicular.

'OK,' she says, smoothing down her hair and shaking the remaining dress back down over her hips, 'now it's your turn.'

In this shop and many – oh, so many – more she pulls confection after confection over my head and stands me in front of a mirror so that we can examine the results together. Time after time, our two reflections gaze unhappily back at us.

'I don't understand it,' says Gillian in growing perplexity as we move further down the high street. 'We've seen some completely munting dresses, *sure*, but we've seen some lovely ones too. Dresses that practically sing with the promise of beauty and transformation. But you just – what do you do? – you just . . . silence them all.'

'I've been telling you for years, I don't suit any clothes,' I say. 'Nothing works. That's why I don't bother. I have a mind for sin and a body for word-processing.'

'Let's give it one more try,' says Gillian, rallying. 'In here.'

She dives through another door that has suddenly materialised between Monsoon and Burger King. I shuffle in after her, to be greeted by blaring Muzak and a shop stuffed full of young women trying on dresses. Really young women. And not trying on bridesmaid dresses but the real, bridal deal. There can't be one of them a day over twenty.

Gillian frowns. 'Call the Office of National Statistics,' she says. 'Because this lot are going to play havoc with the numbers. Let's go.'

Back on the street we take a collective deep breath. This coincides with my ingestion of two Nurofen and Gillian has to thump me on the back until I recover. This takes a long time as it is like being hit by a piece of string.

'That last shop didn't count,' decides Gillian as we walk on. 'We'll try in here instead.'

This is a place with pretensions – crowding the floor is an abundance of fake French-style furniture ('Louise Quatorze,' murmurs Gillian as we enter), swagged chandeliers hang from the ceiling, almost bumping crystals with extravagant sconces crawling up the gold-embossed wallpaper and we sink up to our ankles in the spotless cream carpet. After the interior designer left, however, there was, apparently, no money in the kitty to allow the stocking of decent dresses. Everything is made of Persil-white polyester, eighties lace and net so coarse and stiff that it would be better employed protecting seedlings on the allotment.

Despite this, it is hugely, ruinously, ridiculously expensive and when the owner comes over, she sneers so hard at us that I fear her head is about to fall off. After running a contemptuous eye over me and staring in fury at Gillian, who has once again hurled herself to the back of the shop and is hooting gently to herself as she examines the merchandise and its price tags, she returns to glaring at me.

'Appointment!' she barks.

My early training means that I freeze and start massing apologies to cover whatever I have done wrong whenever a middle-aged woman raises her voice near me. Gillian, knowing what I'm like, skids over to my side. She, fortunately, has no such childhood ghosts to contend with and, despite a physique that would ensure that she was killed by the first blow if things ever reached that point, has always been terrifically ready for a fight.

'I'm sorry?' she says.

'Appointment!'

'No,' says Gillian, giving a soft, polite, I-don't-mean-to-embarrass-you laugh. 'My name is Anastasia Romanov and this is my friend and bride-to-be, Lucy Mangan.'

'You must have an appointment.'

'Ohhh,' says Gillian, her face brightening. 'The sun of realisation breaks through the clouds of my incomprehension! Thank you! Apparently,' she says, turning to me, 'we must have an appointment.' She turns back to the woman, along whose eyelids starts to run a flutter of concern, and says solemnly, 'We do not have an appointment.'

There is a pause. The woman hesitates but stands her ground.

'You can make an appointment now.'

'We can?' says Gillian, clasping her hands together joyfully. 'Are you sure you can take the time' – she throws a brief but sweeping and unmistakable glance around the client-free shop – 'to peruse your diary for us?'

The woman swivels on her heel and marches wordlessly to the counter. Gillian trots gaily along beside her.

'It's just that we would hate to delay you if you've got people coming. Time-travelling refugees from 1982, perhaps. Or a convention of sufferers of rare allergies to natural fibres? In fact,' she says kindly, slowing her pace, 'please don't trouble yourself – I'm sure we'll find another way of spending our money without paining you in this way. I think, judging by her expression and the fact that she is manhandling me towards the door, that my friend wishes to leave. We'll see ourselves out. Tatty-bye!'

I put a safe distance between us and the now-puce saleswoman before I let go of Gillian's arm. 'Why,' I groan, 'why must you do it?'

'(a) Because she was a cow, and (b) because it's fun,' replies Gillian.

'Well, it used up my last stores of energy,' I say. 'I need a coffee and a rest.'

'It shall be so,' says Gillian.

Over our coffee, I remember Gillian's explanation for her in-depth knowledge of the region's wedding-dress emporia.

'You know how you said you like to be prepared for the day you meet your soulmate,' I say.

'Mmm,' says Gillian, although I can't be sure this is to me or to the forkful of chocolate gateau she is eating.

'Do you actually believe in them – soulmates, I mean? Because I don't. I think boyfriends, partners, whatever, are like dresses – you try them on, discard the hopeless, then pick the one you like best and that best suits you out of the rest, and hope that with a few nips and tucks, maybe a couple of larger alterations, it will see you through.'

'No,' says Gillian decisively. 'I believe there's someone out there who's just right. The human equivalent of bespoke, tailor—' She chokes suddenly with excitement and starts gesticulating wildly. Eventually she regains the power of speech. 'That's what we'll have to do with your – you know, actual dress. Because looking for off-the-rack for you is a waste of time, Luce. There is something definitely wrong with you. You look terrible in everything. I always thought you were just being lazy or depressive when you said you couldn't get clothes but now I see that you were, if anything, understating the situation. You'll have to get a dressmaker.'

'How do I get a dressmaker? Isn't that like trying to find a blacksmith or a flint-knapper or something?'

'They'll be in the Yellow Pages or on the internet,' says Gillian airily. 'Although you'd be better off getting a recommendation from someone, I suppose. You don't want to end up with a person who sews like a thumbless monkey. And knowing you, you would.'

I sigh and add another bloody, pain-in-the-arse chore to my list. It is like the hydra monster my dad used to read to me about from our Ladybird book of legends. Whenever you cut one head off, two grew in its place.

I also add a camping stove and another deadbolt to my sanctuary under the stairs.

'Excuse me, dearest Christopher, but would you mind removing your dinner plate and assorted mugs from the coffee table so that I may start tidying the room, please?'

'But of course, beloved fiancée. I apologise for my oversight and will attend to the task forthwith.'

'That would be most marvellous and I thank you from the bottom of the largely calcified organ known as my heart.'

Today is the day of our first marriage preparation

class and we are trying to get in the right frame of mind to face the vicar.

We do quite well until I am in the bathroom and Christopher starts banging on the door.

'What are you doing in there?' he shouts.

'You might want to rephrase that question.'

'You know what I mean. You've been in there ages. Normally, I'd applaud this as an attempt to behave like a normal woman, but we need to get going.'

'I'll be out in a minute. I'm just cutting my toenails.'

'Now? Why?'

'I want to look smart for him.'

Christopher opens the door. 'You're insane,' he says. 'You're not going for a job interview, it's a marriage preparation class with William.'

'But it is a vicar,' I say.

'He,' Christopher sighs. 'He. He's a vicar.'

'Whatever. I've never met one up close. So I feel I need to make an effort.'

'If you're not down in ten minutes, I'm going without you,' he said. 'And that won't look good.'

Nine minutes later, I am down and we set off. Half an hour and a train ride later – most of which Christopher has spent giving me the lowdown on the niceties of Anglican theology ('Don't call him "Father". Don't genuflect. And remember that while Catholics believe the bread and wine is the actual blood and body of Christ, Anglicans believe you should gloss over all that and just have a nice cup of tea and a bun after the service instead') – we are at the church. I start to go in the front door.

'Not in there!' Christopher cries, yanking me back.
'What? Why not?'

'He doesn't live there,' Christopher says. 'He lives –
almost like a normal man – in the house next door.
With his wife and children.'

'Blimey,' I say. 'Is that allowed?'

The vicar's real front door is tucked away in a little
alley running down the side of the church.

'I'm curious,' says Christopher as he knocks. 'Did
you really think that he would just be standing there in
the middle of the church, waiting for us?'

'I sort of think of them as there all the time,' I say.
'You know, in a state of suspended animation between
services, just waiting for the next religious kick-off. I
imagine that a bell rings and then they start saying
Latin and then a congregation appears.'

'You make me want to weep tears of blood,'
Christopher says. 'Try not to say – well, anything – to
William over the next hour or so, would you?'

'Trying to silence the little wifey already, eh?' I say.
'That's nice. That's really nice.'

The door opens and there stands Father – no,
the Reverend – William Anglican-Godsquad. Black
trousers, black jumper, white dog collar, big smile.

'Welcome!' he says, Protestantly. 'Come in, come in!
Can I get you anything? A cup of tea? Coffee? The sal-
vation of your immortal soul?' All right, he doesn't
actually say the last bit, but I feel it was definitely
implied.

I say I am fine, but Christopher says he would love a

cup of tea, so after William has led us through to his sitting room, he disappears to the kitchen to make a pot. 'Make yourselves comfortable!' he says as he goes. 'I'll be back in a moment with some tea and biscuits. And God!' (No, again, he didn't really.)

The room is full of ancient, delicate furniture – survivors from another age. Time, I suspect, runs differently in rectories. We sit gingerly, on a very beautiful but austere-looking sofa.

'Don't fucking break anything,' I mutter to Christopher.

'I fucking won't,' he mutters back.

William returns a few minutes later and sets down a laden tray. After introductions, biscuit distribution and a bit of light chit-chat, he settles further back in his chair by the fireplace and gets down to business.

'So,' he says, smiling benevolently at us both. 'I've had a look through your questionnaires and I always like to spend the first meeting with any couple having a look at any sections where there were a lot of questions that each of them have answered differently.'

He brings forth a disturbingly thick sheaf of papers.

'I think,' he says kindly, 'we're going to be here for some time.'

'All right then,' he says ninety minutes later, finally laying aside 'Effects of Backgrounds' (we have now Discussed the Ways in Which Our Families Solve Problems and How This May Affect Our Problem-Solving) and picking up 'Financial Management'. 'Here

Christopher says he is undecided and you, Lucy, disagree with the statement that "My partner and I agree on how we spend our monthly budget". Could you tell me a little about what's going on there, do you think?'

'Yes,' says Christopher with certainty, 'It means that I think we should actually spend some of it on going out occasionally, buying new stuff now and then and generally not behaving as if we were seventeenth-century mendicant friars, and she thinks we should save all of it, sell all but our most vital vital organs and then open another five-year, tax-free, fixed-interest, twin-carburettor, pine-scented bond with the proceeds. She is – if I may lapse into the vernacular for a moment, William – not right in the head.'

'I *am*!' I protest. 'I just like to feel secure. I wasn't brought up to waste money.'

'By "waste" she means "part with for any reason other than the procurement of basic food and shelter",' Christopher interjects. William motions him to be quiet. I note the gesture carefully for much future use.

'Do you think that you could try to compromise?' suggests William. 'Because, while it is very important that you, Lucy, feel safe and secure, it is also very important, as Christopher, I think, was trying to say, that you build a cache of shared experiences together over the years.'

'But we have,' I argue.

'Watching *Friends* repeats together doesn't count,' says Christopher.

'We've been to Hampton Court,' I remind him.

'Did you enjoy that?' asks William.

'I did,' I say. 'I mean, I think fourteen pounds a head is a bit steep, given that you're not allowed to take any choice pieces of Tudor plate away with you, but it was fun.'

'Why?' asks William.

'Because he,' I say, pointing at my beloved, 'tells me all about history and stuff as we're going round and it makes me fancy him all over again.' Christopher nudges me sharply in the ribs but William is delighted.

'You see!' he says. 'What could be more valuable than a reminder of why you fell in love with someone in the first place!'

The vicar has tricked me, I think. Bravo, vicar. Bravo.

'So,' he continues, pressing home his advantage. 'Perhaps you could make a pact to go out and do something together perhaps once a week? Once a month?' he amends quickly as he sees my appalled expression.

I relax. Once a month is feasible, I agree. 'But he's still not to buy branded noodles,' I stipulate. 'Because they all taste the same.'

'That sounds fair,' says William. 'Christopher?'

'I disagree wholeheartedly with the sentiment,' Christopher said. 'Batchelors Supernoodles embrace a spectrum of delicate flavouring to which Sainsbury's own cannot even aspire, but for the sake of future marital harmony I will bow to the practice.'

'Wonderful,' says William. 'Onward!'

The next section is the one about marital sexuality.

William doesn't read out any of the questions but clears his throat and says, 'I gather from this, Lucy, that you are going to have a baby.'

Christopher and I look at each other. It must have been late in our form-filling and, in our punch-drunk state, we must have ticked the wrong box. 'I'm not pregnant!' I squeak. Oh my God, I can't believe I've just said the word 'pregnant' in front of a vicar. I should have said 'with child' or 'expecting'. A polite cough, comedy sound of a slide whistle, anything.

'Ah! Good, good,' says William, evidently relieved. 'Not that children aren't a blessing, of course, but still – as you've got this far, always nice to get things in the right order, eh?'

The rest of the questions pass by in a blur. He gives us homework – we each have to draw a graph recording our emotional peaks and troughs over our respective lifetimes, before and after we met – that he will look at next time, and eventually we wish him a happy Easter, say our goodbyes, and stagger out into the street, across the road and into the nearest pub.

'Two double vodkas,' I say to the barman. 'And Christopher, what are you having?'

'The latest in a series of small strokes,' he says, leaning his head back against the wall and closing his eyes. We drink until closing time.

Easter Sunday, and the Mangans (Christopher is at home trying to meet three work deadlines he forgot about. Or so he claims) are celebrating in the traditional manner – by working our way through the chocolate treasure trove my sister and I have just found on the annual egg hunt. That's right – although Emily and I have a combined age of sixty-five, Dad will still hide those little chocolate eggs wrapped in different-coloured foils in the garden on Easter Sunday so that we can hunt for them after our meal. When we were very young, we used to collect them in tiny trug-shaped baskets. Emily, being three years younger, never noticed that when she bent down to pick up a new egg, her basket would frequently tip and the previous one would fall out. Thus as Emily hunted industriously for eggs, I would simply follow her round the garden, retrieving the lost as they fell behind her. It is our entire relationship in microcosm.

My parents would stand, weak with laughter, propping each other up in the doorway. Perhaps it is the remembered happiness of these early days spent marvelling at their lazy/idiot children that has kept the tradition alive all these years. All I can say is that it seemed an eminently sensible practice to me. And I always gave her half of them afterwards – it was the labour-saving aspect I was after, not extra chocolate. Now she is older, she is wiser and I have to find the eggs myself but it is still pretty good fun.

This year's hunt is another riotous success – though it does involve a moment of high tension when it looks as if Dad has hidden only one prize Big Egg instead of the two mandated after the Great Creme Egg Controversy of 1983. War is averted when Emily spies a telltale flash of red and yellow under the cotoneaster behind me, although she nearly breaks my legs getting to it.

As we sit gloating over our spoils, Mum insists that we help her clear out the chest of drawers in the sitting room, because it is at least seventy-two hours since she has done something dusty, boring and pointless.

Fortunately, she has forgotten that the bottom drawer contains all our family photos, going back three generations. I don't mean the drawer is full of them. In fact, our entire collection can and, indeed, does fit into one old shoebox, which is what happens when said three generations of family have been (a) remarkably ugly and (b) possessed of the belief that having your photograph taken amounts to a breach of the eleventh commandment, Thou Shalt Not Show Off. We do not even possess a single fancy portrait or professionally posed shot of a proud Victorian clan, just a haphazard assortment of snapshots clearly taken by people rendered daring by advanced inebriation to show for our past and present existence.

'But,' as my sister once pointed out, 'think what we would have to show if only we could box up crippling Catholic guilt and an all-pervasive sense of failure! We'd have to turn Manchester into a warehouse.' So that is some comfort.

Still, we take them out and pore over the sparse collection with pleasure. There's the one of my five-year-old Dad and his three-year-old sister, tiny beaming faces belying the fact that, according to my father sixty years on, they hadn't eaten for four weeks and took it in turns sleeping in the family clog at night.

There's one of me looking mutinous in a leotard. 'All the girls in your class were going to dancing classes,' says Mum, sighing. 'We sent you along in the hope that you'd make friends. The teacher sent you back with a note saying you just stood in the corner going purple, trying to get out the book you'd hidden in your knickers. You'd think we'd have learned to search you after the piano lessons.'

'If you'd wanted me to make friends, you'd have been better off not cramming me into school uniform and sending me to a school that *did not have a uniform* every day.'

'You're not still going on about that, are you?' says Mum.

'On my deathbed I will still be going on about that,' I reply. 'And if not on my deathbed, then certainly on yours.'

Then we find the little booklet of black-and-white snaps from 12 August 1972. Mum and Dad's wedding day – the culmination of ten on-off years of courtship, the story of which Emily and I instantly demand to be told again while we cram our mouths with chocolate eggery.

'Oh, you've heard it all before,' says Mum, busily sorting the rest of the drawer's junk into charity-shop and bin piles.

'Tell it again, tell it again!'

'It were 1806,' says my dad suddenly from the depths

of the sofa. 'Your mother were fourteen, nobbut a slip of a lass wi' blonde hair and laughing, bloodshot eyes. I were fifteen and manly . . . '

'You were fifteen and seven stone wet through,' says Mum.

'Fifteen and manly,' continues Dad, who has long ago learned to ignore such interruptions. 'We lived at opposite ends of the old mill town of Preston. She were the doctor's daughter, I were the clinker-covered son of an offal fettler and a whippet-grinder. Sometimes I'd catch a flash of her blonde hair as she went past our hovel on her pony to Our Lady of Perpetual Succour Convent School for Posh Folk of a morning, but well I knew that our different stations in life would prevent us ever meeting . . . '

'Oh, for goodness' sake,' says Mum, shaking her head as Your Father's Nonsense shows no sign of abating. 'We were boy and girl next door. His father was a bookkeeper and mine – well, mine was a doctor. And there hadn't been an offal fettler in Preston for years.'

Emily and I too long ago learned to ignore these interruptions.

'So how did you meet?' we say to Dad.

'It were the Parched Pea Purveyors' annual winter ball,' he says, smiling dreamily, wreathed in happy memories. 'Me sister, Imelda Mary Philomena Bernadette, had been crowned that year's Miss Black Pudding at the May Fair so she were t' guest of honour and the rest of t' family were invited an' all. Me and me forty-two brothers put on us finery and painted our feet black so no one could tell we'd only one shoe between us. Me mam made herself a beautiful dress out of pigskin, wi' a flurry of burlap ruffles at the bottom so she could clean the floor as she walked. She never like to be idle, did our mam. Her eyes fell out as she put the last stitches in, but we pawned the privy and bought her some new ones before the ball.

'We arrived at the dance hall. Everyone who came were given a piping-hot firkin full of parched peas. The smell of vinegar and promise lay thick upon the air. The magnificent oak doors swung open to receive us, and I stepped straight on to a firkin of parched peas some daft bastard had spilled on the floor and went arse over tit into the grand piano. I broke seventeen bones and had to carry me own arms in a bag to the doctor's house. I rang the bell with my nose and collapsed on the front doorstep. Your mother opened the door, looked down at the poor, crumpled heap of humanity lying there before her and bent over me like a ministering angel. I watched, teetering already on the brink of undying love for her, as her tender lips parted and she said, "What are you doing there, you stupid bugger. Gerrinside and I'll call me dad." I had been teetering on the brink of love for her for years. Now, at last, with the sound of her voice ringing like a belt sander in my ears, I fell. We were married just ten short years later, when her father was dead and couldn't object any more.'

According to Mum, whose head by the end of this is ready to explode with the pressure of the necessary corrections building within, the true facts of the matter are these:

They went out for a couple of years as teenagers, until she went away to university – 'And,' she adds, with a sniff of disapproval that echoes down the generations, 'your father went to drama college in London.'

Then, once they had both graduated – or Dad, as his mother had put it, 'got over that guff' – they got back together.

'And then he proposed,' says Mum.

'How?'

'Can't remember.'

'Dad?'

'No idea. Drunk.'

'You proposed while you were drunk?'

'No, she was.'

'I was not. Anyway – then we got married.'

'But how? What did you do? How did you organise it?'

She looks bemused. 'There wasn't anything to organise in those days. Everybody just knew you were getting married and turned up.'

'What, you didn't even send out invitations?'

'We didn't have to. We had Mrs Beasley. She told everyone. And I made my own dress, bought my hat in Owen Owens, your two grandmas spent the morning making ham sandwiches, we got married in the afternoon, ate the sandwiches, and everyone went home. Dead easy.'

*

Dead easy. The words ring hollowly in my ears for the rest of the day. For, once we have finished clearing out the drawers, Emily has the bright idea that we should start compiling a draft guest list.

'Just the family part, obviously,' she says. 'You can choose your friends yourself.'

'Gee, thanks,' I say.

Mum and I actually made an abortive pass at this a few weeks ago, after I'd made the mistake of telling her that Christopher and I had crunched some numbers and address books, and come up with a figure of a hundred guests as one that could feasibly be fed, watered and accommodated on the day. After watching me hunched with twitching pen over an exercise book, knee deep in scrunched and shredded paper, my mother had sighed and said, 'I don't know why this is so difficult. It's just All Family and Closest Friends.'

'I can't do All Family,' I said through gritted teeth, 'because, technically, that comprises the entire population of Preston, half of Garstang and a fair portion of Grange-over-Sands. Poverty and lung disease just aren't cutting the swathe through the generations they once did.'

'That's true,' Dad had agreed, wandering through from the sitting room in search of either a pie or the lavatory. 'Remember how we had to stop off at the TB clinic to wave at your Maureen's lot before we got to the reception? Eighteen of them in there at the time. Saved us a bomb.'

Then – forgetting for a moment that it is quite

important that I do not sustain any major disfiguring injuries in the months before my wedding – I had made some remark to the effect that All Family and Closest Friends was not a sensible division anyway, because some of my friends were closer than some of my family, at which point the situation quickly degenerated.

But now, as Emily digs out names and addresses, we tacitly agree to put this failure behind us and start afresh.

Two and a half hours later, we have agreed on three names. Emily's, Mum's and Dad's. And at least two of those, in my mind at least, are still up for review.

Another eighteen hours pass and we have the bulk of the task completed.

'OK,' says Emily, as we pop another handful of aspirin each and lean back in our chairs to stretch our cramped and aching muscles, 'let us take the remaining points of contention in turn. First off – are we inviting or banning children?'

It takes us another two hours to decide that children cannot be accommodated. Not of friends, and not of cousins.

'Won't your friend Anna expect to bring Ellie and Peter?' worries Mum. 'Peter is your godson after all.'

I reassure her that this is one person at least whose delicate parental sensibilities we need not worry about upsetting. The first thing she did when she got the invitation was book a babysitter for twenty-four hours so she could come to the wedding and drink herself daft. She was horrified when I suggested children might be invited. She all but backed me against a wall and threatened bodily harm if I said I wanted them to come.

We decide to take this robust attitude as our exemplar. And when I think how boring our wedding will be for children – no dancing, nowhere to run about, no streams or ponds to fall into – I feel less bad about striking them off the list. Let the little buggers stay at home and be happy. Wish I could.

'Second,' says Emily, 'are we going to attach conditions to Uncle Alan's invitation? One school of thought says yes, for health and safety reasons, the other says it would be an infringement of his civil rights, and yet another argues that if a sixty-two-year-old father of three needs to be told not to set his farts alight, he perhaps shouldn't be coming at all.'

We agree that he can come but must be flanked by two of his boys at all times.

'And finally,' says Emily, 'we come to the Great-Auntie Betty Conundrum.'

Now, I am very fond of my Great-Aunt Betty. The name alone is enough to secure my affections, but on top of that she has a variety of personal eccentricities that have added much gaiety to my life over the years. To wit:

1. She's Scottish.
2. She eats only cold toast. By which I mean she eats other things as well – stovies, cullen skink and coal, mostly – but if it's toast, it has to be cold.

This goes utterly against any known form of sense or reason and drives anyone who sees her do it completely bonkers. It is the economy of the gesture I admire. You don't need to make a big song and dance to assert your individuality or independence from the mores of your family, your society or your species. You just have to eat cold toast. It's genius.

3. She has a bosom grown men could ski down. It starts at her neck and just keeps on going. Her GP once told her that she could have a breast-reduction operation on the NHS. 'Och,' she said, hitching the fourteen stone of mammarian tissue off her waist, 'I wouldnae do that, laddie. Could you no just make ma feet a wee bit bigger so I dinnae keep falling over?'

4. Every week she holds a whist drive for seventy in her two-up, two-down house that can barely contain her bosom, never mind guests. Every Thursday you can walk in and see old-age pensioners perching on pouffes, mantelpieces, Formica picnic tables, wedging themselves between bookshelves, and all but hanging on to the light fittings for the chance of winning sixpence and a cruet set. We don't know where she gets the sixpences. We don't know where she gets the cruets.

The problem is, she has eight sons and they would all come with her. You can't stop them. They move as a pack. They eat everything they see, break everything they touch and speak in Glaswegian accents thicker than porridge. Even the family hasn't understood anything they've said since their voices broke.

'I can't have her – and them – Mum. I just can't. Not only would they take up nine spaces on the list, but they'd eat enough for thirty. It can't be done.'

'But if you don't invite her, you can't invite Great-Aunt Eckythump.'

That's not her real name. It's what we call her because that's all she ever says – or said, before she stopped speaking to us when Emily threw up over her signed photo of Frankie Vaughan twenty years ago.

'An invitation might heal the wound,' suggests Mum.

'She's a witch. I'm healing nothing.'

And on and on it goes, far into the night. Dad brings us bacon sandwiches and coffee in relays. As he puts a new trayful down, he says, 'Have you got room to invite all the vegetarians we know?'

We all turn to look incredulously at him.

'The short answer is – no. The long answer is – no, and why would you want us to?'

'Because then,' he says with feeling, 'I wouldn't have to have them round for dinner again for ages. We could do them all with one fell swoop. I'd be free.'

Poor Dad. He is a man of an almost inhumanly small number of prejudices but he cleaves tightly to those he has. And vegetarians are top of the list. 'They expect a separate meal when they come round here,' he will mutter darkly. 'But do they cook normal people a steak when you go round there? No, they do not.'

He articulates few desires as he shuffles through life – I believe he has barely nudged into double figures over the course of his six and a half decades – and I wish I could fulfil this one, but it cannot be done, I say sorrowfully.

He nods his head understandingly. 'It were just a thought,' he says. 'Just a thought. Am I coming, by the way?'

He is, I say.

'You'll let me know what time?'

I will. He nods again and shuffles off to bed. When the tray is empty, we do likewise. I lie in my creaky bed, in my old bedroom (Emily has commandeered the double in the spare room) and think of Christopher, deadlines safely past by now, probably lying content-edly on the sofa listening to the BBC News channel with Patrick on his stomach and I hate him very, very much.

CHAPTER SEVEN

The next morning, however, I see the list lying on the table and am not only flushed with a sense of triumph but seized with a firm sense of purpose. I announce that I am off home to compile the Closest Friends element of the thing, and then the world's most troublesome guest list – or list of the world's most troublesome guests, whichever you prefer – will truly be complete.

They wave me off with shining faces, golden trumpets and pennants fluttering in the breeze. I get home, open the door and step straight on to a pile of catshit someone has evidently waited until after Christopher left the house to deposit, but I do not let it deflect me from my goal. I chuck my shoe into the garden, wipe up the mess, spray some provenly useless disinfectant/repellent combo thing round the place and sit down at the table.

I open my address book, gird my loins and begin the painful process of dividing my friends into the invited and the non-invited. Under normal conditions, appraisals of friendships are carried out unconsciously and with infinite subtlety over a lifetime, as different friends come to prominence or fade into the background according to their and your fluctuating needs. As is becoming clearer to me by the day, however, weddings do not fall under the heading of 'normal condition', and so, armed with a budget and space restrictions, I erupt into the middle of that gracious dance like a sabre-wielding tyrant, hacking down innocents on each side.

As the afternoon's brutality wears on, I begin to long for ye olden days. Then, as I understand it, everyone was born and died in the same place – usually a picturesque if insanitary stone cottage – and the entire village was one big clutch of knottily interrelated peasants, drawing their water and cholera from the same well, and tilling the same wretched soil to tug a living from the reluctant earth. Cousins married cousins, and the resulting five-legged babies could be used to form the basis of a travelling sideshow that gave the family a useful additional revenue stream. But, alas, those halcyon days are gone.

Now, families are scattered to the four winds. People move away to go to university, to get jobs, to take advantage of the million billion opportunities that present themselves, now that the limit of the known world is not circumscribed by how far your donkey can travel before the feudal lord drags you back to help with the annual flint-knapping or the fear of the warty witches in the encircling forest. And once we find our new homes, we start to build new tribes, made up of people we want to be with rather than have thrust upon us by accidents of birth.

And they call it progress, I mutter bitterly as I sit

there hour after hour, scoring through names, adding new ones, making little heaps of definite invites, maybes, and maybe-after-all-not, feeling guilty and liberated by turns. At one point I hit on the idea of drawing Venn diagrams – a circle for friends I have known for over ten years, a circle for friends I hope to know for another ten, and anyone in the overlap goes into the definites pile. Or a circle encompassing all friends and one for 'didn't invite us to their wedding though', and the overlap is banished to the maybe-after-all-not heap. After that, I try the kidney test – if X were to need a new vital organ, how far would I go to help them? Visiting them in the hospital? Fund-raising? Submitting to a blood test? Anyone who gets as far as tissue-typing goes in the definites, anyone I wouldn't do a fun-run for is a maybe.

As I look at my little heaps of names, I fervently hope none of my friends gets ill. It will be a very time- (and organ-) consuming process. I realise that over the last decade or so I have already refined the ore of my acquaintanceship, and gradually got rid of most of the dull, draining, dutiful and occasionally outright toxic friendships you forge in your younger years. This social smelting means that, with a very, very few exceptions, all my friends are proper friends, all are people I like and admire, all people who mean something to me. They are all people I like and in many cases love.

Love is such a stupid word, of course. It is asked to cover such a ridiculous range of feelings that it becomes almost useless. There should be as many words for love as there are people we – uh – love. I love both Christopher and Gillian, for example, but only with the former does the word encompass both 'affection' and 'frequent desire to tear his fucking throat out'. 'I love Gillian', on the other hand, comprises not just 'affection' but 'fascination' and 'occasional heart-stopping concern for her mental well-being and physical safety'.

Eventually I whittle it down sufficiently to allow me to merge it with the family list and still come in at around a hundred guests. I sit back, sigh with relief at a job well done and phone Christopher.

'Read them out then,' he says, so I do. He interrupts occasionally for clarification.

'Uncle Joseph – is he the one who thinks his teeth will go soft if he watches ITV?'

'It's Channel 4, but yes.'

'Auntie Pat – is she the one that's the size of a bean or a house?'

'She's the size of a bean. Emily's going to bring her down in her pocket and we'll only need to pay for half a canapé. Number ninety-eight – Sarah from law school, ninety-nine – Miles from primary school. I thought when I was seven that I would marry him, actually. He had one of those little bits of hair that always stuck up at the front and he never tried to pee on you in the playground.'

'I'm glad you've lowered your sights since then.'

'And finally, I give you Mr one hundred – my friend Greg, from university.'

'Well, that all sounds splendid,' says Christopher.

'Why, thank you, fiancé,' I say smugly. 'It took a while, but I got there in the end.'

'There's just one thing that occurs to me,' he says. 'I hardly like to mention it, but I feel perhaps I should . . . '

'Well, what is it?' I say impatiently. 'I've got other stuff to be getting on with after this, you know.'

'It's just – tiny, tiny thing, I know – but you haven't included a single friend of mine in your drawing-up of the list of people who are going to bear witness to our spiritual union.'

'Don't be ridic—'

I run my eye down the list again. I turn it over. I turn it back again. He is, it seems, entirely correct. Hmm.

'There appears to have been a small oversight at this end,' I say.

'There does, doesn't there?'

'I'll take another pass at it and see if I can clear a few slots for your people instead, shall I?'

'Could you?' he says politely. 'That would be extremely kind, and I won't have to throw you out of the window when I get home.'

I hang up and settle down to work again. By the time Christopher comes home I am able to inform him that I have a new, rebalanced guest list coming in at one hundred and twenty and a new, unbalanced budget that involves me starting a nocturnal dog-walking business and him selling his sperm on the internet.

'Splendid,' he says, taking his coat off and hanging it carefully on the floor. 'And what is our next task now that this Herculean labour has been completed?'

'Let me consult the Good Book,' I say, pulling Emily's folder towards me. 'According to this, it is to visit and shortlist reception venues. But what the Book doesn't know is that I also still have to find someone to make me a dress.'

Ever since I put the word out, after Gillian's high street epiphany, that I was looking for a dressmaker, I have been inundated with suggestions and recommendations. Not one of them has worked out. The first woman I went to burst into tears when I told her I wanted a wedding dress and spent the next three hours clutching my hand and explaining that she had only gone into the sewing business because her husband had abandoned her and their two children and gone back to Skopje with the au pair.

'I mean,' she gasped hysterically, 'have you seen Skopje? All the twenty-two-year-old blowjobs in the world aren't going to make THAT worth while!'

'Maybe she takes it up the bum,' my friend John said when I told him about it later. There are glimpses into the male psyche that I could do without sometimes.

The second woman was a recommendation from my slimmest, richest friend, so it was my own fault for going anywhere near her. She looked me up and down, smiled the thinnest, wintriest of smiles and, waving a pale, brittle hand, said, 'I'm afraid this is not . . . a frame . . . I'm accustomed to working with. You would, I suspect, be better served . . . elsewhere.'

I wish I had had the courage to run round her beautifully appointed shop full of equally pale, brittle women, ringing an imaginary bell and shouting, 'Unclean, unclean!' Failing that, I wish I'd kicked her in the face. But, in an excess of cowardice that I'm sure will haunt me for years, I did neither. I scuttled out and comforted myself with the thought that one day she will crack, eat a cupcake, put on four stone overnight and kill herself. And very nice it was too.

The rest had either been too far away, too expensive, too hesitant ('What is it you want?'), or too scary ('I'll tell you what you want'). So I am stuck.

Christopher says he has already drawn up a reception shortlist. We decide that we will combine visiting them with our trip to John Lewis on Saturday to order invitations.

'Efficiency, thy name is us!' cries Christopher.

I look at the lever-arch file before me, whose three-inch-deep mysteries we have barely begun to penetrate, and I really do hope so.

Saturday dawns. Christopher is in town already, having got up early to go to a lecture on the Suez crisis by Professor Something-or-Other, who is apparently *the* man you want to go and listen to if post-war, canal-based snafus are your thing. As they are not mine, I declined to accompany him. And I'm having it written into my vows that I do not have to do so after marriage either.

I have had breakfast, a shower, fed the cats, found my shoes, dried my hair and am running only twenty minutes late, a personal best.

I get to the station just in time to watch my train pulling out from the platform. With a quarter of an hour now to wait, I wander into the newspaper shop on the concourse for a desultory flick through the magazines, until the proprietress fires me a look that goes some way beyond hate. I contemplate staggering backwards clutching my chest and crying, 'You have killed me, you have killed me! Put away your dagger eyes!' but decide that the few moments' entertainment this would afford me would not outweigh the near-certainty that she would step smartly out from behind her counter and push me under the next train.

So I contemplate the noticeboard outside. Futons for sale. Holiday homes for rent. Painters, decorators and plumbers for hire for whom no job is too small. Yoga instructors who specialise in relieving lower back pain, only to send your entire body into spasm when they give you the bill. Masseuses offering sensuous back rubs and inventive approaches to spelling in the privacy of your own home. And finally, a brown and white printed card that says: 'Local dressmaker Jean Barnett. Wedding and christening gowns a speciality,' followed by a mobile phone number. Well, I reason, why not?

I dial. At the other end of the platform, a phone starts to ring.

'Hello?'

'Hello. Is this Jean Barnett?'

'Yes,' says a friendly middle-aged voice. 'Who's this?'

'My name's Lucy – I'm looking for someone to make

me a wedding dress and I saw your advert on the station noticeboard . . . Listen, you're not the lady I can see talking on the platform now, are you?'

She is. We walk towards each other. I'm taking the echoes of *Brief Encounter* as a good omen. Perhaps she will be my sartorial soulmate. We chat for a few moments and arrange an appointment at her house for the next day. As her train arrives she pushes her business card into my hand.

'Those are my numbers,' she says as she boards. 'Ring me tomorrow!'

The card says: 'Jean Barnett. Dressmaker. I Can Create Beauty With Your Shape.'

'I've been waiting for you all my life!' I shout as the train pulls out of the station. It is at this point I realise that Jean's train is also my train. Ah well. Never mind. Maybe if I hang around for another quarter of an hour the universe will send me £5,000, a florist and a set of trained bridesmaids too.

I regale Christopher with the news when we meet in the Strand. He regales me right back, with a summary of his lecture. When we are sure that we have bored each other equally, we set forth to begin our venue tour.

The first three places are deemed too far away. I can walk only eighty yards at a stretch in heels on my best day – if I am hampered by nerves, a dress and Spanx pants so tight they will be forcing my legs to scissor with every step, the potential for disaster is overwhelming. And we decided weeks ago against all hiring of cars, after the first company Christopher spoke to reeled off a set of fees so vast that he said, quite genuinely, 'I'm sorry, you've misunderstood – I don't want to buy the cars, just rent them for a couple of hours.'

The fourth is fantastic – an enormous hall with a vaulted roof and great stone fireplaces. If it was a wedding for 500 and we were minor European royals, this is where we would come. As it is, our guests would be rattling around like marbles.

'Nobody can afford to fill this place any more,' sighs our guide, a superbly debonair, immaculately dressed fifty-something man whose voice has barely risen above a whisper as he has shown us round. 'All we get' – his face twists in a spasm of disgust – 'are corporate events. Lawyers. Bankers. They try to climb inside the fireplaces, they throw bread rolls at the paintings and pass out in the shrubbery.'

We make sympathetic noises. He gives a small bow of acknowledgement.

'But once,' he says quietly, with a small, coy smile and a sweetly confiding air as we lean in to hear him, 'I spent the week secretly passing water under every bush out there, so I knew that, wherever they fell, they would be lying in my urine till they woke up.'

There is a moment's silence while I ransack my brain for the suitable response. Christopher rallies first.

'Ingenious,' he says, 'and, I would imagine, terribly good for the soil too. Nitrates, you know.'

'Ah,' says the man, delightedly. 'Are you a gardener too?'

'I dabble,' says Christopher, who wouldn't know a plant from a hole in the ground, which is pretty much your basic starting point for gardening, but the subsequent chat keeps us safely away from any more untoward revelations until we are safely back on the street again.

'Well,' says Christopher, as we find a café in which we each hug a reassuring cup of tea to our breasts, 'I think we will decide to regard this incident as a superb example of the idiosyncratic British eccentricity that once made this country great. And hope we never get invited to a corporate event at Micturition Hall. Agreed?'

'Agreed.'

The final place on our list is Dr Johnson's House. We turn down a side street off the Strand, jink right a bit, left a bit, and suddenly we are in one of those tiny, archaic-and-almost-forgotten pockets of London. Flat-fronted Georgian buildings rising serenely around a hushed and cobbled courtyard, graciously blanking out the sight and sound of the vulgar modern world that still rushes on six feet and a million miles away.

'Dr Johnson was the man who wrote the first dictionary,' says Christopher as we mount the stone steps – from where I am already envisioning speeches being made – to the front door and walk in.

'I know *that*,' I say, rolling my eyes contemptuously. 'It was in *Blackadder*.'

A very posh, very beautiful woman shows us round. She and Christopher talk architecture while I try not to break anything. Once we have been all over it, she leaves us to get the feel of the place for ourselves.

'I think this is the one, don't you?' says Christopher.

'Oh yes,' I say. 'It's perfect.'

It really is. It's lovely to look at, it's got a wonderfully calm, peaceful atmosphere, and there are lots of little rooms where people can hive off and talk together, as well as a bigger one where people can gather for speeches if it's raining and we cannot use the court-yard.

We tell the beautiful woman – whose name is Jessica – that we want to hire it. She quotes a price that hurts but does not cripple. 'And when is the wedding?' she asks.

'Sometime in September,' says Christopher. 'We'll fix the exact date with the vicar next week.'

'Will we?' I say.

'Yes,' he says. 'Our second class is on Wednesday, remember. It's easier face to face than by email.'

We make out a cheque for the deposit and, flushed with success ('A church, a guest list and a reception! We're playing in the big leagues now!'), we head for John Lewis.

It should have been so simple, I think to myself that evening as I sit fuming on the sofa. We had discussed the matter beforehand and discovered with relief that we were both firmly anti cut-outs, colours, deckled edging, gold linings, tissue paper, and firmly pro sloping copperplate scrawl on a plain white folded card like you see in films.

Couldn't be easier. And all I had said when we saw one in the flesh, so to speak, was, 'We need to tweak it just a bit – maybe have it on cream instead of white, or a slightly more modern font – so that it tells people, "Yes, it is, technically, a big, central London wedding but it's not grand, or posh, and there's no big dinner, dance or marquee thing going on so everybody can just relax and you don't need to wear a hat."'

Christopher frowned. 'And the invitation is supposed to say all that, is it?'

'Yes.'

'But I thought we were putting a letter inside saying what would happen on the day?'

'We are.'

'So why can't we have exactly this?' he said, pointing to the crisp, copperplate rectangles on which we have notionally agreed. 'Why do we need your "tweaked" version?'

Looking back, I think this is where I first felt the gulf between us – possibly between all men and women – begin to open up. 'Because they have to match – to reflect – what's going on. They have to convey the – the mood of the wedding.'

'If there is anyone on the guest list capable of reading a letter saying, "Church at three, reception fifty yards down the road afterwards for champagne and canapés, everyone out by nine," and then becoming hopelessly confused by its encasement in an invitation bearing an unexpectedly elaborate font, can I suggest we remove them from said guest list immediately?' he said.

'There's no need to be sarcastic,' I said, struggling to get out from under the seventeen enormous ringbinders that had me pinioned to the sofa. 'Let's just look through some more and see if we can find one that suits us both.'

We looked. Minutes passed in increasingly strained silence. We found nothing.

'I don't even know why you're so bothered about the invitations anyway,' I said, in an ill-judged attempt to break the tension. 'They're supposed to be my job. You're supposed to be the groom, remember, regarding me from a safe distance with a bemused yet tolerant eye.'

'They're going out with my name on,' he said.

'But everyone knows they're the bride's domain,' I said. 'If your friends despise them or they're not right in some way, it'll be me that takes the blame.'

'It's not a matter of blame,' he said, loudly. 'I want to have a say in my own wedding.'

'A say!' I cried, standing up in a sudden fury so the binders slip to the ground with a series of slow thunderclaps. 'A *say*? You've got the church you wanted, the vicar you wanted, a non-Catholic service AND you're in charge of the music. I'm just doing the admin. I'm not a bride-to-be, I'm your sodding PA!'

'I've chosen the church, the vicar and the music because you're (a) functionally godless and (b) so

profoundly bereft of all cultural knowledge and educa-
tion that you are virtually indistinguishable from a
mud patch.'

'I want the other invitations!'

'Fine,' he said, stepping over the folders on the floor
and striding to the lift. 'Do what you like. You and your
mother organise our wedding however you want.'

'Don't you bring my mother into this!' I shouted
after him as the lift doors opened. 'She hasn't even
mentioned the invitations!'

The doors closed and Christopher vanished. I bent
down, hiding my tears by picking up the fallen files. A
shop assistant came over to help. 'Sorry about that,' I
gulped.

'Don't worry,' she said. 'Last week, we had a couple
come in here and start hitting each other with the
Letterpress. At least we didn't have to call Security on
you.'

And with that comforting thought, I headed home.
Christopher was not back by the time I got there, so I
busied myself in the kitchen, tidied the house, did some
paperwork and then threw myself down on the sofa to
fret and await his return.

Patrick diverts me from the business of internally
rehashing the argument by jumping up on to my lap
and demanding to be petted. As he rolls over to encour-
age and facilitate belly-rubbing, I hear Christopher's
key in the lock.

'Uh-oh,' I say to Patrick. 'It's ba-ack.'

Christopher comes into the sitting room and bows deeply. 'I am sorry for becoming testy about the ultimately insignificant issue of Invitation Font,' he says, 'and for Bringing Your Mother Into It, especially since, as you point out, this is one of the vanishingly few occasions upon which we have not been delivered of her opinion.'

'I'm sorry for being narky too,' I say. 'But I've baked my apology in the form of a fish pie. If you want some, it should be ready in about ten minutes.'

'Is it a fish pie with pastry on top, like in books, or fish pie with mashed potato on top like in my grandmother's pie? They are almost equally good, but in my mind mashed potato secretly has the edge.'

'It's mash.'

'Ah!' he cries triumphantly. 'We are meant to be together after all!'

He flings himself on top of me on the sofa and does raspberries into my neck until I threaten him with burned pie if he doesn't let me up.

Later, as we are finishing dinner, he asks me if I settled on a choice and ordered the invitations.

'No,' I say. 'I decided on the font and the card and everything but then they asked me if I wanted engraved text – that's the proper, posh one, where you can feel the bumps and see the grooves on the other side – or thermographed, which is a sort of fake engraving. They add a special kind of powder to the ink, heat it and it dries raised. So you get the bumps but not the grooves on the other side.'

'Hmm,' he says. 'How nearly interesting.'

'Or, finally, we can have ordinary printing, which is just – well, printing.'

'So?'

'My brain just shut down. It was one choice too many for that day. And when I couldn't decide on that, I started doubting all my other choices so I told them just to forget it for now and I'd come back another day. With—' I say, bending my head low to my plate, 'my mum.'

The extended disco version of the Great Invitation Row goes on far into the night and includes an extra chorus of 'Why Are You So Dependent on Your Wretched Family' and 'Don't You Talk To Me Like That' that really gets the blood pumping and I think could go straight to number one if we can just get it into the shops in time for Valentine's Day.

When I finally get to bed, Christopher as usual falls asleep immediately – and I do mean immediately. I once watched him carefully every night for a week and he is actually unconscious before his head hits the pillow. He reads sitting up and then he pulls his pillow to the horizontal with one hand, puts his book down on the bedside table with the other, and as he lets go of both he falls asleep. And a fraction of a second later, his head reaches the pillow. My theory is that only men can do this because only men's minds are made of impregnable strongboxes into which they neatly pack the day's detritus, drop the lid and don't open it again till they've had a good eight hours of the dreamless. Either that, or they are like cockatoos – as soon as it is dark, they just instinctively shut up and go to sleep. I must try throwing a napkin over Christopher's head tomorrow and seeing if it works.

Even on a good day I am jealous of this gift of immediate somnolence. Like most of my more-or-less demented gender, I consider the first hour in bed to be a time for anxious reflection – on the things left undone that day, the things to be done tomorrow, the things I have completely forgotten about and should have done last week – after which fretful but necessary time I can begin the welcome task of lowering myself gently down into sleep. At times like tonight, when I know I am in for three or four hours of reliving arguments and building brilliant alternative cases for the prosecution before I am purged of all tension, I want to bash his head in with a brick.

I lie there and work my way through the issue.

There is no right or wrong about invitations. Or canapés, or flowers, or orders of service, or anything else he's planning on having feelings about. But somebody's got to have the casting vote. And it should be me. And why? Because I'm the fucking bride, that's why.

And the accused would say, if he were awake instead of snoring deeply like the thirteen stone of manflap he is, why should the bride get the final vote? And I would say (by this stage I am pacing before the jury in the courtroom in my head) that the word 'bride' by definition means 'woman'. And the word 'woman' means 'Someone who knows, instinctively and without necessarily being able to put it into words, although this in no way lessens the utter rightness of her position, what needs to be done'. Because while men move through a world that seems composed entirely of binary choices – 'X good, Y bad. Like A, not like B. Do X. Choose A' – women (and yes, I generalise hugely, because I think you'll find that at three o'clock in the morning inside my own brain and courtroom I can do exactly as I goddamn please) pick their way through a webby mass of possibilities, consequences real and imagined, subtle contradictions and probable ramifications.

This feminine modus operandi arises, I go on to point out to Imaginary Christopher – who I am pleased to note, looks significantly more contrite as well as more effectively persuaded than the real thing ever does – from the innate and unbreakable habit of seeing things from everyone else's point of view as well as (nay, I add with a flourish that dazzles Imaginary Christopher yet further, sometimes even better than!) our own.

You think we come to our decisions lightly, I say, lowering my voice to compel the court's attention, you think we make our choices – of anything, from clothes, to train seats, to invitations – whimsically. And in fact we have ourselves so well trained that we almost think it too. But actually, ladies and ladies of the jury, if you take a moment to unpick the next decision you make

– be it ever so large or small – you will find that you
have automatically factored in dozens, possibly hundreds, possibly thousands of actual and potential
variables, considered the opinions of and impacts on at
least ten other conscious entities from pets to parents,
via the neighbours, the milkman and the frog doorstop
which always seems to regard you with a malevolent
and judgmental eye, before voicing the results.

Meanwhile, I say, my voice gathering in volume as I
move towards the climax of my speech, men just point,
say 'Want that' and fall asleep. It is a wonder anyone
gets married at all, but while they do, all that which I
have laid before this courtroom is why women should
get the final say in all matters pertaining to The Big
Day. Thank you. I rest my case.

CHAPTER EIGHT

Somehow, *somehow* it is May before I manage to fix an appointment with Jean. Blame can be laid, I suspect, at the door of my continuing secret terror of The Dress.

But today is at last the day when I face my satin nightmares and meet my dressmaker. I am running around the house trying to remember where I last saw the hairdryer and my shoes. Christopher is peering out of the kitchen window at our next-door neighbour. She has seventy-two children and is busy screaming at them to get in the car to go to school. 'Don't make me effing come up there!' she shouts in a voice that could wake the dead. The kids' eardrums must look like Swiss cheese.

'I've never wanted to be a Victorian Methodist social worker more,' he says as I pass through the kitchen for the fourth time. 'I would walk in there and tell her I'm taking the children to New Zealand.'

'You can't blame her for losing her rag sometimes,' I say. 'Look at me – I've only got to get myself down the road for half ten and I'm already running late. Have you seen my shoes? Or the hairdryer? And have you fed the cats?'

'I haven't seen your shoes, the hairdryer is in my study because I tried to use it to blow the dust off a yard of books, and the cats and I are involved in a silent struggle for dominance so I am refusing to feed them until ten-seventeen. The arbitrary nature of the time being a vital part of my authoritative stance.'

'You can't assert your dominance by refusing – oh, look, there are my shoes – to feed the damn . . . I really haven't got time for this. I've got to go. With wet hair. Feed the animals or you'll be dealing with decapitated mice all day.'

Half an hour later, I am at Jean's house. She whisks me upstairs to her room. 'This is my den,' she says.

There is an enormous bed, on which are set out a variety of wedding magazines. A half-dressed, flesh-coloured dummy stands in the corner. Although I know I am in one of the few places where this is to be expected, even desired, the effect can never be less than unsettling. There is a trestle table covered in swatches and towers of tiny plastic drawers, some of which are neatly filled with hooks, eyes, press studs and other bits and pieces which my lack of haberdashery qualifications prevents me from naming, and an array of slightly larger boxes from which spill a million different-coloured threads, ribbons, pieces of lace, brocade and bindings. It looks as if everything knows its place but is more interested in what's going on next door.

'Right,' says Jean. 'Sit down and tell me this – do you know anything about what you want?'

'No,' I say helplessly.

'Well, do you know if you want it to be white?' she asks.

'Yes! I mean – I don't. I mean – I don't want it to be white.'

'You see!' Jean beams delightedly. 'You do know something! Now, let's have a look through these magazines and see what else you might like.'

We sit and stare at page after page of fatless freaks. Most of them are sheathed in incredibly simple – and simply incredible – close-fitting dresses that make them look like shards of ice. Shards of ice broken off Nicole Kidman. Shards of ice broken off Nicole Kidman after she'd been on a 180-day lemon juice fast. One breaks with convention by wearing a fishtail skirt so tight that I hoped someone on the shoot had been appointed to check her feet for gangrene.

'You have to be able to walk,' I said, peering at it. 'That's pretty much your only job on the day.'

There are a few that provoke gasps of horror rather than awe. One looks like a cross between Bo Peep and an explosion in a tissue factory, and another is sporting a huge, frothing dress with red satin roses scattered all over the skirt – not just a meringue, the full pavlova. But by and large, my problem is the exact opposite of the one Gillian and I had in the high street shops. Everything looks too good. I cannot begin to imagine anything on any of these women looking right on me. Whether this is a failure of imagination or a laudably realistic attitude, I do not know, but either way I am beginning to fret.

Jean interrupts my unsoothing reverie. 'Look at this,' she says, showing me a photograph in which someone appeared to have confused a diamanté bikini with appropriate bridal attire. 'That's a wedding dress, can you believe it? I think,' she says, shaking her head and sighing, 'her mother must live abroad.'

There and then I hitch my wagon firmly to Jean's star. Because my grandmother used to do this – make up stories about people she saw in pictures or in cafés and, in the instant of saying them, coming to believe they were true. I think it comes with age, or maybe boredom, this capacity to conjure up twenty little parallel lives a day and I'm quite looking forward to when it's my turn. Anyway – I loved my grandma and she always steered me right on important matters. A blaze of hope, nay of certainty, that Jean will do the same rises up inside me and fuels a sudden spurt of mutual decision-making.

By the end of the session, we have decided the following:

1. Because I am a midget, we will keep things very simple. No lace, no embroidery, no nothing.
2. There will, however, be a corset. Because I am a midget with a noticeable tummy and an un-noticeable bust, and because Jean assures me that a corset is the means by which these positions can be reversed.
3. There will not be a veil.
4. Mum will come with me next time and help me choose between pale gold, pale oyster or pale

coffee-coloured materials because I have been staring at swatches for forty minutes now and my eyes have gone funny.

5. There will be an A-line skirt and a broad band of material running across the top of the dress and around my shoulders, thereby effectively inverting my body shape and making me look like a Proper Woman.

'It's the right kind of dress for a London wedding,' says Jean, when we have completed our decision making.

'But I'm not having "a London wedding",' I say. 'I'm just having a wedding in London. My family aren't from London, and they may assault me if I look as if I am.'

'It's not their day,' says Jean. And that is the end of that.

I set off home. Before I even reach the bus stop my mother rings to find out how the fitting went. She is delighted to learn that her presence is requested at the next one.

'What date will that be?' she says, and I hear her mighty diary swing open. This time next week, I tell her. 'I was going to buy my new bra then,' she says. 'But that can wait till Thursday.'

'Are you sure?' I say with concern. Mum's annual bra purchase is a big day for all of us.

'Aye,' she says. 'I had to buy extra knickers after our luggage got delayed on holiday, so my whole schedule's off anyway.'

That's a relief.

On the bus, I decide to ring Anna, my best friend from university. When I told Jean she wouldn't need to make a bridesmaid's dress, she had looked very surprised. I explained that my two first choices had turned me down and that as I hadn't been too bothered about having one in the first place, I had given up the idea. She nodded understandingly but said that in her experience most brides were glad to have some company down the aisle.

'Even,' she added, 'if it's just a little 'un.'

And that got me thinking. Jean knows more about brides and weddings than I do. And I do have a goddaughter – well, she's my godson's sister so it amounts to the same thing – Ellie, Annas's firstborn. She is very young – three, I believe – but she will be at least six months older in six months' time, so maybe it would work?

So I ask Anna if Ellie wants to be a bridesmaid.

'Not at the moment,' says Anna. 'She wants to be Daddy's briefcase so she can go to work with him in the morning.'

It is then I remember that it is still less than three months since Anna had another baby (Peter) and she can right now therefore respond usefully only to direct questions. Questions like 'Where have you put the baby?' and 'Do you know you have a bra on your head?' and 'Did you mean to leave your shirt/front door open?'

I rephrase. 'Would Ellie like to be a bridesmaid at my wedding in September?'

'Oh, oh I see! Oh, gosh, well, do you know, thank you, that's so lovely, but I don't think – hang on, if I can just get him latched on to my – where did I put my boob? – that's better – I don't think she could cope. I think she's just a bit young. And trust me, you don't want to be worrying about anyone other than yourself on your wedding day. I had two tiny ones, do you remember? And they were fine, actually, but we didn't know that and it was just too much stress. So although I'd love to see her do it, I think you shouldn't have her. Does that sound bad? You can have her, she'd be delighted, but she might wreck everything. But I shouldn't take the chance away from her, should I? I'm being a terrible mother. But if she never knows, it won't matter, will it? Unless she finds out years later and really hates me for it. It could undermine the whole basis of our relationship if she finds out I lied to her – sort of lied, I mean, it's lying by omission isn't it . . . '

This continues for some minutes before I can get a word in. But eventually I manage to tell her that she is right, Ellie probably is too young and she is very kind to think of me rather than her daughter. 'You may be a terrible mother,' I say, 'but you're a very good friend.'

'Oh, thank you,' she says gratefully. 'As long as I'm managing to be something, somewhere, other than a milk-dispenser and shit-scooper, I'm happy. See you in September. It'll be nice to leave the house.'

I sit back, pleased. Overall, it is a weight off my mind. OK, I won't have the comfort of a friend travelling behind me, but neither will I have the expense or the bother of coordinating extra dress fittings for everyone or worrying about anyone other than myself on the day. And Christopher. And Mum. And the light sprinkling of functioning alcoholics on the guest list. But not bridesmaids. So that's good.

'So,' says William, smiling as we settle ourselves carefully into the spindly sofa thing once again, 'how are the preparations coming along?'

We agreed between ourselves beforehand not to mention the invitations. Or the guest list. Or the music. So Christopher just says that everything is fine and we hand over our life charts, plotted with the emotional highs and lows as best as we can remember them, as promised.

'What on earth is that?' I say as Christopher gives his to William.

'What's this?' Christopher says incredulously as he catches sight of mine. 'What's *that*?'

Mine is an intricate mass of annotated dots and crosses in all the colours of the rainbow, several of each decorating every year of my life. Every significant emotional event is there, large or small, good, bad or ugly. From the death of Frisky my pet rabbit when I was seven, to the first time I realised that, contrary to Mum's insistences, I *could* have a drink with soup (I was twenty-seven), to buying my own flat. From the terrible hiatus between the withdrawal of the old Milky Way and its replacement by the Flyte bar, to the sight of Gillian being used as a bridge between two desks so that Lauren McMaster could practise the high jump indoors, all had been diligently marked, ranked and analysed.

Christopher's, on the other hand, is a strikingly minimalist affair. At zero to five years old, he was, apparently, 'Happy. Enjoyed countryside.' At five to ten years, he was neither happy nor sad because 'Still living in countryside but disliked school. Also disliked children. And being child.' At eleven to fifteen he was unhappy. 'School no better. Still child.' Twenty, happy. 'University. Full of pricks but was also prick so felt at home.' Twenty-five, very happy. 'Working. Still prick, but competent prick.' And at thirty-two he has added another ranking by hand to describe himself as very, very happy. 'Met Lucy. She only sometimes thinks me prick.'

'Is that it?' I ask. 'Seven points? How long did that take you? Seven seconds?'

'We see this a lot,' says William soothingly. 'Women tend to put more detail in. They seem to have either better recall or a greater willingness to write down emotional things.'

'Excuse me,' says Christopher politely. 'But the woman you have before you is the most emotionally illiterate female it has ever been my misfortune to adore. She hasn't done the world's most comprehensive chart because she's in touch with her feelings. She's done it because it was homework and her *über*-swot instincts kicked in.'

'That is true,' I nod sadly. 'All of it.'

'I do see that Christopher has added a "very, very happy category" in order to accommodate how he felt about thc two of you meeting,' says William, holding the two charts side by side and peering closely at them. 'While you – well, you have marked your meeting but it seems to rank equally with getting the cats and slightly below negotiating your first pay rise.'

'You've got to remember I was working with a very small scale here,' I say. 'Our meeting is probably actually above the cats if you get a ruler and draw a line. I can't promise anything about the pay rise though.'

'Well,' says William brightly, putting the papers aside and fixing us with a determinedly optimistic stare. 'It doesn't really matter who the "emotionally literate" half of the partnership is, does it? Couples are supposed to complement each other, so as long as there's someone who is open about these things to go with someone who is – perhaps, more . . . practical and less demonstrative, that's a perfectly good recipe for success even if those attributes aren't distributed in the traditional way.'

'He's telling you it's OK to be dead inside,' says Christopher.

'He's telling you that you'd be dead without me to solve your problems for you,' I say.

'Let's talk a little bit about how you're both feeling about the big day,' says William hurriedly. 'Christopher, how are you doing?'

'Fine,' says Christopher, clearly baffled by the question.

'And you, Lucy?'

I review the situation. 'My sister has bought every dress in Bristol and still has nothing to wear on the day. She has gone into therapy, which I expect I will be paying for, after being told by a lady in the millinery department that her head was so big she'd have to have a special hat made and that her hair wasn't thick enough for a fascinator.

'I have, at the last count, 83,000 cousins coming down from the North on the day. It's going to look like a re-enactment of the Jarrow marches, but with flimsier shoes. And it would have been more, but we offended 30 per cent by putting the word out that children won't be invited and there's a further 14 per cent who have never been to London and don't want to start now.

'My mother is in daily communication with her five siblings, still trying to solve the equation that pits speed and ease of travel between two of England's largest conurbations against the cost. At the moment, one wants to catch the train, but only if it can be guaranteed that the buffet car will sell tuna mayonnaise sandwiches without sweetcorn; one wants to come by National Express coach if someone will teach her how to use her son's iPod so she doesn't have to listen to anyone's mobile phone going off all the way down; one is driving and could give three others a lift but that would leave one left over and if that's going to create a stink he'll just get the train but could people let him know how much of a fuss they are going to make if they don't come in the car because he'll need to book his ticket soon because he's not paying more than it would cost in petrol. And the other one wants to walk here barefoot and offer his suffering up to God as penance for coming into a Protestant church.'

'I see,' says William cautiously. 'And your father?'

'Dad has said nothing since Easter. I presume he's fine. It's possible he doesn't yet know I'm getting married. He still calls Christopher "Jonathan" half the time, you know.'

'Ah,' says William, shaking his head gently. 'It can often seem that way with fathers. But I'm sure there is a lot going on beneath the surface.'

I've known my dad a long time – though admittedly never well – and I'm equally sure there's not. But I don't say anything.

'I married a couple a few years ago,' says William, 'and the father of the bride was completely unflappable in the weeks leading up to the wedding, and at the rehearsal the day before, but afterwards he went completely to pieces. And he said to his daughter – "I get it now. I gave you away. You have your own family now. You belong to someone else." He was quite overcome.'

Christopher nods, evidently moved by the story which he sees as William does – as a tale illustrating the spiritual import of the service, the profundity of the journey we are about to undertake and a way of focusing our minds upon it amidst the extraneous noise and bustle of organisation, practicalities and other secular distractions.

Me, I'm torn between wanting to laugh and wanting to squawk with indignation. I want to laugh because the idea of my father, much as he loves me, doing any-thing other than waving me off in the taxi at the end of the day and then turning to my mother to ask what she wants for her tea is – well, laughable. And I want to squawk indignantly at the idea that any father might still secretly view his daughter as – what was in that guy's head, do you think? Was she a chattel? Burden? Novelty keyring?

I settle for smiling politely. And thanking God-even-though-he-doesn't-exist that my own papa is unlikely to follow this horrible nameless man down the same route. I like to think that even after I am married, if I turn up on the doorstep wanting a hot meal and a bed for the night, he will still greet me with the same vague, amiable smile that he always did, check quickly which one I am again ('No, don't tell me. Is it Emily?') and potter off to put some leftover pie in the microwave. I'm nobody's novelty keyring.

'Now then,' says William, 'I think it's time we set the date, don't you!'

We dig out our diaries and turn to September.

'I take it you are aiming for a Saturday?'

'Oh yes,' I say. 'If my uncle Joseph has to lose a day's pay as well as buy a train ticket and get his suit dry cleaned, there'll be merry hell to pay. Sorry for saying hell in front of your vicarness, vicar.'

'That's quite all right,' he says. 'We don't think of it so much as a rude word, anyway, so much as a very nasty place.'

'Oh, good.'

Christopher looks very pained next to me on the sofa. I must tell him not to worry. Me and the vicar – we're really coming to understand each other.

So – there are four Saturdays. We can make all of them. The vicar can do two of them. We wait with bated breath while Christopher rings Dr Johnson's House ('Is he allowed to use a mobile phone in here, vicar? Because I'll make him go and stand outside in the real world if not?' 'No, no – again, it's quite all right') to find out if the place is free on either date. It is. He books it. It is the simplest moment of the entire wedding so far. We all breathe again.

Then I stop as I realise that I will now be getting married on the last Saturday in September. On a real day. In a real church. With a real vicar. I have a small choking fit and Christopher says goodbye for both of us and carries me out.

Outside on Fleet Street, I manage to take in a few restorative lungfuls of lead pollution and recover.

'We've got one more meeting with William left,' says Christopher. 'If you could try to get through it without having convulsions whenever the reality of the situation is forced upon you, I think we would all feel a lot happier.'

I promise to try to do better next time.

A week later, I am making pizza while I wait for Mum to come and pick me up so that we can go to Jean's to decide on material. Christopher is watching me closely. He has a list of things he wants to know how to do, 'so that if you die or divorce me, my grief is not compounded by a precipitate drop in the living standards I have come, during the course of our cohabitation, to enjoy'. Home-made pizza is top of the list, followed by 'Those sliced potatoes' (boulangère), 'Those shredded potatoes' (rosti), 'That egg and potato thing that I pick the peppers out of' (tortilla) and 'Those mashed potatoes that taste better than usual' (mashed potatoes with cream instead of milk).

The pizza took pole position after I set him the task of peeling potatoes so they could be grated for a rosti.

'Do you know how?' I said doubtfully, as I handed him the knife.

'I am not totally devoid of culinary skills,' he replied with dignity, which, given that when I first turned up at his flat unannounced I found him gnawing on a stick of raw spaghetti, seemed a touch optimistic, but I said nothing.

I returned to the kitchen twenty minutes later to find him, red-faced and slick with sweat, carving centimetre-thick slices of peel off the potatoes.

'You're not going to end up with much potato to eat if you carry on like that,' I observed.

'Like sex,' he said through gritted teeth, 'it is an infinitely trickier task in practice than it appears in theory. And,' he added as another sprout-sized spud dropped into the pan, 'the rewards for a beginner are not as fulsome as promised by those with experience in the field.'

'Do it like this,' I said. 'Take potato in left hand.

That's it. Now, insert knife – slightly, at an angle, not vertically, you are not trying to kill the potato, and run it under the skin. That's the way. Now go back to the top and do it again. And again. And again.'

'But it's harder this way.'

'It is at first. But it will get easier. It's like touch-typing – in the long term you will be faster and more efficient.'

'That was always my aim with sex. Oh, this is making my hand hurt.'

'It hurts women's hands too, but somehow they manage to peel on through the pain.'

'Nonsense. Women's arms are configured differently.'

'No, you're thinking of genitals. Our genitals are configured differently.'

'If I peel all these potatoes, can I have a look at your genitals tonight?'

'If the potatoes you put in the pan weigh more than the peelings you put in the bin, yes you may.'

'I set to work with renewed vigour!' said Christopher, bending to his task once more.

Alas, he attacked the hapless veg again with such enthusiasm that I knew my genitals and I would go unmolested that night, and so it proved. Since then, he has solved the problem sufficiently in his own mind by determining that when I leave him – via death or decree nisi – he will pay a woman to peel a hundredweight of potatoes every Monday morning so that he can slice, shred and dice them according to whim for the rest of the week.

So, here I am, showing him how to make dough in the breadmaker and now rolling it out on the chopping board.

'Can pizza be square?' he asks.

A faint but familiar weariness lays itself like a mantle across my shoulders.

'Do you want the pizza to be square?' I ask.

'No, I'm just interested. I suddenly realised that all the pizzas I've ever eaten or seen or read about have been circles.'

'It's because when you roll them out – as I am doing here, look – they naturally roll out into a circle.'

'Couldn't you cut bits off it and reincorporate them into the – now square, or possibly rectilinear – base, thereby retaining both the original dough volume and the new, four-sided shape?'

'No, because when you "reincorporate", you would have to roll it out again and it would, despite all one's best efforts, strive with some success to take on a circular shape once more. A bit like this conversation.'

'I see,' says Christopher, gazing in fascination at the roundel of dough before him. 'And, of course, the costs – of time, effort and money, particularly if mass-producing the item on a commercial rather than domestic basis – involved in tampering with what is a perfectly serviceable item with even the minimum of intervention, quickly render said tampering unviable. How interesting. A rare example of a natural proclivity's efficiency being unimprovable by human hand. Thank you very much.'

'You're very welcome.'

I'm not quite sure what I contributed to this debate, which as ever seems to have taken place largely within his head, but I'm glad he's happy. Though somewhere deep in my soul I know there is a yearning for a simpler life with a man whose entire panoply of personal needs can be met with a can of lager and a weekly dose of *Robot Wars*.

'Now,' I say, transferring the pizza to a baking tray, dusting the flour off my hands and tying an apron round his waist. 'You add whichever of these toppings you like – tomato first – and bung it all in the oven at 220 degrees half an hour before you want your dinner.'

Just then Mum pulls up outside and I hurriedly kiss Christopher goodbye. 'I'm so glad you're going to see Jean again,' he says. 'It gives me hope that you will actually be wearing a dress down the aisle and not denim dungarees and a thick sweater. I'm really hoping to marry a woman that day. Bye!'

I rush out of the door before Mum starts up the drive. We try to keep her out of the house if at all possible, for much the same reason as I do not keep full-length pictures of Eva Mendes or Angelina Jolie in there – there are certain things a girl learns to do over the years to protect her mental health. Of course, Mum knows what I'm up to, and fires questions at me instead of carrying out her domestic inspections, until the quota of disapproving looks she had planned for the day is fulfilled.

'Have you cleaned the hob?'

'No.'

'Got the cat hairs off the sofa?'

'I did, but they were replaced overnight. I don't know yet by whom – neither of the cats has cracked under questioning.'

'Have you mended the blind?'

'Mum, let me save us both some time – all the domestic, mechanical and moral failures you witnessed last visit? Not one of them mended yet.'

The subsequent delivery of the fully annotated and footnoted treatises on How I Can Bear to Live Like This and Why Am I Not Ashamed takes us neatly up to Jean's door. She welcomes us in and spreads the shortlisted samples out in front of us.

Pale oyster hits the skids first. 'We don't want pink,' says Mum.

This does not come as a great surprise to me. This is, after all, a woman who was so scared of having 'girly' girls when we were growing up that she made us wear trunks to school swimming lessons instead of costumes. Not a costume instead of a bikini. Trunks instead of a costume. For our entire primary school careers. I almost admire her limitless capacity for taking the germ of a reasonable idea and running with it to the outer edges of lunacy. Or I would if my own capacity for any kind of positive or generous thought had not been crushed by the weight of the years of ridicule I endured throughout my formative years.

Next up for consideration is the beautiful pale coffee

colour, like a very, very milky latte or a very, very expensive truffle chocolate, or—

'Diarrhoea,' announces my mother.

I open my mouth to protest, but do you know what? It's not worth it. Because once someone has put the concept of diarrhoea in your mind, nothing is going to shift it. Now and for evermore, that particular shade of satin will remind me of liquid turd, and I'm not walking down the aisle feeling that I am effectively swathed in shit. This much I know.

Pale gold – thank God, even though you don't exist – meets with her approval. 'Oh yes,' she says, 'this is the one for you. It goes with your hair and your eyes. Even though they don't go with each other. Isn't that clever?'

'Genius,' I agree.

'Now come downstairs and I'll show you both the type of material I want to make it with,' says Jean.

I follow her, confused. I thought all bridal gowns were made out of Wedding Satin and that was that. There can't be another decision to make, I think. No wonder brides go mad.

In the sitting room, Jean hands us a square of fabric. It is slightly shiny and slightly stiff. It is, she informs us, zibeline. 'For the kind of dress you're having – this is what it should be made of,' she says firmly. 'It will hold its shape better. It's stiffer than satin. Everyone has satin.'

The words are out of my mouth before conscious thought has formed. 'But I want a Petra dress.'

Now it is Jean's turn to look confused. Mum simply looks astounded. She can join the club. I don't know what just happened.

'What's a Petra dress?' she asks.

While I try to take command of my brain again, Mum explains that Petra was the daughter of the people next door and my babysitter for about five years, until I was about ten and she got married and went to live somewhere else. 'And when she got married, all the Mangans were invited. But this was in the early eighties and her dress was a huge meringue . . .' She turns to me in horror. 'You can't be wanting one like that?'

'No, no,' I say, having at last re-established the connection between conscious thought and speech (I tell you, you don't know how much you need it till it's gone). 'I just mean – the look of it, the feel of it.'

For the first time in decades, absolute decades, I remember sitting on Petra's lap at the reception, and the worry of crushing its magnificence beneath my weight disappearing as I felt the wonderful, cold, richness of the dress under my legs and stroked its heavy softness with my hand. More than seeing it, the tactile sensations made me understand that this was a special dress for a special day.

I don't tell Mum or Jean this, of course, for fear that it will make the former violently sick all over the carpet. I give them a reasoned, rational case for the non-zibeline version. I liken it to the invitations – I just want to take the edge off the formality of it all wherever possible. A stiff 'London' dress is for the kind of stiff London wedding I am trying to avoid.

Jean understands and nods. My mother does likewise. A Petra dress, sans meringue pouffage, it will be.

Our choice made, Jean hands me a sample slip of the material. 'To help you choose matching shoes and whatever you're wearing on your head,' she explains helpfully and, I notice, firmly. Evidently my reputation as a woman lacking all bridal instincts is now preceding me.

Then the final task of the day is at hand. Jean whips out a tape measure and starts to advance meaningfully towards me. Oh, joy! Oh, rapture unconfined! It is time for me to strip down to my underwear and let her take my measurements. I hadn't realised I had so many. Shoulder to shoulder, shoulder to elbow, round my boobs, under my boobs (a dispiritingly close figure resulting), head to toe, hip to ankle, you name any two points on my body, Jean measured between them. When she gets to my waist, my mother mutters, 'She's not going to like that one.'

Jean undoes the tape and rewraps it eight inches lower, round my thighs. 'No,' she says gaily. 'This is the one she's not going to like.'

Great, I thought. Now they're working as a team.

'You have a classic Victorian shape,' announces Jean, sitting back on her haunches.

'Classic pear,' translates Mum.

'Classic Weeble,' I moan inwardly. The only difference is that not only do I wobble but I increasingly feel that I will fall down.

Jean gets up to do the final measurements – shoulder to shoulder, then up and down across my back, and then again across my front. 'That's odd,' she says, looking puzzled as she checks her numbers again. She measures. 'They don't come out nearly the same,' she says. 'I mean – there's often some minor variation, but this . . . '

'Oh my God. I'm a hunchback! You're saying I'm a hunchback? How do you propose we design a dress that disguises that?'

'It is strange,' Jean says, turning me round by the shoulders so she can perform a 360-degree examination of the carnival freak in her bedroom. 'Because you look all right to the naked eye.'

'I must say, I've never noticed anything amiss,' says Mum, gesturing for me to keep turning slowly so that she too can examine my form for Quasimodo-ish signs. 'And it's too late to do anything about it now. We'll just have to keep on with the dress as planned and hope for the best.'

I think I might have that made up as a T-shirt to see me through the rest of this wedding. Just keep on as planned and hope for the best.

CHAPTER NINE

I do not know how this happened but it is June. Four months to go before W-Day. As I balance on top of a stool on top of a chair to change a light bulb in the hallway, I try to work out whether I am within hailing distance of being on schedule. I have a church and a friendly vicar. I have a reception venue that doesn't smell of wee. I have a caterer willing to cater for some of the stupidest dietary requirements known to man. My dress – or at least its draft form in calico – is being put together as we speak. These are all good things.

On the other hand, I have not yet ordered the invitations, booze or decided on a cupcake provider. Despite almost daily and increasingly shrill requests, Christopher has not yet got round to asking his friend Richard to be his best man. I still have preparation classes to go to, work to do and relatives to placate/inform/disabuse of fanciful notions on an almost hourly basis. I do not know what I am doing about flowers. We have not yet drawn up a definitive guest list. And, above all, I have not yet thought about shoes.

This is more of a problem than you might think. As a midget I of course need, on my wedding day above all other days, a pair of gorgeous, sophisticated, glamorous, high-heeled shoes that add inches to my height and sweeping grandeur to my dress. As a midget, however, I take a size thirteen shoe. That is the size the average six-year-old takes. And the average six-year-old, alas, has little need for gorgeous, sophisticated, glamorous, high-heeled shoes, and especially those that might go with, say, a pale gold dress. If I were getting married in pink diamanté or Clarks patent leather, I might have more luck.

Ah well. At least I have Anna's party to take my mind off the wedding palaver for a few hours. She sent us an email a couple of weeks ago, inviting a few people round for lunch and drinks to celebrate the weaning of Peter and the concomitant return of her pre-pregnancy brain. Naturally, a few people round for lunch in these beFacebooked times has metamorphosed into something of a cross between a university reunion, a three-ring circus and – given the number of my friends who have pulled so far ahead of me in this adulthood game that they have already reproduced and must therefore bring the results with them – a crèche.

Some of these friends Christopher has met before, some he hasn't. This means I can relax slightly and enjoy myself, safe in the knowledge that if he says or does something strange out of my earshot, there will be someone around who can explain him away to whoever has been perturbed or offended. Sometimes I do not feel too different from my parent-friends.

Just then Christopher wanders into the hallway reading out – I don't know why – an article about the

Welsh assembly that has caught his interest. 'Strange to think that the Welsh have their own administrative system,' he says as he turns the page. 'I spent most of my life assuming that Tolkien had made them up.'

Finding nothing boring enough to engage him in the rest of the newspaper, he eventually looks up and realises what I am doing.

'Why, I wonder out loud, is the shortest entity in the house – bar *none*, the cat's taller – doing that?'

'Because the last time I left it to you, you electrocuted your hand, fused the downstairs and smashed the bulb so widely across the lino that I am still picking bits of it off the floor even today.'

'You should keep them safe,' observes Christopher. 'As we enter a new, low-energy age, those shards will take on vital historical significance, one day to be accepted as antiques and share museum honours with spinning wheels, mangles and casual racism.'

'Instead of talking,' I say, as the chair and stool begin to shift beneath me as I reach to the furthest prong of the unnecessarily complicated light fitting installed by the previous owner, 'could you perhaps hold on to the furniture beneath me so that I don't plunge to my death?'

'You underestimate me,' says Christopher, laying down his newspaper and taking hold. 'I can do both. But first, tell me what I really came in to ask you – what do you want me to wear for this thing today?'

'What were you planning to wear?' I say cautiously, as I descend with the help of Christopher's hand from my perilously unsteady tower.

'My lime-green cords, my red checked shirt and a tweed jacket.'

'Fine,' I say after a moment's pause.

We haven't got time for an argument, I reason, and at least it will give those who don't know him fair warning as to what they are about to come up against.

We are, unfortunately, driving because although Haywards Heath is only about twelve miles away as the crow flies, to get there by public transport requires a four-day train ride, a boat trip and a short biplane hop at the other end. I say unfortunately because I cannot drive, so Christopher must, and he treats the kerb as if it was a childhood security blanket ('Move out! Move out! Stop hugging it! Why are you this kind of dick?') and every other person on the road as if they were a long-standing personal enemy. We both arrive at any destination crippled by nervous exhaustion, and swearing that next time, however far we go, we will take a taxi – each.

When we arrive at the house the hostess, Anna, waves energetically at us from an upstairs window. 'I'm just dressing some infant wounds!' she cries. 'Front door's open, let yourselves in, drink's on the decking, guests are in the garden, children are everywhere!'

A wall of sound hits us as we walk in. A four-year-old boy gloms instantly on to Christopher's leg. 'Come and play ships with us!' he says.

Christopher brightens. 'All right,' he says amiably.

The child drags him off to the playroom/ocean to

effect introductions to the rest of the crew. I head on through to the garden. I am just effecting my own introduction to a glass of wine and a handful of crisps (I'll move on to the olives later, when I'm talking to people and have to try to pretend I like them – the olives, not the people) to restore my travel-shattered equilibrium when a cry from the far end of the garden splits the air as only a ululation of utterly false delight can.

'Omigod – Luuuuucy!'

'Oh *my* God,' I mutter into my wine glass as a woman in shorts and stack heels comes tottering towards me. 'It's Siobhan.'

Anna, who has discharged her nursing duties and her patients and joined me by the Chardonnay, murmurs back, 'We didn't invite her. I don't know how she's here.'

We both roll our eyes. That is Siobhan's great skill. No one ever invites her to anything. And she is always, always there.

She is one of those stubborn impurities that remain after the social smelting of your twenties has occurred. Life gets busy, time gets short, and your boss wants you to stay late again. You must meet up with X, Y and Z because they're such fun when you do – but the restorative effects of a bit of comfort TV and an early night would last longer. Gradually Monica, Ross, Rachel and Co. win out over real life friends. Coupledom and kids spirit others away to bigger houses in – where was it again? The friend whose consistently disastrous life once claimed your sympathy or *schadenfreude* becomes a drain on your limited resources and is quietly dropped. Whatever did happen to her, do you suppose . . . ?

So peripheral friends start to . . . disappear, until all that you are left with is the real thing – friends whom you regard with true affection, people with whom you have lots in common, friends for whom you would go to bat in times of trouble, who would support you through your own and who can generally be relied on to add to, rather than detract from, the sum of your personal happiness over the years. And vice, of course, versa, otherwise you will be the one getting shunted off into the sidings.

Individuals like Siobhan, however, go nowhere. Individuals with the impregnable self-confidence of the spoiled only child. Individuals you couldn't rebuff with a bulldozer. Hints, avoidance tactics, outright insults glance off her like ping-pong balls off a tank.

Oh come, I hear you say, surely 'tis but a brittle veneer of confidence that she perhaps maintains better than most but which nevertheless masks a bleak, howling pit of insecurity within, as it does for the rest of us? To which I, Anna and the rest of her awed and resentful coterie, who amongst us must be able to account for most of her waking life and whose collated reports over the years have never yet yielded evidence of a moment's self-doubt, reflection, hesitation or unhappiness ever disturbing the pool of Siobhan's consciousness, would have to reply with a resounding 'Not this time.'

She is not malicious in any way – I suspect because this would demand a level of effort and empathy of which she is simply not capable – merely entirely focused on what works best for Siobhan.

Things just have a way of becoming arranged in the manner that most greatly benefits – Siobhan. Invite her to dinner (and remember, you don't really need to – if she wants to be there, she'll be there regardless) and you will somehow find yourself cooking exactly what suits her current diet, allergies or detox regime. Over the hors d'oeuvres she will truffle out the lawyer who can help her with a 'tiny legal problem' (which he will end up working on for six months pro bono). Over the main course she will inveigle the interior designer into sourcing 'a few pieces' for her new house, or the gardener into landscaping her lawn for next to nothing, and over pudding she will find the couple best placed to give her a lift home, because it's only five miles out of their way and taxis are so unreliable, don't you agree? I sometimes think she sees people as a butcher sees a cow – etched with dotted lines dividing them up into their choicest cuts. A prime professional skill here, a nice chunk of valuable talent there. Perhaps she doesn't so much have friends as a larder full of semi-filleted carcasses. Who knows?

What I do know now is that she is heading fast towards me and that I need to rearrange my face into something resembling pleased surprise.

'Siobhan!'

'Youlookamazinghaveyoulostweight,' says Siobhan,

which is not a question but her way of saying hello. You could be covered in tumours, eight months pregnant and cyanotic and she would still say exactly the same thing.

'How have you been?' I ask.

She launches immediately into a twenty-minute monologue that tells me in great detail exactly how she has been.

She is actually a very restful companion when you are in the right mood – that mood being 'knackered and incapable of contributing to a meaningful conversation'. She is always the star of any story but she always tells it well and has plenty of them to hand. She launches into her latest batch, of deals she has brokered while dealing feminist hammer blows to the corporate bully boys who would seek to destroy her (she does something in the City, but I don't know what and it is now years too late to ask), the parties she has been to, the half-marathons she has run the day after and the planets she has realigned in between times.

It is an account that takes us all the way through Anna calling for us all to help shove the little tables together to make one big one to eat at (Siobhan tugs half-heartedly at a tablecloth or two as they are thrown over the coalescing counter tops and stakes her claim to the success of the operation by breathing a sigh of satisfaction as we sit down and saying to no one in particular, 'Didn't we do well!') as well as the arrival of the plates full of barbecued pork and chicken and cheerfully enormous bowls of salad.

While Siobhan chunters on I look down the table for Christopher. He is sitting at the children's end of the table, flanked by rows of four-, five- and six-year-old boys, and appears to be holding court. When Siobhan pauses for breath and barbecue, odd phrases float up to me, 'poop deck' foremost amongst them. Cap'n Christopher and his happy crew aboard the HMS *Sofabed*, I think, and reach for some salad. My ring catches the light and Siobhan squeals again. 'Omigod! You're engaged!'

I cringe and nod. It is a testimony to the known paucity of sentiment in all Siobhan's exclamations that instead of looking up with even momentary, instinctive interest when she makes these noises, a gathering will generally just bow its collective head and wait for the moment to pass. She has basically inverted normal human response/communication. She shouldn't be denounced. She should be studied.

'What are you doing where are you having it what are you wearing,' she says.

I don't answer, because again, it's not a question, just a synaptic trigger pulled by sight of a ring.

Then she says, 'And who are your bridesmaids?'

From somewhere high above and outside myself, I can hear the faintest of voices telling me to think more quickly. To realise that a question mark from Siobhan signals danger. Unfortunately, down on the earthbound plain, I am three glasses to the bad and my senses are catastrophically dulled. Instead of being warned, I am flattered. Siobhan actually wants to hear something about me! The world must be right – marriage is indeed a momentous and powerful event. So I tell her about Gillian and my sister turning me down, and about Anna and I deciding that Ellie was, in the end, too young. 'So,' I am about to conclude happily, 'I've saved myself all the bother and all the expense without offending anybody!'

But the breath I take to deliver my denouement with suitably triumphant glee is my undoing. Into the pause she leaps. 'Oh,' comes another ringing cry – the air must be rent to shreds by now, I note in the corner of my mind that has not yet filled with horror at what I realise now is to unfold with the crushing inevitability of a Greek tragedy – 'but you must have a bridesmaid! Allegra can do it! She's always, always wanted to be a bridesmaid! Oh, you must let her – she'll look so beautiful!'

Oh yes – did I mention that Siobhan has a daughter? It's easy to forget because she doesn't often intrude on her mother's thoughts or conversation, but her name is indeed Allegra and, it turns out, she is sitting halfway down the table gazing expectantly back at me. The tableful of guests stunned to silence by Siobhan's boldest manoeuvre yet wait to see what I am going to do. Siobhan beams with delighted satisfaction. I stare at Christopher mentally begging for help. But he has barely emerged from his battleship haze and has no idea what is going on.

I stutter briefly, but what can I say when six-year-old Allegra – a sweet child who should be blamed neither for her name nor her mother – is looking at me with wide, bluebell-coloured eyes peeping out from beneath a bruncttc bob, styled – but of course – exactly like Siobhan's, and waiting for me to grant her her heart's desire?

I make one weak effort to point out the hassle of bringing her for fittings. No problem, says Siobhan, she will be only too happy to bring her down whenever necessary. I hesitate again, and Siobhan leaps to fill the void once more.

'If it's a question of expense,' she brays kindly, 'I'll pay for her little frock.'

I am now well and truly trapped. I cannot reject my putative bridesmaid without becoming known as England's Champion Child-Dream Wrecker, and if I shilly-shally any longer I risk being branded as either poverty-stricken or mean.

I take back everything I said about her not being malicious, inwardly doff my cap to her evilly manipulative genius and give in. I smile grimly, and say that of course she can be my bridesmaid. Love her to be my bridesmaid. Don't know how I didn't think of it before. What a wonderful idea. Et cetera, et cetera. The talk around the table gradually resumes and I choke down a chicken wing or two along with my fury.

Siobhan leaves the party before the rest of us, yanking Allegra off the trampoline and trotting her round the guests to say goodbye.

'Goodbye then, Allegra,' I say, giving her a kiss. 'I'm sure we'll be seeing each other soon.'

'Oh, you will, you will!' promises Siobhan cheerfully, as Allegra gazes mournfully at the children still bouncing their tiny idiot selves all over the trampoline. 'We can't wait!'

They leave, and Anna shoves another glass of wine into my hand. 'Well, you've done it now,' she says. 'That woman will be all over you like a fly on shit from now till the wedding.'

'I know,' I say miserably. 'But it's not Allegra's fault and I couldn't upset a six-year-old.'

'You wait,' says Anna, draining the rest of her glass. 'Three months from now, you'll be wishing you'd thrown the child down a well, never mind momentarily crushed her spirit.'

'We should have staked Siobhan through her black, black heart years ago,' I say ruefully. 'But it's too late now. Oh well. I'd better get going myself now. Have you seen my fiancé anywhere?'

'He's judging a face-pulling competition in the playroom, last I heard.'

Indeed he is. I stand at the door and signal intent-to-leave.

'Splendid efforts and I commend you all,' he says as he stands up and returns his paper crown to the adoring throng. 'I only wish this country still had a thriving music-hall tradition where Rory, Emma and Ryan in particular could parlay their talents into long and successful careers. Good day to you all, and may your fizzogs always be flexible.'

They cheer him all the way down the road.

'That was an excellent party,' he says on the way home. 'And some woman came up to me and told me that you'd made her daughter your bridesmaid. I'm glad you changed your mind about that.'

I look at him. I am very tired. 'Yes,' I say. 'So am I.'

A few days later, I am round at Gillian's. I am supposed to be helping her type out end-of-term reports. They are not due until the end of July and she is supposed to type them herself straight into the school's database, then print them out and give them to the kids. However, she is so technologically incompetent that every time she touches a keyboard, half of south-east London fuses. So she handwrites them all in advance, I type them up for her on my laptop, give her a disk to take to school and she gets a kindly colleague to upload the contents for her into the database. It is a convoluted route, which is why we have to start early.

'"Charlene has problems concentrating and is quite . . . " What's this say, Gill?'

'Evil. Charlene is quite evil.'

'No, it's longer than that. Stop wandering around the room and come and sit here where you can be useful.'

She comes over. '"Difficult". It says difficult. We're not actually allowed to say "evil" any more.'

'Speaking of difficult,' I say, as I peck away at the laptop, 'I was up Googling till one in the morning yesterday, trying to find somewhere that might sell suitable shoes for me, bridal freak. There's a shop in Marylebone, apparently, called The Little Shoe Shop, which does exactly what it says on the tin. When we're finished here, do you want to come with me to have a look?'

She agrees readily.

'There's nothing I like better than a futile mission, Luce,' she says, lying back down on the couch while I try to decide whether Michelle Baring is generally 'conscientious' or 'unconscious' in the classroom.

Gillian, incidentally, has taken a size nine – nine! – since she was twelve. When she was bored in history class, she used to slip off one of her shoes under the table and make me fit both my feet inside it. Then she would rock her chair back, take one quick look at me crammed into one giant shoe and start laughing so hard Mrs Meehan would send her out of the room. Gillian used to go out waving her hands above her head like a madwoman so that Mrs M wouldn't realise she had only one shoe on and I would reunite her with her footwear after class.

Gillian has evidently been reminiscing about our misspent youth too. 'Do you remember that we once decided it would be a very good idea if all brides came down the aisle on rollerskates?' she says.

'No,' I reply. 'But I like it.'

'It was that summer when everybody was mad about rollerskating,' she says. 'We weren't very imaginative children, were we?'

Three hours, twenty-three reports and a train, tube and bus ride later we arrive at what I hope will be wedding footwear Shangri-la. 'It's like a shoe shop for dolls!' says Gillian as she bounds round trying the shoes on, on her hands.

I explain to the assistant that I am hunting for bridal shoes and show her my material sample. She gets a beautiful, a perfect pair, in my size, down from the shelf.

'Ooh, they're lovely!' says Gillian.

'Aren't they!' I say and kick off my shoes to try them on. I stand up. I take two steps and collapse in pain.

'Get up!' cries Gillian. 'They're perfect! Get up!'

I drag myself to my feet and take three more steps before going down again.

'I can't,' I moan despairingly from the floor. 'They're agony!'

'No, they're not!' Gillian insists. 'Pain is all in the mind.'

'It's not. It's in my feet.'

I pull myself up on to the chair and tear off the shoes. 'Look!' I say, pointing to my toes, so savagely squashed that they are retaining the shape of the shoe. 'That's not right!'

'Could she try a larger size?' says Gillian.

'I'm sorry,' says the assistant. 'That's the only one we have left. They've stopped making this design.'

'Of course they have,' I mutter. 'Of course they have.'

'Shoes can be stretched, you know,' says the assistant.

'Can they?'

'Yes – you just take them to a cobblers and they do

it for you. They put them on a last and stretch them slowly over a couple of days.'

'Are you sure?' says Gillian suspiciously.

'Why would she lie?' I ask her.

'I don't know,' Gillian shrugs. 'But it just sounds like one of those ancient lost arts, like flint-knapping or thatching.'

'Well, I'm sure it's true,' I say to Gillian, while glancing apologetically to the woman trying to help us. I feel I have to buy the shoes now, so I hand over my card and hope for the best.

A hundred quid lighter, we leave the shop.

'What do I do if I stretch these bloody things and they still don't fit?'

'We have to get you a back-up pair just in case.'

'But I'll have wasted a hundred quid!'

'You can put them on eBay,' says Gillian. 'If you word it right, I bet there's a paedophile shoe fetishist out there who will pay through the nose for them. You'll probably make a profit.'

'I hope so,' I say morosely.

'Where do we go now, then?' says Gillian.

'My only other possible sources are shops that sell bridesmaid shoes and things,' I say.

This rapidly turns out to be a bust. The only things in my size are either white sandals, diamanté slippers or satin ballet pumps. And if ever there were a day when I need heels, this is it.

'Let's give up, Luce,' says Gillian as we traipse wearily out of our seventeenth store. 'You're a fucking freak and you're just going to either have to get married in the ones you've bought after they've been stretched on the rack or go barefoot.'

When I get home, I take them to the local shoe repair shop.

'Can you stretch shoes?' I ask, handing mine over.

'Yes,' the man says, taking them out of the box. 'But not these ones. They're too small. They'll not fit on the thing. It only starts at a size three. Sorry.'

Just occasionally I get the feeling that the gods are trying to tell me something. Perhaps that I should learn to sacrifice comfort for beauty. Perhaps that I shouldn't marry Christopher and breed another generation of peg-footed children. Or perhaps—

'It's OK,' I say, brightening. 'I think it just means it should be rollerskates after all.'

CHAPTER TEN

'You should take a notebook in case it gives you any ideas,' says Christopher authoritatively.

'I would take your commands more seriously,' I say, lifting my head from the feline shenanigans, 'if you weren't delivering them to me naked.'

'Don't look at it,' he says, covering his penis with his hands. 'It shies away from publicity.'

'Then what is it doing parading itself publicly in front of the sofa?' I ask, not – I feel – unreasonably.

'I can't find any clean underpants.'

'Did you look in the drawer?'

'Yes!'

'Did you look in the other drawer?'

'No!'

'Go on, then.'

A trudge, a thundering upstairs, followed by a thump and a distant cry of 'Eureka!'

I sigh and return to my task of dragging Henry-the-well-known-terrible-cat out from under the coffee table so that he can join his brother outside for the day. He yowls in protest.

'Too bad, Henners,' I say. 'We're going to be out all day at my friend Andrea's wedding, so you have to be too.'

He yowls again.

'I'm sorry,' I say. 'But look at it this way. You've got the shed, you've got water, you've got food and you haven't got to spend all day making small talk with people you've never met.'

I know the bride, Andrea, and her husband John from a temp job I had in the City a few years ago – neither of them well enough to know any of their current circle of friends but, by virtue of my double bond to the couple, they have generously invited both me and a guest. Which will be Christopher if he ever finds his trousers.

We are on the train back from the wedding. I have given in to the mounting hysteria that I have been suppressing all day. Christopher is gazing at me with fascination.

'Amazing,' he murmurs under his breath. 'I think it might be female after all.'

Let me explain. By some miracle we arrived at the church on time. We slid into our pew with a sigh of relief. That is my last happy memory of the day. From the moment I looked up and saw the artfully decorated church – flowers, candles, ribbons, serried ranks of buttonholed ushers – I knew I was in trouble.

Usually, I pride myself on the fact that I am one of life's stable sorts. Present me with a difficulty, a problem, an unexpected situation, nay, even a crisis and I will remain calm. Did I have a meltdown when a bridesmaid was foisted upon me by a brunette tyrant on a juice fast? I did not. I rang Jean and calmly ordered a dress to be cobbled together from whatever is left over from the ten yards of fabric already ordered, 'because I'm buggered if I'm spending any more than that on dressing a total frigging stranger'. I am a woman, you see, who strives always to find a solution via the application of calm, well-ordered thought.

But there, in the church, at this first intimation of *über*-organisation I embarked, unstoppably, on a compare-and-contrast exercise that soon had me hyperventilating into a paper bag while Christopher searched his pockets for Valium and a cosh.

Throughout the day, all around me evidence of our matrimonial failings piled up so rapidly that by the end of it I could barely see over the top.

1. The bride had lost, at a conservative estimate, eighteen pounds in the weeks leading up to her wedding. I have cut my sugars in coffee from two and a half to two and am still feeling resentful that this has not caused the fat to drop from my body in giant lumps.

2. They have matching ushers. Who all know what they are doing. We are having no ushers and I have no idea what we're doing.

3. They have a photographer. We do not have a photographer. We do not have disposable cameras resting on tables for guest use because we do not have tables and I suspect strapping them to the canapé-delivering waiters will meet with legitimate resistance.

4. There are six bridesmaids in pale blue dresses perfectly styled to fit their perfectly graduated heights and ages. I have one bridesmaid, forced upon me, who is going to be dressed in left-overs.

5. The bridesmaids each receive a perfectly wrapped, matching present. My gift to Allegra will be not kicking her mother in the head as I go past for her unwanted interference in My Sodding Day.

6. They serve a three-course meal on damask table-cloths, bone china and time. 'We're not even sitting down at ours!' I cry in low but anguished tones to Christopher as he guides me to our snowy island. He crams a bread roll into my mouth before my panic can gather in volume. As I choke it down, he picks up one of the little pale blue voile bags that reside by everyone's plates.

    'What are these?' he says with interest.

    'They're party favours.'

    'Are we having these?'

    'No.'

    'Why not?

    'Because (a) *we're not sitting down to a meal* so we'd have nowhere to put them and (b) I do not have time or inclination to make 120 drawstring bags full of sugared almonds.'

    'You could ask Gillian to do it.'

    'If I left it to Gillian, we'd find half of them full of tampons and the other half full of Ecstasy tablets.'

'Well, if we gave your mother one of the latter it might help her enjoy the day.'

7. Before the meal, the bridegroom and the father of the bride speak, afterwards the best man – a full complement of speeches, full of compliments. At our wedding there will be speeches only if the weather is good enough to gather everyone outside in the courtyard. Otherwise, we're not bothering. Even so, I have a small seizure every night at the thought of what Christopher and my dad might be saying on the day, and the best man's speech is an even more unknown quantity than usual because a best man has still – still! – to be appointed.

8. Everything matches.

'Everything matches!' I hiss. 'The party favours, the waistcoats, the dress, the flowers, the table-cloths, the bridesmaids. The presents for the bridesmaid. I bet even the roast beef is going to be pale blue with silver accents! Nothing at my wedding is going to match!'

My fiancé urges me to stay calm. 'Remember what Frasier said when Marty complained that nothing in his apartment "matched"?' he says. 'He tells him that as long as everything was of good enough quality, they don't have to match, they will simply "go" together. That is what will happen at your wedding.'

'But nothing I've ever done or bought has been of good quality,' I say.

'That is a flaw in the plan, certainly,' Christopher says, gazing serenely before him and sipping a glass of champagne. 'We can but hope that my impeccable taste in music, wine, friends and ecclesiastical architecture will be enough to counteract your ability to drag us down to the level of swine, and yoke the day together into a relatively harmonious whole.'

Despite these kind, supportive words, I am gibbering with worry by the time we leave – early. When Andrea kisses me goodbye and mentions that they are off for a six-month sabbatical in Africa, it is all I can do not to fall to my knees, clutch hers and sob with gratitude that she will not be able to attend my wedding and witness the debacle.

I gibber ceaselessly as the train chugs home.

'They're ending with an evening of dancing to a live jazz band,' I read from the order of service. I must remember to get some orders of service. We probably need some of those. 'Our day ends with the house closing at 9 p.m., us hopping into a taxi home and leaving a hundred guests to do likewise or head out into London to please themselves for the rest of the night.'

'So?' says Christopher, who is trying very hard to read a book about interwar Egyptian politics, with little success.

'So, my wedding is going to look like a Communist rally. We're doing nothing! We're providing nothing! We are nothing!'

'I don't mean to be rude,' says Christopher eventually, closing his book and catching me by the ankles as I attempt to climb out of the window and throw myself on to the track. 'But you are, as I believe the young folk call it these days, talking the absolute bollocks. It won't be a worse wedding. It's just going to be a different kind of wedding. Listen to my list, a list of important facts derived from male science instead of crazy lady spew:

1. 'They did all that out in the country. If we were to reproduce it in London, that size of dining room alone would require us to work till we were eighty to pay off the loan.
2. 'They were five crucial years younger than us and so were all their friends. If we had dancing at our wedding, we'd have to have joint-lubricant and ambulances standing by.
3. 'You couldn't organise such an elaborate affair – ever. You have many fine qualities, but your brain is not built for party planning. It's all you can do to pay the milkman on time and remember to change the loo roll in the bathroom. And I cannot help because, as you so rightly point out on a roughly thrice-hourly basis, I am even worse. I do not even know where we keep the loo roll. I do not know how it gets to wherever we keep it in the first place. It is one of many tiny miracles upon whose magic I prefer never to let daylight look.'

He stops. I sigh resignedly. There is, after all, not much I can do about it now. Removing any one of the basic building blocks of the wedding now would cause the whole fragile edifice to collapse. We would have to redesign and start again from scratch. And I'd rather have the winner of the 2009 All Comers Shittest Wedding of the Year competition than do that. Once again, sloth saves me from total convulsive panic. We will just carry on as planned. And I will get that T-shirt made.

Christopher may claim to love me 900 but I have decided not to put the theory to the test today. I shout my goodbye and quickly hare off down the road to catch the train into town before he can question me too closely about my plans for the day. Andrea's wedding proved a spur to action and today I have decided to sort out the invitations once and for all.

Mum meets me at John Lewis. We travel up to the wedding department. I find the lever-arch file that sparked the problem last time and open it up.

'The choice is between Option A,' I say, presenting her with Christopher's preference, 'and Option B' – mine.

She picks, unhesitatingly, B.

'Ayethangyew!' I say triumphantly. 'And why did you pick this one, frequently unfairly traduced mother of mine?'

'Because the other one will give folk the wrong idea,' she says, puzzled that I should need to ask when it is so abundantly clear to all right-thinking people.

'Ayethangyew once again,' I say, gathering up the file and taking it over to the order desk. 'Now follow me. We have printing choices to make.'

She cuts through that Gordian knot with equal efficiency.

'Would madam like the flat printing, the thermo—'

'She'd like the cheapest,' says Mum and we are home in time for lunch.

Her home, of course, as not being surrounded by six roomsful of evidence of my various forms of ineptitude is easier on the nerves for both of us.

I am just about to turn on Dad's computer to start drafting the letter that will, God willing, accompany the invitations that are to be sent out in three weeks' time, when I realise that it will have to include details about a wedding list. Which means deciding whether we are having a wedding list. And, if we are, what should be on it.

I unfortunately utter some of these thoughts out loud and within earshot of my parents.

'I remember our wedding list,' says Dad.

'What was on it?' I say, because I fall for it every time.

'A pair of shoes,' he says mournfully. 'Some winter kindling. An egg.'

'No, really,' I appeal to Mum. 'What did you ask for?'

She tells me they did not have a wedding list at all. 'For a start, people would have thought it was rude. And the other thing was – we needed everything, and everybody knew it. It wasn't like today, when you all live with each other for years and years and have quite enough stuff to be getting on with. We both went from living with our parents to moving into our own home. So people gave us whatever they could – new or second-hand. His mother gave us the bed from her spare room—'

'It were no hardship,' says Dad. ''T' pigs never used it anyway.'

'My mother gave us a pair of rugs to do until we could get carpet, my brothers and sisters clubbed together to get us a dinner service and his sister bought us a kettle. Well, stole. She stole us a kettle. The local bobby came and took it back during the reception, but still, the thought was there.'

'Mrs Beasley gave us her secret family recipe for horse liniment,' says Dad.

'Give over,' I say.

'That's actually true,' says Mum with a sigh.

'It is that,' says Dad. 'Used to rub your mother down with it throughout her first pregnancy. She stank like a medieval midden but her trotting action were a pleasure to behold.'

'Now you can give over,' says my mother, swatting at him with a newspaper.

I leave them to fight it out and ponder the wedding list conundrum some more. I had always vaguely thought that, on the whole, we probably wouldn't have one. My sister and I were never allowed, as children, to write out wish lists for birthdays or for Father

Christmas because it looked greedy. The assumption that there would be presents at all always summoned looks of reproof from the sterner members of the family – maiden aunts, the more horrible of my uncles and so on – and early training dies hard.

(Although, however horrible those uncles were, they didn't come close to my friend Ian's Uncle Roger. He used to give him and his brother a begrudged 10p each at the end of his annual stay with them. Just how begrudged this munificent sum was became clear the year Roger's visit coincided with Sam's birthday. When Roger discovered this, just after giving his nephews their coins, he leaned forward and took 5p back from Ian and left. Aren't families great?)

But my vague anti-list sentiment only lasted until I started going to weddings as a guest. And as a guest, I bloody love wedding lists. They are the single, shining light of simplicity in the whole affair. If we grant – as I think we must – that nobody feels right about turning up to a wedding empty-handed, no matter how graciously and genuinely the bride and groom have declared their desire for your presence alone rather than your presents, then a list is a blessing. You don't have to trek round shops for weeks beforehand, trying to find an item that successfully embodies your degree of friendship and disposable income, suits the couple's combined and individual tastes while demonstrating that your own is superior to all, and which above all is small and light enough to carry halfway across the country and between B&B, church and reception thereafter. This is a tall order, although it is remarkable how often it can be fulfilled by a glass vase for twenty-five quid.

Wedding lists remove all such traumas. You log on to johnlewis.com or somethingmoreimaginative.co.uk, or you'resurelyhavingalaugh.com, run an appraising eye down a list of desired items, choose one and, click, you're done. After the hours spent ringing round the hostelries on the list of accommodation, and trying to work out train routes and fares with the troglodytic morons manning the booking lines on Network Arse End of Nowhere ('I can do you a Supersaver Return, but you have to have left a week last Thursday and you can't sit facing direction of travel'), I love it. Love it.

That's not to say I don't become narked on occasion. Couples compiling their lists do sometimes get carried away and interpret the opportunity as a chance to upgrade their entire lifestyle and service their personal hobbies and interests. No, I am not buying her a year's supply of Clarins or him his rock-climbing equipment or sailing gear. What are you doing marrying the kind of ponce who goes rock-climbing or sailing anyway? Nor am I buying video games, computer software or anything else that has been invented within the last thirty years or so. At least maintain a semblance of decorum and only put things on the list that pay homage to its origins as a means of furnishing a newly-wed couple with the necessities of life and enabling them to set up home together. Glass, china, cutlery, rugs, cushions, towels, the odd kitchen appliance (not including espresso machines and the like – they break both the thirty-year and the ponce rule outlined above) are all fine. Anything else – you'd better think carefully.

It is fortunate, of course, that I held these particular beliefs before the prospect of compiling my own list hove into view. For they accord so well with my household situation that I might otherwise have been accused of justification after the fact. The fact being that Christopher and I still live like students. Over the last few years we have had – almost unconsciously – to stop reciprocating dinner party invitations because we have simply fallen so far behind in our ability to emulate the standards set.

The Great Dinner Party Revolution happened almost overnight. One moment people were inviting you over for curry on mismatched plates and scrabbling hopefully around in cupboards for forks and enough unchipped vessels of any shape, size and material to hold your booze, and the next it was all expensive crockery, elegant wine glasses and full sets of crockery laid out on tablecloths and punctuated with napkins and place mats. I'll never forget my first sight of side plates at a contemporary's house. Only parents have side plates. I felt as if I had simultaneously gone through the looking-glass, back to the future and into a flat spin.

Ever since, it has been becoming gradually more embarrassing to have people round. Sometimes I try mentally billing us as bohemian, but it never works. It is all too clear from the rest of the house – not to mention our personalities – that we lack the laissez-faire charm such a pose requires. And it is particularly hard to pull off when the host is dressed in tweed.

Back at home, I try to explain all of this to Christopher.

'So,' I conclude, 'I thought we could ask for the simplest dinner service and cutlery set from John Lewis. And I'd love a decent frying pan. You know, with a handle. And maybe even a jug of some kind. The last time I made gravy, I had to put it into an empty coffee jar. I think people noticed.'

'Our pan has a handle.'

'I mean one that's still reliably attached to the pan, not sitting in a drawer awaiting a miraculous visitation from a messiah with a soldering iron.'

'Do I have to come with you to choose these things?' he asks.

'No.'

'Then that all sounds like a very good idea.'

'So . . . you wouldn't let me choose the invitations on my own, but you're happy for me to have sole charge of picking out the domestic accoutrements we'll be using for the rest of our lives?'

'I have learned my lesson. Your odd emotional investments should be left to play themselves out without interference.'

I test that theory by telling him that I have ordered the invitations. He closes his eyes for a moment, passes a hand across his face and says, 'What's done is done.

Make me another fish pie and I will forgive you with my heart and not just my head.'

Fair enough. I'll tell him another time that Mum and I went back to John Lewis this afternoon and chose everything. Maybe tomorrow, while Allegra's here. He won't kill me in front of a child.

We had our first visit from Siobhan and Allegra within days of Anna's party.

Siobhan drew up outside and barely came to a stop before turfing the child out with some smiling rubbish about us getting to know each other before the big day ('Loosely translated as – my childcare arrangements have broken down so she's yours for the afternoon,' said Anna when I rang for advice about what to do with a strange six-year-old for the next four hours) and a variation on this theme has been played out every week or so since. Before I can say, 'Don't you think you could take care of your own daughter for a morning/ afternoon/evening?' Siobhan is gone and Allegra is on my doorstep. I realise now that I have permanently mutated in Siobhan's mind from busy bride-to-be to worker-from-home-and-therefore-precious-untapped-babysitting-resource and can expect to be deployed to cushion her yet further from the vicissitudes of childbearing and, indeed, life.

Fortunately, my house holds two great attractions for Allegra. All the delights of artistic endeavour with poster paints, junior tennis and Angelina Ballerina classes apparently pale into insignificance beside the chance to play with a pair of giant ginger cats. Mummy, of course, does not allow pets and we have fallen into a minor but comforting routine whenever she comes to stay.

When she arrives, I give her the cats' different tins of treats so that she can choose their daily allowance – six each – and she spends a good ten minutes pondering which combination will best suit today's needs. It is a ritual of great solemnity. I always watch her face, set in concentration, and wish I could narrow my own focus so effectively to whatever task I have in hand.

It is then her great delight to roam over the house, dispensing her chosen bounty, two nuggets at a time, at intervals while Henry and Patrick trot devotedly at her heels. Then, if the weather is good, we will go out for a walk round the patch of wasteland at the end of the estate and Patrick – rarely Henry, fat flump that he is – will follow us. This is, Allegra informs me, almost as good as having the dog for which she longs.

If the weather is bad, she will spend her time in the sitting room, making beds for them with various cushions and the old towels and blankets I have dug out over the weeks to aid this increasingly impressive project, which involves much moulding, rearranging and careful padding to fit the carefully observed curvatures of their intended occupants. If the planets and feline whimsy align – and I periodically find myself holding my breath and hoping, after so much serious infantile industry, that they do – Henry will curl up in one and go to sleep, making Allegra's happiness complete.

Today, however, we have to vary the routine a bit as Jean had asked me to take Allegra's measurements and send them to her. Actually, she asked me to ask Siobhan to take Allegra's measurements and send them to her, but it seemed sensible to cut out the middle man and do it myself.

'Will Henry and Patrick be at the wedding?' asks Allegra, as she jumps up on to the coffee table so that I can wield the tape measure more easily.

'That's a good idea,' I say. 'One of them could be a page-boy and the other could carry the ring.'

'We could tie the ring to Patrick's tail.'

'Not Henry's? He's more handsome.'

'No,' says Allegra decidedly. 'His tail is too fluffy. The ring would get lost. Patrick has a thin tail. You could put the ring over it.'

'That's another excellent idea. I could make Henry a cape instead. Turn round a bit – no, the other way – I've always thought Henry would look good in a cape.'

'Would they walk straight down the aisle, though?'

'We'd have to put them in harnesses, I think.'

Allegra looks puzzled.

'They're like special cat leads,' I explain. 'We bought them when we first moved here, to walk them round outside until they got used to this being their new home. Otherwise they wouldn't have known where to come back to when we let them out on their own. OK, lift your jumper up so I can try to decide where your waist is.'

'It's where I bend,' she says helpfully, doubling over to aid me further.

Christopher galumphs downstairs from his study and discovers us in the sitting room. 'Hello strange child that comes here sometimes,' he says to Allegra, who giggles as she straightens up again. She likes Christopher, although naturally he comes a distant third to the cats.

It is very reassuring to me to see the two of them together. My most enduring concern after Christopher and I 'got serious' was how he would cope with children if we had them. I knew he wanted them and, although I wasn't entirely sure then whether I did or not, I knew I didn't want to be with anyone who would take the choice away from me. But I did worry about how he would *be* with them. When a man habitually pops a blood vessel every time a car goes past playing music too loud, or he hears an underinformed answer from 'some monkey-brained twunt' on *Newsnight*, you have to wonder how he would react to a screaming baby or a mind that has yet to master puréed pea-eating, never mind the history and politics of Great Britain.

Gradually, over the years, as I watched him (always readying myself to leap into protective action and hustle the babe out of harm's way the moment a situation looked like unravelling) with friends' children, my fears lessened. He *is* clueless (I once watched him study a two-year-old, who was standing inches in front of him with an expectant look on his face, and his arms upstretched for thirty or forty seconds, before he bent down and said with a frown, 'Do you want me to pick you up?'), but entirely patient with and fascinated by them. He treats them, because he knows of no other way, like miniature adults and, of course, they love it.

'I'm Allegra,' she reminds him, as she turns to allow me to measure her shoulder width.

'I almost didn't recognise you,' he says. 'Don't you normally stand on the ground?'

'I'm on the table so Lucy can measure me for my bridesmaid dress.'

'Ah, I see. Would you like a drink to fortify you?'

'What does fortify mean?'

'It means "give you the strength to get you through your ordeal".'

'What does "ordeal" mean?'

(It is at times like these, however, that I still wonder whether it wouldn't be safer just to have him sterilised.)

'"A thing you must put up with", like having your measurements taken.'

'I don't mind having my thingies taken,' Allegra says, fairly. 'But I am thirsty. Can I have a drink just because I'm thirsty?'

'You can,' says Christopher. 'Shall we have a glass of Ribena each?'

'Yes, please.'

'Potential wife?'

'Yes, please.'

He comes back from the kitchen a few minutes later.

'There you are,' he says, putting down the glasses. 'Spotty glass for you, Allegra, tiny glass for tiny fiancée, large but boringly plain tumbler befitting my great age and status for me. Cheers!'

Allegra takes a mouthful and cocks her head to the side. 'Someone's phone is ringing,' she says.

'Dammit,' I mutter and race upstairs to hunt for my mobile, which turns out to be in my dressing-gown pocket, a place I have no memory of ever putting it. It is, to the surprise of no one, my mother.

'I woke up at four o'clock this morning and made a list,' she begins.

'And hello and how are you too, Mother dearest?' I reply.

'Number one – what are you going to do with your hair?'

'I was going to tuck it all up under a swimming cap and paint woodland scenes on the top . . . Well, what do you want me to say? I dare say I'll have it cut a couple of weeks beforehand, wash it in the morning, maybe let Emily have a go at it with a bit of mousse and hairspray and hope for the best. That's at least three more interventions than it normally gets before it goes out in public.'

She sighs.

'Number two – what are you going to do with your face?'

'I'm sorry – did you just ask me what I am going to do with my face?'

'Yes.'

'I don't understand the question.'

'Well, are you going to wear make-up?'

'Could you hang on a second, please, Mum?'

I switch the phone to silent, and bash my forehead with it. Hard.

'OK, I'm back, sorry about that.'

'So are you?'

'Yes. Yes, I shall be wearing make-up. On my wedding day. On my wedding day, I shall be wearing make-up.'

'Well, I wanted to make sure. I know what you're like.'

'Is there anything else?'

'Will you be getting someone to do your make-up for you?'

'Like who?'

'A person.'

'Oh, a person. No.'

'I think you should.'

'I'll take it under advisement.'

'Number three – do you think it will be all right if I put Alan in a single bed?'

'Alan, my uncle?'

'Yes.'

'Alan who is – correct me if I'm wrong – just one man? He doesn't have a conjoined twin of considerable proportions hanging off him like a giant, fleshy pendulum that has somehow escaped my memory?'

'Don't be ridiculous.'

'So why should there be any problem with him having the single bed?'

'It just seems odd to be putting a grown man in a single bed.'

'I'm going now.'

'Don't forget it's my birthday on Saturday. Emily's coming for the weekend and you've to be here for your tea.'

'The first of July, I know. It is engraved in my diary and on my heart. See you then.'

'Byeee!'

I hang up and go downstairs to see how the Ribena posse are getting on. Christopher is standing on the coffee table while Allegra loops the tape measure round his knees. 'You have very good knees,' she says.

'That's excellent news,' he replies.

'Now sit down on the floor so I can measure your head.'

'"With one fluid motion",' says Christopher, lowering himself into position with much huffing, puffing and the occasional small grunt of exertion, '"he complied".'

'You talk funny,' says Allegra, wrapping the tape several times around his head. 'People can't understand you.'

'Ife been htold,' says my fiancé with difficulty through his gag.

'Oh dear,' says the seamstress manquée, 'I'm afraid your head is too big. We will have to make you a smaller one, otherwise you won't fit down the aisle.'

As I am musing upon this vision of someone with an even foggier understanding of the wedding than my mother, I hear a car crunch into the car park behind the house.

'Allegra, your mother's here.'

She quickly gathers up her bits and pieces, says goodbye to Christopher and the cats, and goes reluctantly to the back door. 'Can I play measuring again next time?' she asks.

'Of course you can,' I say, as Christopher extricates himself from the tangled tape, knocking a glass still half full of Ribena over the sofa and smashing an empty one to pieces on the floor. 'And if you're very lucky, I'll teach you how to strangle him. If I haven't got there first, of course.'

CHAPTER ELEVEN

Today is Mum's birthday. Mum's birthday.

In previous years we have attempted to take her into town for a meal if we could find one cheap enough (there is nothing more deadening to the appetite than the cry, 'Chicken risotto for how much? Your father could feed us for a week for that!' And by the time you have gone, for the eight-billionth time, through an explanation of overheads, modern Western capitalism and the notion of dining as a pleasurable experience rather than a pitstop for simply refuelling, you're lucky if you're not battling rising waves of nausea and despair) or a show if we could find one crap enough (Mum being one of those rare people who wants to go in rather than out humming the tune), but in the end it was the journey itself that became impracticable. And by impracticable, I mean too dangerous. It was one thing to pacify the hordes of outraged commuters whose feet she had slapped down off the seats as she moved through the carriages. It was quite another to attempt to soothe the multitudes who had been told to turn their music down, to wait until they get home to speak to their friends on the phone, not to drink so much, not to eat in public and to move their bags and let old people sit down.

For the sake of her – and our – mental and physical safety, therefore, we have determined that this year the celebrations should be kept entirely at home. Even though it is in fact a double celebration, as we are marking both her sixty-fifth birthday and her retirement from the family-planning fray. After forty years of plugging coils into south-east London uteri, fitting caps to recalcitrant cervixes and throwing pills down the throats of anyone from schoolgirls to septuagenarians, provided they could count to twenty-one and had a vagina that was open for business, she is stepping down to spend more time with her gin and tonics.

She is a little worried about what she will find to fill up her time. We are all a little worried about what she will find to fill up her time. I fail to see how there cannot be any fallout nor how it cannot fall disproportionately on me, as the only immediate family member currently embarked on a meaty undertaking simply crying out for a project manager. The best I can hope for is that she might at least start ringing me with the day's list of questions at a less ungodly hour than seven o'clock in the morning, once she no longer has to get to work.

Our festive itinerary looks like this:

Friday evening
Emily arrives from Bristol. Emily spends rest of evening in the kitchen constructing a needlessly sophisticated cake – with me acting as handmaiden to her Jane Asher manquée – that will ensure neither of us gets to bed

before 2 a.m. This tradition began when we were teen-agers and, through some strange, synaptic misfire, my mother conceived the desire to have a set of studio photographs taken of her two grease-slicked, acne-spattered daughters – whether for posterity, blackmail or just a good laugh we never determined because we both refused outright. To make up for it, Emily decided to make her a sponge 'n' icing model of the two of us – taking particular delight in pitting my fondant face with the end of a cocktail stick to represent my black-heads – and we haven't looked back since. This year, in honour of the retirement element of the celebration, she is tackling a scale model of a speculum. And if you think that's in slightly bad taste, you should have seen the stuff I vetoed.

Saturday

9 a.m.   Don earplugs and join Mum for the opening of the presents.

9.30 a.m.   Give Mum all the receipts to her presents so she can take them back next week.

10.30 a.m.   Mum's secret present arrives.

Do you know about Colour Me Beautiful? It was a great craze in the eighties – amongst well, I was going to say, amongst women of a certain age, but I have just realised that it must have been amongst women only very slightly older than I am now, so I'm going to move swiftly on – which involved a woman coming to your house, draping swathes of material around your shoul-ders and telling you which colours suited you best. You got classified as either a Winter, Spring, Summer or Autumn, depending where in the spectrum of hues your hair and skin tone landed you, and then you could go forth and rebuild your wardrobe. Nowadays it would be a reality show, but back then the made-over (or 'revamped' as we called it then, kids!) clientele had to make do with it simply being reality.

Naturally, Mum – as she had taught us to do with all things creative, colourful or feminine, never mind anything that was an unholy combination of the three – despised the idea. But clearly a seed was planted and over the next thirty years a sigh would occasionally escape her as she saw the lasting benefits reaped by those who had indulged, or when she stood before her own wardrobe and mentally compared the smorgasbord of more-or-less appalling shades with the neat blends that hung in the closets of the CMB elite.

So, at last, Emily and I have decided to take matters into our own hands. We have booked one of the reps – who rejoices in the name of Silvana Borg – to come round and Do Her. In fact, she is going to Do all three of us as a job lot.

'It only cost a little bit more,' said Emily. 'So I thought – why not? And she's throwing in a make-up session for each of us too. I warned her Mum might try to break her hand off if she comes at her with a mascara wand but she says she's willing to take the risk.'

It all unfolds pretty much according to plan. As soon as I see Silvana's car pull up outside, I engineer a towel emergency in the bathroom to get Mum out of the way ('Come quickly – I've forgotten which way round the blue, non-emergency, guest mediums go!') and Emily swiftly ushers our visitor through to the sitting room. She is a tiny, tiny Mauritian woman, a little pocket person, as immaculately groomed and coiffed as you would expect, with olive skin and huge brown eyes in a small, sweet, heart-shaped face.

'I could wear her as a badge,' Emily mutters as I come downstairs and we usher her through into the sitting room. 'Is Mum still busy up there?'

'Don't worry,' I say. 'I disturbed the Imperial Leather stockpile under the sink before I came down. She's probably taking the entire cupboard apart by now.'

Silvana accepts the offer of a cup of coffee and starts to lay out the tools of her trade. The armchair is filled with mountains of gorgeously coloured swatches and on the coffee table she lays out equally gorgeous palettes of eyeshadows, lip tints and blushers. 'There!' she says, sitting back on her heels in satisfaction. 'Everything ees ready! Now, who goes first?'

'The birthday girl,' says Emily. 'I'll just go and get her. Brace yourself, everyone.'

She brings Mum down and flings open the door of the sitting room. 'Surprise!'

'Oh my God,' says Mum, looking round the room, which looks like a cross between a small branch of Boots and a bazaar. 'What have you daft ha'porths done?'

'It's a term of endearment,' I explain to Silvana who

is looking a little bemused. 'She's just trying to express her pleasure at the thoughtfulness of our gift.'

Emily explains who Silvana is and what she is here to do.

'You little buggers,' says Mum, as Silvana seats her in front of the mirror, fastens a white tablecloth around her neck and brings forth the first batch of scarves. 'What a good idea.'

The rest of the morning passes in shrieks of delight and horror as we all throw into the ring our amateur opinions about what suits who, along with Silvana's professional judgment. Mum is declared a Summer, Emily a Winter and I am a Spring.

We break for lunch before embarking on our make-up session.

'She's getting married in September,' says Emily, pausing in her sterling work of uncorking a couple of bottles to point the corkscrew at me.

'How – just half a glass, please, I'm driving – loffly!' says Silvana, beaming.

After most of the first bottle has disappeared down Mangan throats while Silvana questions me politely about the wedding, Emily says, 'What colour dress do you, Silvana, a trained professional, think she should choose? And please, bear in mind that (a) she's a fool and (b) she has already chosen it.'

'We-ell,' she says, squinting at me critically, 'not white, that I think is for sure.'

'So far so good,' I say, raising a glass.

'I think because you have blonde hair the temptation

would be to go for a pink, but thees—' says Silvana shaking her head, 'thees I would not do.'

'Hurrah!' cries Emily, draining her own glass and pouring us all another.

'I would say . . . on the whole – maybe a very pale coffee or perhaps gold,' she says.

We all shriek with delight. And drunkenness.

'It's pale gold!' says Emily. Silvana looks deeply relieved. So do I. As long as I've remembered correctly, of course. It's been a very long time since I saw anything to do with my dress. Oh well.

Emily and I manage to stay quiet while Silvana starts on Mum's make-up. Our mother has gone six and a half very happy decades without ever wearing more than a slick of lipstick (frosted pink, disgusting) and, during the heady eighties, a solid block of sky-blue or leaf-green shadow above her eyes, and she is not looking forward to this part of the 'fun' at all. Despite the wine, she is so tense that she flinches at every movement of Silvana's delicately wielded brushes towards her face. Any sudden movement or laughter on our part would undoubtedly cause her to bolt like a skittish horse.

Watching Silvana adding blusher, lipstick and eyeshadow to our mother's never-before-foundationed-and-powdered face is like watching Rolf Harris work. Each brushstroke brings it more to life. 'Can you tell what it is yet?' I murmur to Em under my breath. Eventually, Silvana pronounces herself satisfied and steps back to allow Mum to look at herself in the mirror. She leans forward. The nation waits.

'My God,' she says. 'I'm GORGEOUS.'

We all cheer and Emily leaps into the hotseat for her turn. This does not take long because one of the many reasons Emily is not being my bridesmaid is that she has one of those faces that barely requires any make-up. She has skin like a baby's, a big, ripe mouth that you can't put lipstick on without making her look like a blow-up doll, and eyes the size of headlights, fringed with ridiculously dark, ridiculously long lashes. When she was very young and still had her little fat hamster cheeks, her lashes used to rest on them when she slept. If you add mascara to them now, it looks like two crows flying down her face every time she blinks and you have to protect any old people near by from the draught.

'There,' says Silvana after ten minutes' minor improvement upon what nature has already wrought. 'You are done!'

Emily admires herself casually in the mirror – hey, all in a day – and then picks me up by the scruff of the neck and dumps me in the chair.

'Thank you,' she says to Silvana. 'Now try and work some magic on this.'

Silvana kneels down to examine my face more closely. 'Hmm,' she says, unscrewing the top of what looks like a pot of Polyfilla and starting to smooth it on, 'you have quite open pores . . . '

'Open!' shrieks Emily. 'You'll need a harness and a potholing degree to sort them out!'

' . . . and we need to get rid of these dark circles under your eyes . . . '

'I've got half a pot of white emulsion left over from doing the kitchen,' offers Mum, who since her facial transformation has become far too chipper for my liking.

' . . . and we will even out your skin tone with this . . . And reintroduce the contours with this . . . And add a little bit of highlighter to this . . . '

'To what?' asks Emily. 'Have you found her A-levels at the bottom of one of her pores?'

I wonder if I can get myself adopted by another family before the wedding?

Silvana kindly attempts to come to my rescue. 'You are awful,' she scolds the two of them. 'Do not be awful!'

'Thank you,' I say resignedly. 'But alas you are thirty years too late.'

Once the groundwork is laid, my mother and sister crowd forward to watch as Silvana's hand hovers over her Spring palettes.

'Ooh – will it be Lobster?' cries Emily in mock, or possibly by this stage down the second bottle real, excitement. 'Rosebud? Hint of Grape? Or should we just trap your lips in a mangle and hope that they colour up naturally?'

'Why don't you get out of the pigging way so that Silvana can get to work?' I snarl.

They tiptoe exaggeratedly back to their chairs. Silvana sweeps shadows and glosses across the appropriate features, then invites me to open my eyes and inspect her handiwork.

I look. I turn to my mother and sister with great calm. 'I see now,' I say kindly, 'why you were kicking up such a fuss. You were jealous. Jealous because I am now a Beautiful Laydee and you are relegated to mere reflections of my greater glory. I'm so sorry. I thought you were just being twunts.'

'You look so lovely!' Mum exclaims.

'You really do. Almost not ugly at all,' says Emily.

It is true. I thank Silvana effusively and buy everything that she has used to create the vision that is now Me.

'Sit down,' she says, after I have bundled my magical goodies into my bag. 'And I will give you instructions on how to do everything that I have done.'

I grab a pen and Mum's pad and start taking notes as Silvana co-opts Emily's head and starts tracing lines with her fingertips over it to show me what she did where and why. Whenever her eyes are open, Emily rolls them at Mum, who is standing behind me but, I am sure, is reciprocating. All the same, I figure this is information important enough to require them to endure a little boredom.

After a few moments of taking Silvana's dictation, however, Emily opens the eye our artiste is not using to demonstrate sweeping eyeliner techniques and says: 'Here's a mad thought: rather than attempt a cack-handed version on the most important day of your life, why don't you hire Silvana to do your make-up for you?'

'What a Good Idea,' says Mum instantly.

I look from one to the other. Light dawns. My family has many faults – many, many, many faults – but being natural liars is not one of them. 'You set this whole thing up, didn't you?' I say.

'Yes,' says Mum.

'No,' says Emily.

'Well, yes and no,' they say together.

'I had the Colour Me Beautiful idea, and then Silvana mentioned that she could do our make-up too, and that got me thinking that you would never agree to hire someone for your wedding day unless you'd met them and actually seen what a difference it could make, so I told Mum and Silvana everything so they could help persuade you today. But you were so slow on the uptake that my cleverly laid plan has crumbled into dust and we just all have to say: Hire Silvana, she will make you look properly nice for your wedding day, you should not go down the aisle coated in three-year-old Body Shop foundation and a freebie lipgloss from the cover of *Cosmopolitan* like you were planning to, Jesus Christ, it just won't do, now please see sense.'

She stopped, lung capacity rather than depth of feeling having run out.

I pause. She is right, of course. My lack of experience in this kind of thing, plus my lack of imagination, is such that I would never have appreciated what a difference it could make and I would never have agreed to lay out money on an entirely untested theory. But now she's here, and my new face is here, I can see that of course I should book her, and immediately. But there's no need for them to know any of that, so I pause a bit longer before capitulating.

'Go on, then. Silvana, are you free on—'

'On the last Saturday of September, yes, I know.' She grins.

'Of course,' I say. 'Emily wouldn't have booked anyone for today without checking that they were around to complete the job.'

'That would have been a rookie mistake,' says Emily, bowing low.

'Right then,' I say. 'See you in September. And remember – I need to look like this. But I want you to make the other two look like burn victims, OK?'

'You are awful too,' says Silvana decidedly, as she leaves.

It's true. But it's why we get along.

Tomorrow I have a dress fitting with Jean, in which I will be trying on a preliminary version of my dress, done in calico, for approval. Christopher is aware of this appointment, even though I have not told him anything about the dress, and he is becoming increasingly concerned about what I am planning to wear down the aisle.

'Just tell me roughly what it looks like,' he says as he grips Henry firmly in his arms so that I can embark on a careful flea patrol through our risibly fluffy cat's pelt.

'No.'

'Why not? It's because she's making you a bridal

Slanket, isn't it? You're going to get married in a white satin Slanket and woolly mittens because you think it's going to be cold in the church.'

'She's not making me a Slanket.'

'But has she given you any advice, or have you just told her what you wanted?'

'Why are you so bothered?'

'Because how are you going to manage if you haven't had anyone to give you advice?' he says. 'You don't know how to dress. I mean, there are plenty more hoggish women out there who look a lot better than you do.'

I mentally added this to my Big Book of Backhanded Compliments from Assorted Boyfriends and Now Fiancés Over the Years, somewhere between Ian (my first boyfriend at university), who once told me, after I had been shopping for a skirt for graduation day and came home complaining about being too short for everything, that he was glad I wasn't a normal height, 'because if you were five foot six or something, I'd have no chance' – a comment that has intrigued me more and more as the years have gone by, and Jason (random man from a friend's party), who once looked hard at me and said, 'You know, if you were in a photo or something with nothing to show the scale, you'd have quite a nice figure.' A comment that has intrigued me less and less as the years have gone on.

'But,' Christopher adds, 'you don't have any self-confidence when it comes to clothes and you've no common sense.'

'Mother?' I cry, staring into his eyes in mock-bafflement and patting his face with my hands. 'Is that you? What have they done to you?'

'Made me slightly less masculine and gently bearded,' he says, backing away while Henry yowls and squirms at my antics.

I abandon flea patrol and go downstairs, claiming a prior appointment with *The O.C.* I scroll unseeingly through the menu, while I muse upon what my horrible fiancé has said and come to the reluctant conclusion that the man has a point. I do not know how to dress. When I put on the mocked-up dress tomorrow, I cannot be trusted to know whether it looks right or not. And I will certainly be unable to suggest improvements or changes. I do need help.

I pull the phone towards me. 'Who ya gonna call?' I mutter. (Do you realise it's now twenty-five years since the film was released and it is still impossible to use that phrase without at least mentally adding 'Ghostbusters' to it? That line may be the one thing that outlives cockroaches after a nuclear war.)

My mother has gone to her sister's for a second birthday-cum-post-retirement holiday – which is to say, she has gone to Eileen's to do all the things she normally does (drink gin, eat fish fingers, chips and beans for supper, watch *Coronation Street* and alternate wildly between cackling laughter and swift, brain-stunning fury for no reason any external witness can perceive) but with even less regard to her mental and physical state now that she no longer has to keep a steady hand for coil insertions on her return. So she can't accompany me. And even if she could, she would be of little help. Although she always looks good, she has no more clue about clothes than I do. She gets away with it because she can still, despite a six-decade diet of butter, full-fat milk, bacon and chocolate, throw her clothes on an enduringly fatless, five-foot-ten-inch frame that still sports thighs like an Indian brave's. It is a wonder I haven't imploded with jealousy years ago.

My sister is busy coordinating a special work project 'involving even more computers and even more fuck-wits than usual' and cannot come to London for the next six weeks. I'm going up there in a couple of week-ends' time to make sure she has not killed herself or injured anyone during the process but, until then, we are effectively incommunicado.

But it's OK. For I still have Annie, Rosie's mother, who, I realise suddenly, is exactly the woman I need for the job. I put down the phone. I know she will be reluc-tant to tread on what she sees as Mum's turf, but I also know that she will deny me nothing face to face. I have proved that with many a Mr Kipling's fondant fancy over the years.

'Pleeeease, Annie?' I beg, sitting on her squashy sofa with a chocolate biscuit in one hand and a cup of tea in the other. 'I need a fresh eye. Preferably in the head of someone who knows how to dress.'

'Oh,' she says, waving an embarrassed hand. 'I don't know how to dress.'

As she is sitting in front of me wearing a beautiful black wool dress that she has had, to my certain knowledge, for thirty years without it ever going out of style, artfully accessorised with a single silk scarf and enormous agate ring that she 'just picked up in Greenwich market the other day', while I am lying on the ground (the better to beg for her assistance) in ill-fitting second-hand jeans, limply overwashed T-shirt, fetid trainers and despair, I do not bother to reply to this.

'Pleeeeeease, Annie? Just come and tell me if it will do or if it's the worst idea anyone's ever had in the history of clothes and/or weddings? You wouldn't want to see me coming down the aisle looking like a giant satin nightmare, would you, knowing that you could have stopped it right here, today, with just half an hour of your time, not including the drive to Jean's and back?'

'But I don't want the responsibility of helping you choose your dress,' she says. 'You should just have what you want. I don't want to put you off something you love. You shouldn't listen to anyone.'

'No, no!' I cry. 'That's exactly wrong! I must be told if I'm making a mistake. I can't trust Mum because we're related and we could be genetically predisposed to liking the same, wrong thing. I sort of trust Jean but I don't really know her well enough. And I can't trust myself because my brain has broken under the stress. And you're the perfect person to help me, because you have style, you love me and you couldn't tell a lie if Rosie's life depended on it. Which, I may as well make clear to you now, it does. I've got her strapped to a petrol drum at home and she's under strict instructions to drop a lighted match into it if I think for one moment you're not telling me the truth.'

Annie gives up. 'Let's go,' she says, taking her car keys from the hall table.

Forty minutes later, Jean is twirling in front of us the dressmaker dummy that is sporting the calico draft of my dress and I am quizzing Annie on everything. She likes the shape, she likes the collar, she approves of the corset and the A-line, and she loves the colour and the fabric. I scrutinise her closely and can tell that Rosie is safe.

'Right,' says Jean, 'let's try this on you.'

I shuck off my clothes and, with my back to the giant mirror, step carefully into the pin-stuffed folds. It is like stepping into a very dangerous linen cupboard. Jean and Annie lift the dress up around me, I slip my arms through the holes and Jean starts lacing me up at the back.

'Breathe out,' she instructs, and yanks me in another inch. 'Are your boobies in the cups at the front?'

'Technically, yes,' I say, looking down at the two forlorn little mounds drifting about in the two padded domes arching across my chest. 'But we could still hire the rest out to Centre Parcs and use the rent to pay for the wedding.'

Jean peers over my shoulder and down at my chest. 'That's amazing,' she says thoughtfully. 'I made them as small as I could.'

'Great. Perhaps you can hire some elves for the next go.'

'Don't worry,' she says reassuringly. 'I can always make some extra pads to go in. I've just' – she peers down again – 'never had anyone who couldn't fill . . . Never mind. Let's pin up the skirt and then you can turn around and have a look at yourself.'

She pins the skirt, gives a final tug on the corset and I turn around to face the mirror. Annie, Jean and I stare. I cannot believe it. I look completely and utterly dreadful. I look – and it may not seem, written down, like the worst word in the world, but imagine, please, if it were the first description to come into your mind as you saw yourself for the first time in the dress that is supposed to transform you into something between queen and deity for a day – stout. You know, like a middle-aged woman. A middle-aged woman in the fifties. A middle-aged woman in the fifties who is leaning over the fence of her back-to-back to talk to her equally stout neighbour while her ten kids play around her ankles. Pasty flesh oozes from the top of the corset, and my upper arms – not yet hidden by the collar, which will be added after the rest of the dress is made – have swollen to the size of hams. Pale, unglistening hams. I am mortified. Annie is frozen in horror and Jean is dumbfounded.

I don't, to be honest, quite recall what happened next. Scraps of memory are all that have made it through the protective barriers that my mind immediately threw up between me and the Pillsbury Doughboy in the mirror. Jean leaping to loosen my stays and me collapsing, sobbing, on to Annie like a hysterical Southern belle. Annie trying to tell me that it would be much better when it was properly fitted and the collar was on.

'No, it won't!' I bellow into Annie's bosom. 'It'll still be me and I'll still look disgusting!'

'No, no, no,' Annie soothes as she rocks me back and forth. I have evidently, I notice only then, climbed into her lap at some point. 'It will all be fine in the end.'

'No, it won't!'

'Yes, it will.'

'No, it won't!'

'I'll go and get her a drink of water,' says Jean, as she slips out of the room.

'Is it just the dress that's upsetting you?' asks Annie.

'No, it's . . . EVERYTHING!' I howl, unleashing a fresh storm of sobs upon her patient and now entirely sodden shoulder.

'Like what?'

'Like – Christopher still hasn't asked Richard to be his best man, like I've got a bridesmaid I don't even want . . . she's really sweet, but I don't want her . . . and I don't understand about the music . . . and I don't know what to do about flowers . . . and Mum still thinks we should be serving everyone a roast ox each instead of canapés, and I haven't sorted out the booze yet . . . and . . . and . . . '

'And . . . ?' says Annie encouragingly.

'And Christopher's WEIRD!'

Annie looks puzzled. 'Do you mean you're having doubts about marrying him?'

'Only because he's so WEIRD!'

'What do you mean? Of course he's weird. But you've known that all along, haven't you?'

'Yes, but . . . '

'But what?'

'But . . . I always thought I would marry someone normal. But he's going to be weird for ever! I'm too tired to cope with him being weird for the next forty years.' I hiccup myself to a stop and start sniffing instead.

'Oh, you're too tired to cope with anything right now,' says Annie, kissing me and pushing back the hair from my face with one hand and wiping away my tears with a tissue in the other. 'Don't you worry. Everyone has these kinds of feelings before they get married.'

'Do they?' I say hopefully, as Jean comes back into the room carrying a glass of water. I take it gratefully and slide off Annie's lap on to the sofa beside her.

'Oh yes,' says Jean, coming to sit next to me and starting to unlace the offending dress. 'All brides get so stressed by everything that's going on that the fiancé just starts to look like another problem that's got to be sorted.'

'That's right,' nods Annie. 'And you have a daft idea in your head of what a bridegroom should look like and how he should behave, and then when your own one just carries on behaving just like he's always done, it can all get a bit too much.'

'Exactly,' agrees Jean. 'Now, let's get this thing off you—'

I stand up and let the dress fall to the ground.

'That's it,' Jean says. 'Now step out. Good girl.'

'And remember,' Annie says, as I put my clothes back on, 'you're weird too.'

'Am I?'

'Of course you are,' she says with certainty. 'I've known you since you were three. You were a very unsettling child. And Christopher's an unsettling man. But I love you both. And I know you love each other.'

'We do,' I say, pulling my T-shirt over my head.

'And the dress will be fine,' adds Jean. 'I just pulled it a bit too tight.'

'It wasn't you, Jean,' I say. 'It was me. But it's OK. For the next three months I've just got to remember to love Christopher and hate chocolate, and not the other way around.'

On the way home I meditate upon the task before me. I have been very lucky in the past. Three formative moments served to protect me over the years from yo-yo dieting, eating disorders, body dysmorphia and all points in between. As a teenager, while my friends were experimenting with black coffee and laxatives, worrying about how many calories there were in mint Tic Tacs and whether swallowing after you-know-what counted as breaking your diet, I sailed merrily through unscathed, thanks to a trinity of prophylactic experiences, to wit:

1. Reading a copy of *Just 17* when I was about twelve in which there was – this being the height

of supermodel fervour – a four-page interview with Claudia Schiffer. And in it she proclaimed there was no such thing as the perfect body – why, she added, even she had a terribly uneven hairline. It sowed deep within me the seed of knowledge that the fight into which women throw themselves every day was essentially unwinnable and that the easiest thing might therefore be not to bother. Ever.

2. Reading an article in one of my grandma's teetering piles of *Reader's Digest* one summer about hand, foot, hair, mouth and bottom models. That's right. So few women were deemed perfect enough in all parts that advertisers sought out specialists instead. The Fairy Liquid advert, I seem to remember, used one woman to do the laughing mother bending to decorate her child's button nose with bubbles, but another one entirely to be the hands that had done dishes but that were now gently caressing themselves in close-up. Once again, I was armed against the lie.

3. When I was thirteen I had flu and lost my appetite – wholly, utterly and completely – for six weeks. I went down to five stone. My limbs were like sticks. My ribs were countable. When I lay down, you could see my pelvic bones jutting up like mountain ranges round the deepening valley of my stomach. And my fat thighs remained absolutely unchanged. I looked down at them

and realised that I would literally have to starve myself to death to get this most hated part of me to change. And if I did, I could probably be exhumed ten years later and still the saddlebags would be there, as ugly and defiant as ever. It surely wasn't worth it.

Added to this, however, was another saving grace. I was a naturally skinny (apart from the thighs, which appeared to have been stuck on as an afterthought by a malevolent god) child and adolescent. If I never got breasts – well, I never got puppy fat either, which seemed to be the main trigger for my friends' flights to green salad and ProPlus.

So I was able to develop an array of bad eating habits and stick determinedly to a stringent non-exercise regime without any difficulty or deleterious side effects. Alas, nobody told me that youth's the stuff that allows your body to endure these things without complaint, or that after twenty-five it starts to seek its revenge.

After this age, your body's *raison d'être* seems to become, not the efficient carrying of you through life, but to search for new and interesting ways to let you down. You get fatter, hairier, and before you know it your highest hope for aesthetic appeal lies in getting your spots to clear up before the first wrinkles arrive. What a life.

Add to this DNA-determined disaster the inactivity that comes with working from home for the last three years and *voilà* – you arrive effortlessly at the awful images just apprehended in Jean's Giant Mirror of Truth.

So now, just like every other bride in history, I must give in. That evening, I sit on my hands to stop myself shoving Twix into my mouth like logs into a sawmill. I concede that I must undo the well-padded work of a lifetime's sweets and sloth. I must over the next three months break my bad habits and shift some of my accrued avoirdupois, which is French for 'having too much arse'. Because I am not walking up the aisle looking like Mrs Pepperpot. I am not. Call me weak, call me shallow, call me anything you like, as long as it's not – Christ on a bike – stout.

CHAPTER TWELVE

'So,' says Mum as she whizzes round the bedroom unpacking her suitcase. 'What have you been up to while I've been away?'

I tell her about the new regime that has been established during her ten-day mission to drain the North-West of its gin reserves. No chocolate. No cheese. And some exercise.

'Exercise?' says Mum, confused. 'But you don't. You won't.'

'Aha,' I say. 'But I do. And I will. And I am.'

I tell her how, after Annie told Rosie about my little meltdown at Jean's, Rosie rang me up to suggest that we start playing tennis together every evening at the park that lies between her flat and my house.

'There are three courts,' Rosie said. 'One of them has markings, one of them has a net and one of them has both. And you don't have to pay.'

'It's like a dream come true,' I said.

And so began what quickly became a very rewarding evening ritual – an hour of bashing out the day's frustrations on an intriguingly uneven surface with a partner who perfectly matches me not in terms of skill (for Rosie can both hit the ball and make it go roughly where she wants it to) but in temperament. We are both fantastically uncompetitive. We lose track of the score, the number of games, whose turn it is to serve and neither of us cares. It is brilliant. It is not only making me feel thinner and fitter already, but it is also doing great work in erasing all sorts of traumatic, early, PE-based memories that have done so much over the years to cripple my already profoundly non-athletic instincts.

Occasionally rain or an inescapable social engagement stops play, but soon we are pressing on through drizzle and feeling vaguely restless if we miss a game two nights in a row. If I get nothing else at all out of being married, I explain to my mother, who is now changing out of her travel clothes into a new outfit that she has evidently bought while away, at least I will have, at last, a Sensible Exercise Regime with which to stave off obesity and Type 2 diabetes. Hurrah.

'Ta-daaah!' cries my mother as she twirls out from behind the wardrobe door towards me. 'What do you think?'

'What is it?'

'What do you mean, what is it? It's my outfit for the wedding!'

There are thoughts, Wordsworth once said when he wasn't going demented about daffodils, that lie too deep for tears. I'm having some now. For my mother is standing before me in a pale blue sleeveless chiffon two-piece (yes, of course, with pleated skirt. Of *course*) of such unremitting hideousness that for a moment I am speechless.

'Well?' she says.

How can I put this politely?

'Hmm,' I say slowly, 'tell me . . . while you were out shopping with Eileen – did you experience any discomfort? Dizziness? Any kind of searing pain in your head that sent you temporarily blind and could explain this purchase as the after-effects of a minor but significant stroke? Because it's absolutely disgusting.'

'What do you mean?' Mum cries in disbelief, turning to the mirror again and lovingly smoothing down the chiffon folds that are doing so much to make her look like an ambulant sofa.

'I mean – it's the wrong colour for you – it's the wrong colour for anyone not gumming a rusk – and it's the wrong material for you – or for anyone not engaged in an interpretive dance recital – it makes you look wider than you are tall – it flattens your bust, hides your legs and yet displays your bingo wings as if they were the choicest cuts on the counter. It's extraordinary.'

It really is. As previously noted, my mother has always been distressingly tall, slim and – although I naturally cannot see it myself, but deduced the truth of it over the years by the number of times I have seen her slap tipsy and opportunistic male friends round the head for trying it on – attractive. We have photos of her on the beach in the sixties that look like something from a magazine shoot. She used to make her skirts out of a single yard of material and was known throughout her early hospital training days as Dr Legs Livesey.

None of which bounty she made any use of, of course, because she married my dad when she was eight, but still – she always seems to recall it with pleasure. So why is she choosing to swathe herself in this powder-blue nightmare?

I stop. A thought has suddenly occurred to me. A thought so strange, so entirely foreign to our family's mentality that I have to search my mind for the words before I can voice it.

'You're not . . . ' I say hesitantly. 'You haven't . . . you haven't chosen this deliberately, have you? To be kind, because you think I'm going to look like a bag of shite on the day and you don't want to pull focus? Because you don't have to, you know. I'm quite used to looking like a bag of shite. I don't mind.'

'Don't be ridiculous!' says Mum, looking horrified at the thought of anyone attributing such sentimental motives to her actions. 'I want to look great!'

'Then why this catastrophe in chiffon?'

She looks at herself anew. I wait in vain for the first flickers of doubt to cross her face.

'I don't know what you're talking about,' she says stubbornly.

I sigh. I didn't want to have to do this. I take a picture of her with my phone and send it to Emily with a text saying, 'Mother of the bride in grip of terrible delusion. Please help.'

Seconds later the phone rings. 'Put her on,' says Emily tersely.

I hand Mum the phone. I hear Emily shouting at her.

She looks again in the mirror. I see the doubts form. I take the phone before they turn to tears.

'Thanks, Em,' I say. 'Your work here is done.'

'Thank God,' she says. 'Thank God. Let us never speak of this again.'

Ten minutes later she rings back.

'We're speaking of this again,' she says.

'OK,' I say, as I watch Mum divest herself of the azure atrocity and hang it sadly and still uncomprehendingly back up in the wardrobe.

'A girl at work looked over my shoulder and saw the picture,' Emily continues. 'And, after she had been sick, asked me what was going on. I told her and she said that near here there is a shop that sells nothing but mother-of-the-bride outfits. It's called Battleaxe Galactica or something, and you need to bring her with you when you come up at the weekend so we can drag her in there and Sort This Out.'

Bloody hell. Another weekend chewed up by the wedding.

'Do we all have to go?' I whine.

'Look what happened when we didn't,' she replies simply, and there's no arguing with that.

Battleaxe Galactica is in a chocolate-box village, from some points of view, forty minutes outside Bristol, but from theirs, 'in the heart of the Cotswolds'. On the ground floor the walls are lined with severe satin suits, glamorous but sturdy gowns, and serious hats floating above them on unseen poles, like miniature UFOs. At the back, there is a tiny café where bustling, matronly waitresses are serving coffee and cakes to waiting husbands and exhausted, matronly women. Upstairs, there are even more hats floating above even more clothes and in the middle there is an open space where a number of women are trying on clothes. There are, in fact, two changing-room cubicles on the back wall, where one suspects the management had hoped to corral the customers, but these have long since been abandoned in favour of the communal approach.

All of human life is here. A thin, expensively high-lighted blonde woman is trying on everything pearl and oyster coloured in the shop. Staff are bringing stuff to her in relays. She plucks out a few and waves away the rest – 'I would say that was salmon pink, wouldn't you?' – with disdain. She's Siobhan, thirty years on. Where do they get their confidence from, these people? Is it money? Looks? Or just luck? She looks as if she has never been visited by a moment's self-doubt. I bet she never says sorry automatically when other people bump into her in the street. Once again it becomes shiningly clear that all that stuff you hear about the most confident people on the outside being the most quiveringly neurotic wrecks on the inside is just something neurotic people say to make themselves feel better.

Other fatter, redder, more normal specimens of mature womanhood are using their daughters as staff. The air is thick with hissed instructions – 'Get me this in a size sixteen!' 'Tell your father I'm going to be late!' 'Take that look off your face!' – and flying HRT patches as dresses are whipped on and off. One woman – who is neither fat nor thin nor, interestingly, just right – is having great difficulty choosing between a pale-purple suit and a pewter-coloured dress. We all do our best to keep quiet, but everyone knows that it was in the communal changing room that the phrase 'a critical mass' was born. Soon everyone is lobbing their two-penn'orth at her. She looks first startled, then grateful, then confused.

'OK,' shouts someone at last above the sound of the sartorial mêlée. 'The basic feeling in the room is, I believe this—' she glances quickly round us all. Speak now or for ever hold your peace, I think. 'The pewter dress, though more expensive and only wearable on special occasions, makes you look fantastic.' There is a general murmur of agreement. 'The purple suit, however, though cheaper and would do for Sundays, makes you look only so-so. Yes?' Another murmur of assent. 'Therefore, the winner is – the pewter dress. Case closed.' I think she banged a gavel as we cheered but I can't be sure.

Although she has two daughters running to the rails for her, my mother cannot find anything she likes.

'Too small!'

'Too big!'

'Too posh!'

'Too casual!'

'Too expensive!'

'Too cheap-looking!'

'Too tiring,' her daughters eventually conclude. 'Too pointless.'

On our way out, my sister stops at a bargain bin by the door. It is mostly full of the kind of underwear that looks as if it has been made by retired Govan ship-builders. 'Wait a second,' she says, tugging at a bit of chocolate-brown satin poking out of the top from underneath the Playtex girders. She unearths a fish-tailed skirt and dives back in to find a matching fitted jacket. 'Try these on,' she commends. 'We'll just order a cup of coffee and come back up in a second.'

We collapse in the café while Mum heads back upstairs to the changing room. The waitress gets our order wrong and as we wait for the right drinks Em suddenly starts nudging me hard.

'What? Stop that! What?'

She nods towards the stairs. I look up. A vision of loveliness in chocolate satin is descending the stairs.

'Dr Legs Livesey, I presume?' says my sister.

'Tell me you like it?' I beg.

'Tell us you can see this is The One.'

'I can,' says Mum. 'I can. I don't know what I was thinking with that awful blue thing. I'm quite upset to think I could have been so stupid.'

'That's OK, Mum,' I say kindly. 'You're very old. It happens. Now, go home, put a stake through its heart and burn it.' And she does.

I stay on in Bristol for the next few days, relishing the opportunity to get away from the wedding for a while. The house is empty all day while my sister is out writing computer code and periodically banging people's heads off desks. I get lots of work of my own done, and in the evenings we sit peacefully in the front room, her answering emails on her BlackBerry, mc reading a book and occasionally marvelling at the fact that I have a sister who owns a BlackBerry.

'That's interesting,' she says one evening, squinting at her tiny screen.

'What?'

'That girl who told us about the Battleaxe Galactica shop has just emailed to say did we also know about the shop in the market that does bridal accessories.'

'No. No, no, no, no, no, no.'

'Yes. It does mostly veils and things for your hair, apparently.'

'I'm not having a veil. I think they make you look like a ghost. Or a fish trapped in a net.'

'So you need something else on your head. We'll go tomorrow. We're running memory checks all morning so I've got nothing to do.'

'Why don't you just go and choose one for me, and I'll stay here and read. I mean, work.'

She continues to read the email.

'Brilliant. They will even make headbands and stuff for you. So you will have to come for them to work out what goes with your hair and colouring. In your case, I'm sure they'll just tie a beige pop-sock around your head, wish you luck and boot you out the door, but still, you've got to try.'

*

Evangeline's – I hope that really is the owner's name – is an explosion of fur, feathers, buttons, sequins, silk and flowers. It makes Jean's room look like a hospital ward. Emily dashes in and begins sifting through what is evidently to her a treasure trove. I start going cross-eyed.

'What do you think?' says Emily, holding a combination of petrol-blue and gold, sparkly, feathery, dangly things against her beaming face.

'I think I need to go and sit in a very, very empty room for a very long time,' I say faintly, staring at the array of frills and furbelows tumbling down from every shelf.

I wonder, briefly, as I watch Emily dart around the shop, scooping up bits and pieces with hoots and whistles of delight, whether my frivolity instinct has been crushed under the burden of being the sensible older sister all my life, or whether I never had one to begin with. That's what I should have spent my money on instead of the extra sausage canapés – frippery lessons. Or Xanax.

As I try to get my bearings, a woman comes in to collect a veil. Evangeline – or, possibly, 'Evangeline' – who is a soft maternal mass of bosom and scarves, brings it forth and lays it reverentially across the woman's outstretched arms. They admire it in silence for a moment before the women starts digging out her credit card to pay.

'How should I store it once I get it home?' she enquires anxiously as Evangeline packs her creation tenderly in a long white box.

'When's the wedding?'

'The twentieth.'

'Take it out and hang it up on the third,' instructs Evangeline. The girl bows her head in acknowledgement of the oracle's words and leaves. Evangeline turns her attention to me. 'Can I help you?'

I look for my sister, who is at the other end of the shop, creating a nest for herself amongst her favourite baubles and emitting little squawks of happiness as she lifts them up to the light. 'I'll wear this for the wedding,' she murmurs. 'And – ah, yes – this to the reception. And this – yes, this one on the train home. And this to bed. And this to breakfast because then I will be happy all day.'

I have clearly lost her for the moment. I turn back to Evangeline. 'I need a . . . headband sort of thing,' I say weakly.

'Are you golding or silvering?' she asks.

'Either . . . neither . . . I'm not sure . . . I'm not bothered . . . I don't know.'

'What jewellery are you wearing?'

'None. Well, apart from my engagement ring. Which is platinum. But it doesn't match my dress. But my dressmaker says that doesn't matter. But I don't know if she'd thought as far as the impact on headbands at the time.'

'No necklace? No earrings? A bracelet?'

'No. No. And – no.'

'What's on your dress?'

'Nothing.'

'No seed pearls? Embroidery? Diamanté? A coloured sash?'

'No. No. No. And no. It's not white though. It's a sort of really pale gold colour. I think. I didn't remember to bring a sample.' I never remember to bring a sample.

Evangeline seems rather at a loss now. At last my sister realises what is going on and joins us.

'She doesn't have any nice jewellery,' she explains to Evangeline sunnily. 'And look at her, anyway – no neck to speak of, no earlobes, and look – ' she grabs my wrist and raises it to Evangeline's eyes – 'do you really want to be calling attention to these stumpy little things? It's a bad enough waste of a ring. You might as well try to accessorise a boiled egg. But she has got a head, and quite nice hair when it's cut, so Mum and I thought we'd try for a doodad there.'

'We'll try her with pearls,' says Evangeline after staring at me intently for a few minutes.

She drags me over to a mirror. Fortunately I have removed my glasses in anticipation of just such a dastardly move and can see almost nothing.

She jams something opalescent and tinkly on my head. 'Pearls and crystals,' she explains.

We all stand there, looking in the mirror. Well, I think we're all standing there. I think we're looking in a mirror.

'She doesn't like it,' says Evangeline to Emily. 'I can tell by her face.'

'No, no,' says Emily soothingly. 'Her face looks like

that all the time. That's why we've booked a make-up artist and puppeteer for the wedding instead of a photographer. But I don't think she should have pearls. I think she's a gold.'

'Or maybe bronze,' says Evangeline thoughtfully.

'Oh, yes!' cries Emily, as if Evangeline has just stumbled across the answer to Fermat's Theorem. 'That's what she is, of course! Why didn't I think of that?'

Seized with new purpose, they buzz round the shop, periodically returning to force so many arcs of bronze, gold, goldy-bronze and bronzy-gold on and off my head that I begin to worry about skull furrows.

After forty minutes, they have narrowed it down to two choices. Well, two headbands. Do they constitute one choice or two? You surely need at least two things to choose between, so that makes one pair = one choice. Or are you choosing between having Thing A and not having Thing A, and between having Thing B and not having Thing B? That would be two choices. Or are you choosing between all those things, in which case you have three choices? It is possible I should get out more.

'We've lost her,' says Emily, clicking her fingers in front of my face to bring me back from the world of sub-mathematical imponderables through which I am wandering.

'Sorry,' I say. 'What do you need me to do? Pay?'

No. First I must choose between:

Small calla lilies and occasional pearls on curls of bronze wire or slightly bigger calla lilies and similarly sized but slightly more frequent pearls on curls of bronze wire. I cannot decide.

'It is tricky,' muses Evangeline. 'Because although she's small, she's got quite a big head, hasn't she?'

'Only in profile,' says Emily, less out of sorority than a desire for accuracy in all things. 'From the front, it looks quite normal. It's like a rugby ball on a stick from the side. So—' she says, turning to me as if suddenly remembering that I am still there. 'Which do you want?'

'I want the smaller one. But I suspect that I am wrong.'

'The smaller one is nice in and of itself,' decides Emily. 'But once you've got a dress on, you're in a big church, a big day, you've had your hair done –'

'I'm not having my hair done,' I interrupt to point out. 'I'm having extra sausages at the reception.'

'– it will look *too* small,' Emily continues without pause. 'So we will take the bigger one, thank you. And I will do your hair on the day.'

I stare at the two headbands. Who would have thought a brace of accessories could cause this much trouble? But I remain hamstrung, unable to decide between the one I want and the one they assure me will look right on the day. This continues until Evangeline suggests that, as she makes everything in the shop herself, she could, quite easily, make something in between. Something, you might almost say, that was just right.

'Some callas,' she says, opening her order book and starting to write, 'a few spirals. And just a couple of crystals – there!' She closes her book and caps her pen. 'Dainty – but elegant.'

'That's me,' I say as we bid farewell and head out of the shop. I walk straight into a display of diamanté tiaras as we leave, but you knew that, didn't you?

By the time I get home, the invitations have arrived. I have 125 of the folded cards, 135 envelopes (in invitation-writing as in life, you are allowed ten fuck-ups and no more), a fountain pen full of ink and I am good to go. But first Christopher must pass judgment on the letter to be enclosed.

He peruses it carefully. I wait with bated breath. He hands it back wordlessly.

'Well?' I say.

'It's fine.'

'But . . . ?'

'But you haven't got anyone for my people to ring.'

'What do you mean? You're there on the list, look: Lucy mobile number and email, blah, Lucy's parents' number, blah and – ta-dah! – Christopher Dingbat's mobile number, email address and landline. The people you're inviting do know who you are, don't they?'

'Can't you wait for me to pick my best man?'

I wait. I gather myself. I am calm. I am speaking in strangulated tones, but I am calm.

'But I have asked you to pick your best man several billion times over the last six months and you have not done so. I have waited as long as possible. I can wait no longer.'

'It's going to be Richard.'

'But you haven't asked him. Therefore, he hasn't said yes. We cannot put his name and phone number down on this letter and send it to 125 people if he hasn't said yes. That would be extremely presumptuous and potentially catastrophically embarrassing. Tell me you see that.'

'No.'

I make one last attempt. I channel my friend Claire, who once told me that the secret to a happy life was never to compromise a single iota on one's choice of husband but to compromise with him a little bit every day after that. He's not my husband yet, and the way he's going, he may not ever become so, but Claire is a wise woman and, not incidentally, very happily married. I draw a deep breath.

'Why don't you give him a ring now – right now – and if he says yes, right now, today, we can add him to the letter.'

'I can't get hold of him today. He's on his way to China.'

'Then that's too bad. People will have to make do with just the seventeen hundred email addresses, landline and mobile numbers provided.'

'What difference do twenty-four hours make?'

Sorry about this, Claire. '*But I've been asking you to get hold of him for six months!*' I shout. Actually, no, I'm not shouting, I suddenly realise. I'm shaking with fury but only a whisper – less biased souls might call it a hiss – is coming out. '*It's not my fault that I can't delay these sodding invitations any longer. They're a week fucking late as it is.*'

'Then what's another twenty-four hours?'

'But it won't BE another twenty-four hours. I'm busy all day tomorrow, it will be Wednesday before I can get to the photocopying place – on the bus, because you haven't sorted out the car tax in time – whereas if I do it now, Mum can give me a lift to the photocopier's and back, and I can have them all in the postbox by this evening. Enormous weight off my mind, giant tick in box of jobs done – versus unnecessary information addition about a best man who, let me just remind you, lives in Glasgow, knows nothing about our wedding arrangements and, while he will doubtless be marvellous on the day, cannot help but be bugger-all use at helping anyone beforehand, i.e. in fulfilling the sole purpose of this letter.'

He rolls his eyes. This does not calm me, not one bit.

'Do you think I just decide that this is the time I want to do things?' I ask him. 'Do you think I wake up in the mornings and say to myself, "Hmm . . . what do I *feel* like doing today? Stroking kittens in a basket or sending out invitations? Hot monkey sex with George Clooney or negotiating discounts on canapés?" No. I wake up knowing that I've got to do D, E and F because yesterday I managed to sort out the A, B and C on which they depend, and because tomorrow I have to do G, H and I so that I can get to X, Y and Z before I finally run out of time. This – ' I say, flinging my arms around in a gesture that I think is meant to indicate 'a working example of a certain but not specific moment in time', 'is when I can fit something in. This—' I repeat the eloquent gesture, 'is how I can give everyone who needs it the most notice. This' – once more with feeling – 'is how I can create if not the greatest amount of happiness for the greatest number of people, then at least the least amount of shit for the fewest. These fewest, never, at the moment, including me. So please don't think I am in any way enjoying or making life easy for myself because I really, really, really am not. Does that help?'

'Have it your own way,' he says, which makes me suspect the point has eluded him ever so slightly. 'Just like the invitations.'

'Not this again! No! I've told you – someone had to have the casting vote! Someone had to decide! And that someone had to be me! Because I'm the fucking bride!'

I'll spare you the rest, I think. Suffice it to say that the invitations are being sent without best-man details, I'm going without sleep tonight and Christopher will be going without a home-cooked meal until further notice.

I escape to Mum's house to write them in the end. She moves all food, drink and spillable liquids out of the vicinity and I sit down at the dining room table. I feel as if I am fourteen again, ready to start on the day's homework. Interestingly, I note that twenty years on I still have spots, greasy hair and, it's possible – I pull out the front of my jumper and look down – yes, it's definite, the same Marks and Spencer bra on. I really must clear out my underwear drawer one day.

Mum wanders through, chatting, though not necessarily to me. 'Now, where did I put those – oh, there they are. I must remember to tell Eileen about the oven, otherwise it'll soon be Friday . . . Did I put the stuff down the sink? Yes, I did, because that's why the Vim's out . . . Shall I put some more on the list or wait till I'm going to Savacentre? Which does the lemon?'

My mother's verbal stream of consciousness can be quite helpful, enabling you to keep track of her position in the house and making it impossible for her to sneak up on you if you were, when young and foolish, trying to embark on a nefarious scheme like extracting a second chocolate biscuit from the Tupperware box, sitting on a recently bumphled cushion or hoisting your sister up to the tap so that she could snatch a quick post-soup drink without having to leave a telltale glass behind. But at other times it can be quite distracting.

'Can you stop saying everything out loud, please, Mum?' I say politely. 'I've just addressed two invitations to Eileen Oven and Lemon Vim. And I haven't spoken to them in years.'

'Ooh, sorry,' she says, clutching my shoulders and giving me a big kiss on the cheek as she goes past. 'I'll try and be quiet. No, I'll go upstairs and make the beds. I forget I can do them first now that I've given up ironing the bottom sheets! Isn't that good? . . . ' The rest of her external monologue is lost as she finally makes her way up the stairs.

I sigh with satisfaction, just as I did when I was fourteen. My after-school domination of the dining table was the only way I could get a minute's peace when I was growing up. No wonder I did well in exams.

Half an hour later, she is back down and sits at the table to stuff and seal the envelopes I have addressed. This mindless industry makes us both very happy – I enjoy the mindlessness, she enjoys the industry – and we sit in companionable silence. By which I mean, I sit in silence and the white noise of her chatter envelops me comfortingly. It is the sound of childhood.

Fifty neatly piled envelopes later, Dad comes home from work.

'Hello, love,' he says when he sees me, and then, although it has been nearly a quarter of a century since he has asked the question, adds from long-buried habit without missing a beat, 'what time do you want your tea?'

'Six o'clock?' I say, because I always did. 'What are we having?'

'Chicken and ham pie.'

'Can I have lots of peas?'

'Aye, we've plenty.'

'You'll clear this lot away before we start eating,' says Mum, gesturing at the cards and envelopes still strewn about the place.

'Dur – d'you think I'm going to eat right on top of all my hard work?' I say. 'I don't *think* so, Mum!'

Thus, with my triumphant reclamation of adolescent sarcasm, is our journey back to 1988 complete, and we all spend a very happy evening there until it is time for me to go home and rejoin the real world.

When I get home, Christopher is shouting at *Newsnight*. Every night, he comes down from his study at half ten intending to watch the programme in its entirety and every night he lasts about eight minutes before he turns puce with rage and has to return to his book-lined sanctuary before he has a stroke. I watch him literally shaking his fist at Jeremy Paxman and reason that at least our children too will be able to hear him coming from afar.

CHAPTER THIRTEEN

Friends warned me this might happen. The wedding is now just two months away and I think I'm going mad. It started with occasional phone calls to Jo, the caterer, to amend my canapé choices. Then it became daily calls to Jo to amend my canapé choices.

'Can we swap the pumpernickel ones for asparagus and cheese sauce, please?'

'Of course.'

Forty-eight hours later. 'Sorry, Jo – just had a thought. Can we halve the number of asparagus and cheese and double the number of mini-roast-beef-and-Yorkshire-puds? Vegetarians are generally too weakened by lack of vitamins to make a fuss, but we'd better keep the carnivores happy.'

'No problem.'

'Hi, Jo – I know we spoke yesterday, but I've been thinking about the average size of my uncles. Could we keep everything the same but quadruple the number of sausages and mustard sauce? And napkins?'

'Leave it to me.'

'Jo, it's me again. Did I mention napkins? As a family, we're given to slobber.'

'You did. Don't worry.'

Then came the day when the only thing I had to accomplish was ordering the cupcakes. That's all. It's the simplest part of the entire wedding plan. I was almost looking forward to having such a manageable task to do, compared to the great, sprawling, interdependent undertakings that every other sodding aspect of the day involves. And anyway, who could not love the idea of ordering a hundred cupcakes, full stop?

There is something entirely unEnglish about the cupcake. We are a nation that still, deep in our hearts, views the addition of chocolate to the digestive biscuit as an immoral advance. Until a very few years ago, people used to purchase Jaffa cakes with the same furtive air as they did porn magazines. Both were felt to pander to depraved appetites and signal unforgivable self-indulgence. The absolute height of sugar-based decadence, the greatest treat available – nay, the greatest extravagance of which the mind could possibly conceive – was the butterfly cake: a fairy cake decorated with a splodge of butter icing with two tiny sponge wings stuck into it. Butter icing! And a square inch of extra cake atop a cake! It was seen only at the best birthday parties and told the world that the chocolate cornflake's days were numbered.

To my mind, the advent of the cupcake, which almost by definition comprises a piece of sponge surmounted by almost twice its depth in icing, is both the greatest invention of the last fifty years (not excepting the internet or the George Foreman grill) and the surest sign yet that Western civilisation is doomed to certain collapse under the weight of its own spiralling excess.

On the grounds, however, that this is unlikely to happen before September, I'm ordering a hundred of the delicious little buggers. The question is – from where?

I was going to order them from the woman who had a stall at the local Christmas fête in December. Suddenly, amidst the tables full of dusty bric-a-brac, raffles, home-made cards and decorations for those who prefer exuberant amateur enthusiasm to aesthetic appeal, was an enormous spread of heavily iced delights. It was terrifically exciting.

I have tasted her chaotically arranged wares and they were delicious. Although I didn't know then that Christopher would be proposing in a matter of weeks, I filed away for future reference the memory and her business card.

However. When I emailed her a few weeks ago, to ask if she had any pictures of a hundred of her cakes arranged in some kind of impressive tower formation as the one and only ornament at a standing-up-and-eating-canapés reception, she sent me a picture that was clearly taken in her sitting room of a dozen cupcakes piled randomly on top of each other and standing on a grubby table that itself stood on the most unsanitary-looking square of carpet I have ever seen outside a nightclub. I do not know precisely the disease for which cupcakes would prove to be the ideal vector, but I do not wish to find out.

I also think you must have to be slightly unhinged to send such a picture to someone preparing to order from you, which makes me worry about reliability. Although I suppose if she is effectively delivering a hundred doses of Weil's disease (that's probably it), a last-minute delivery foul-up could work out for the best.

So yesterday I searched for alternatives, and came up with Crumbs and Doilies – mainly because that is what appeared at the top of my Google search for London cupcake makers. They have a fearsomely professional-looking website, teeming with brilliantly lit photographs of towering – uh – towers of cakes on snowy-linen-draped tables that suggest delight instead of disease.

On the other hand, I haven't got the time or the money left to order a sample, so they could taste like shit. But they probably don't, do they? You wouldn't be able to afford such a fancy-dan website if they did. And there will probably be a few lacklustre comments floating around the internet too – 'I ordered three dozen cupcakes and they all tasted of poo. Even the vanilla ones. Disappointing.'

Although it feels wrong to be ordering untested – or untasted – food, the pretty pictures sway me and I plump for Crumbs and Doilies. High on the feeling of decisiveness and accomplishment, I then sent this email:

Hello! I'd like to order a hundred cupcakes for my wedding on 27 September if you think a hundred is enough for a hundred guests? I don't know whether to order slightly more, slightly fewer or the exact same number, because of course I don't know how many people are on diets, or how many don't like cupcakes and actually would prefer fruit cake although I have never met anyone who honestly does. But you must have more experience in this than I do, so please advise. And can I have them all different colours (I don't mean a hundred different colours, just a mixture of colours, you know) but all pastel colours, please? And some decorationy bits on top of some but not all of them, but no hearts, because – well, I just don't like them. But I like hundreds and thousands, and those little silver balls, and the little stars. Ooh, but not jelly tots either – I do like them, but I think they look too young for what's effectively a wedding cake.

And can I have mostly just ordinary sponge cake but some lemon and maybe some chocolate, but only if brown icing can go with the pastel of the rest without looking like poo. I'm sorry, I didn't mean to suggest you would make anything that looked like poo, I just seem to be a bit obsessed with the whole issue at the moment. But definitely no red devil cakes, please, they sort of slightly scare me. I don't think cake's meant to be red. Pink's different, although I don't know where you'd draw the line. Dark pink would look strange, but not frightening. Anyway, sorry, I'm getting off the point. And I don't want any pink cakes by the way, thanks.

Hope that all makes sense. Look forward to hearing from you.

Best wishes

Lucy x

PS But I would like some cakes with pink icing, please, but not too many. Just in proportion to the other colours, please – I don't want an overall pink-looking collection, it's not a pink wedding, do you know what I mean? Great, thanks.

Such is my state of mind that I honestly believed as I sent it that this was a masterpiece of clarity. The first inkling I have that this is not so is when Christopher, whom I had copied in on the missive to prove that I was working at maximum efficiency, comes downstairs with a concerned look on his face.

'Are you feeling all right?' he says.

'Yes,' I say, puzzled. 'Why?'

'Read this again,' he says, pushing a printout of the email towards me.

I read. I take his point. My brain is clearly weakened by stress and then further addled by proximity to cake when I haven't eaten sugar in any form since I saw myself in the Mirror of Truth. But there's nothing I can do about it now.

'If they're in the wedding cake supply business,' I tell him, 'they will understand. And translate.'

And tonight, as I got ready for bed, I decided to wear my wedding shoes overnight. I am still trying to break them in so that I don't hobble down the aisle and it seemed a sensible thing to do – eight hours of gentle expansion as I slept. Multi-tasking at its finest. It wasn't until Christopher came to bed and looked down at me, lying there in flannel pyjamas and high-heeled, gold-brocaded shoes, that it dawned on me that I am going nuts.

I have to pull myself together the next day, for I am in charge of a child.

'OK, Allegra,' I say. 'Put your shoes on, find your jacket and off we go to Jean's. You're actually going to see your dress for the first time today.'

There is the sound of muffled protest. A few moments later she emerges from the pile of blankets, towels, cushions and duvets from which she has been attempting to construct the most elaborate cat dormitory yet seen in Western civilisation.

'Do we have to?' she asks.

'Yes. We do.'

'But I thought you sent her all my mearum . . . mezza— . . . sizes so she could make it without me?'

'She has made it without you but she needs to see you in it before she absolutely, finally finishes it so that it fits you perfectly. Come on. We can go for an ice cream afterwards.'

Ice cream is still a working bribe with modern children, isn't it?

Evidently it is. Allegra sighs and starts reluctantly to pull her shoes on and search for her jacket, which is eventually discovered to be doing duty as a cat pillowcase.

'Shall I go and wait by the car? That's what I do when Mummy is looking for her handbag,' she says, as I dash round muttering dark imprecations to the malevolent spirits who had hidden mine.

'That would be difficult,' I say, trying the cupboard under the stairs. 'Because we don't have one. We're going by bus.'

'Bus!' says Allegra, beaming. 'I've never been on a bus before!'

'Really?' I say, coming out from under the stairs on all fours, which ungainly position at least allowed me to spot the strap of my handbag poking out from behind the kitchen table. I snatch it up. 'I used to go on the bus with my grandma all the time at your age. It was the only way we could eat sweets without my mother punching us both to the ground.'

'Is that true?' says Allegra, wide-eyed.

'Well,' I say, pondering, 'it's truer than you might hope. Right – got your shoes on, got your jacket, got my handbag. I think we can leave. Let's go.'

We walk the five minutes to our stop in companionable silence. Once on the bus, we make our way to the top deck and Allegra alternates between gazing down the pseudo-periscope to the driver below and gazing around her in delight at the panoramic view from on high. I had forgotten how exciting it is when you are six to see the traditionally distant branches of trees brush your window and look down from your exalted position on the crowds of people on the street who usually jostle you mercilessly as they go about their adult business.

'Look!' she cries as the bus turns down the road behind our house. 'It's Patrick!' I catch just a glimpse of ginger fur and sinew pouring itself over a fence.

'So it is!' I say. 'Aren't you observant?'

'What's observant?'

'Good at seeing things.'

'Yes, I am,' she agrees. As if the sight of Patrick had reminded her, she turns in her seat and asks, 'Will Jean be making Henry's cape too?'

'Henry's cape?' I say, nonplussed.

'Yes. For the wedding. You said Patrick would have the ring on his tail, and Henry would have a cape instead.'

'Oh. Oh, yes, I see. Well, the thing is that, actually, that was a kind of joke. Not a joke, exactly, it was a nice idea – but cats don't really come to weddings in churches. It might be different if we were getting married at home. But on our day, they won't be there.'

'Oh,' says Allegra, in a small voice.

We sit in silence for a few minutes. She gazes fixedly out of the window until I spot another cat and – hoping to distract her from what I presume is her embarrassment at her misunderstanding – start a game of hunt-the-feline. Gradually she joins in and the rest of the journey passes quite happily.

By the time we alight at Jean's we have seen sixteen

other (lesser, we hardened ginger-nuts agreed) cats and a possible fox. As we walk up the path to Jean's, Allegra falls silent again. I squeeze her hand reassuringly, remembering how shy she had been with us at the beginning, and ring the bell.

Jean answers and takes us into her front room. 'I thought we'd just pop it on down here so you could see yourself in the big mirror,' she says cheerfully to Allegra, who is looking more than a little apprehensive.

'It might still have some pins in, but Jean will make sure they don't scratch you,' I say.

Allegra doesn't look any happier. Jean slips the satin tunic, with its little cap sleeves, over her head and smooths it down to her knees. I had been slightly worried that Siobhan will be expecting her daughter to sport some extraordinarily complex creation – cascades of frills, perhaps, or a multi-layered tulle confection strewn with a thousand winking sequins – but now that I can see Jean's handiwork on her, I know that she and I made the right choice, that the colour suits her and that she is going to look lovely.

'And when I've made the little sash, it will tie around here,' says Jean, nipping in the waist slightly. 'And when I've taken – yes, this little seam in here a bit more, and' – stepping back and looking critically at the tiny figure for a minute – 'I think, the hem up just an inch, everything will be perfect.'

'There you go!' I say to Allegra. 'You're going to look just brilliant!'

Another big job crossed off my list, I think thankfully. Which is exactly when Allegra's eyes suddenly fill with tears and she flings herself blindly towards me, hugs my knees and starts sobbing. I look down at her and then across at Jean in horror. Jean shakes her head, clearly as taken aback as I am.

I sit down on the sofa and pull Allegra on to my lap so that she can cry more comfortably into my chest. Even my meagre cleavage is better than a pair of knees, I reason, while I wait for the worst of the storm to pass.

'Could I have a glass of water, Jean?' I ask, as I rock my putative bridesmaid back and forth and the sobs gradually quieten.

'Of course,' says Jean. 'I'll get some biscuits too. There are tissues just by the sofa there if you need them.'

She disappears to the kitchen.

'Tissues,' I say to Allegra, who has lifted her head during our exchange and is sniffing and hiccuping her way back to normality. 'That sounds like a good idea.' I pull one out of the box and wipe her face. 'Now – blow?'

She nods and blows. I resettle her more comfortably in my lap and say, 'Now, my love – what was all that about?'

'I don't . . . ' She stops.

The bottom lip trembles briefly but is bravely steadied.

'I don't . . . ' She stops again. I wait. She pulls another

tissue out of the box, scrunches it up and digs at her eyes with it.

'Whatever it is, you can tell me,' I say. 'I won't be upset, or cross, or whatever else you think I might be. I don't want you to be unhappy. I'm sure we can sort everything out, but you have to tell me what's wrong.'

'I don't want to be a bridesmaid!' she wails, as tears burst forth anew. 'I don't want to walk all down a church with everybody looking! Mummy wants me to do it and she thinks it will be fun but I don't like people looking! I want to be sick when I think about doing it and Mummy just laughs and says I will love it on the day, but I *won't*!' She buries her head in my chest again and cries.

I give her a few moments to recover, which I spend mentally cursing her stupid mother. Gradually, the relief of confession calms her.

''M sorry,' she mutters.

'Don't be daft,' I say, hugging her. 'I'm the one that should be sorry.' I should never have let your mother ride roughshod over both of us, I think. 'I should have checked with you instead of just assuming it would be something you would enjoy. That was silly of me. But you seemed quite happy every time you came round, so I never thought . . . Why didn't you say something before?'

'Because . . . ' The lip trembles again. 'Because – I always want to see Henry and Patrick. And I thought they were going to be at the wedding, and that would have been my last chance to see them, so . . . '

Oh my God, who would be a child again? The agony of it all! I make a mental note that no matter how much I might resent the remorseless passage of the years, the alternative – being busted back to pre-adolescence – would be so much worse.

'I see, I see how everything was now,' I say. 'Blow your nose again for me, while I have a little think.'

She does, amateurishly but effectively enough to allow us all to breathe comfortably once again. It also gives me a few minutes to come up with what I hope will be a workable compromise.

'How about this?' I say. 'As Jean's more or less made the dress now, it would be a shame to see it wasted, especially as you look so nice in it. So why don't you come to the wedding with Mummy and sit in one of the pews near the front. Then when I get to the altar and need an order of service – that's like a list of all the things that are going to be happening at the wedding – you can just nip out and give it to me if you're feeling brave, or I can just share Christopher's if you're not? And that will be a very important job but almost no one apart from me, Christopher, our mummies and daddies and your mummy will see you. But if you would rather not wear the dress and not do anything at all, that's absolutely, completely fine too. In fact, you don't even have to come to the wedding if you don't want to.'

'But Mummy . . . '

'You just choose,' I say firmly. 'And whatever you decide, I'll talk to Mummy about it and I promise you it will all be OK. The best thing about getting married, you see, Allegra, is that just for that one day, everyone has to do as the bride says. So Mummy will just have to like it or lump it. Trust me.'

Allegra gives a small smile.

'So,' I continue, 'the important thing is that you decide what you want to do, about the dress and about what you get up to on the day.'

Jean reappears, bearing drinks and a plate of biscuits.

'Here you go,' she says, putting them on the table beside Allegra who has slipped off my knee at the sound of her return.

'Go on,' I say, motioning towards them as the child hesitates. 'I always need a drink before I make tricky decisions.'

'I do want to come to the wedding,' she says after a restorative draught of orange squash. 'And I do like my dress. It's better even than my party dress and that's my best dress. So can I give you your order of service when you get to the front?'

'That would be just brilliant,' I say. 'Doesn't that sound brilliant, Jean?'

'It does,' she says, drawing her sewing box towards her and beckoning Allegra over. 'So why don't I just make the few little changes I need to make here . . . and here . . . and – turn round for me, pet – maybe just here . . . and everything will be just right.'

'Will you need to see me again?' says Allegra.

'I don't think so,' says Jean. 'You're not planning on growing eight inches in the next four weeks, are you?'

'No.'

'Then that's OK. I'll give the dress to Lucy next time she's here and she can give it to you before the wedding.'

'Excellent,' I say. 'Now, let's all have a celebratory jammy dodger – and then head home for ice cream.'

'I thought you were on a diet,' says Jean.

I hold up a silencing hand. 'Excuse me,' I say politely, 'but I think you'll find that I'm the bride and can do exactly as I please. Isn't that right, Allegra?'

'Yes,' she says, trying to smile but looking tearful again. Something is still up.

'What's wrong, funny child?'

'If you don't need me for the dress any more, I won't see Patrick and Henry any more either, will I?'

'I think,' I say carefully, doing some rapid mental calculations of quite how much I am going to be able to get away with when I do pluck up the courage to speak to Siobhan, 'that your mum will probably still let you come and see me now and again so that you can keep in touch with them if you want to. Perhaps we can make it a regular thing – once a month, say – so that everyone has something to look forward to?'

Her face clears properly at last. She nods vigorous agreement.

'Great,' I say with relief. 'Now, let's say goodbye to Jean and catch the bus home. I'm in severe need of some chocolate ice cream.' I turn to Jean. 'Not a word, thank you. Not a word.'

When we get home, Allegra plunges gleefully back into her bedmaking pile while I dig the box of bribery out of the freezer. Christopher comes out of his study and finds me in the kitchen.

'You're eating two bites of ice cream for every one that goes into a dish,' he observes.

'Yes. Yes, I am. And do you know why?'

'Enlighten me.'

'Because (a) I have this afternoon lost a bridesmaid but gained a regular infant house guest and (b) I have taken it upon myself to explain to Siobhan why Allegra, having not inherited her mother's mercilessly attention-seeking, self-aggrandising gene, does not, will not and shall not be forced to walk down the aisle behind me but is to be allowed to visit me once a month regardless so that she can still see the cats.'

'How are you going to do that without seeming to criticise both implicitly and explicitly her and her parenting skills?'

'I don't know. Therein lies the problem.'

'Would you like me to do it?'

'What?'

'Would you like me to do it?'

'Would you? Could you? How could you?'

'I have a mighty brain,' he says, pulling himself tall and striding round the kitchen in an approximation of a manly fashion. 'I believe it can be done. And it is what husbands are for, to relieve their wives and almost-wives of repugnant tasks, like dressing hogs, digging privy pits and breaking unwelcome news to disliked but unaccountably feared acquaintances.'

I look at him. It is undoubtedly tempting. But there

is no telling what damage he could do unsupervised in such a situation. All the same, we could, I realise, at least share the burden. I lay out a plan of execution before him. He – with his mighty brain – grasps it immediately, which is lucky as just then we hear Siobhan's car pull up.

'Why don't you go upstairs with your ice cream and Christopher,' I say to Allegra, pushing the bowl at her. 'And have a look through our photographs and choose one of Patrick and Henry to keep with you in between visits, while I have a chat with Mummy?'

Allegra looks only too pleased to be getting out of the way and bounds upstairs. 'I warn you, I don't have many of Henry,' says Christopher as he trudges behind her.

'Why not?'

'I'm not sure,' he says. 'I think I'm trying to punish him for his beauty.'

It will be a miracle if she doesn't come back down those stairs with either her brain or her spirit broken, I realise, but then the doorbell rings and more urgent concerns take over.

'Come in, Siobhan. How are you?'

'I'm fine, thanks. I don't really have time to come in, though, can I just grab Allegra and go? I've got an appointment with the nutritionist.'

One part of my mind wants to ask her if this means she has forgotten how to feed herself. But another prompts my hand to reach out and close the kitchen door to hide the evidence of ongoing ice-cream consumption on the premises.

'Come into the sitting room,' I say. 'I just need a quick word.'

She follows me through. I take a deep breath.

'Allegra and I have decided that she will stand at the front of the church and just give me my order of service before I step up to the altar,' I say. 'She's not madly keen on the idea of traipsing down the aisle with everybody looking at her and, as it's a feeling I well understand, I've said she needn't do it.'

Siobhan opens her mouth to protest. I continue without pause. If there's one thing I've learned from living with Christopher, it's never to let your opponent get a word in when you've got something important to say. And over the years my lung capacity has increased threefold, so I'm nowhere near needing to take a breath yet.

'So we worked out the compromise – she's going to wear the dress, by the way, and she looks lovely – and now everybody's happy. Including' – and I include a light, tinkling laugh here to show that I really mean business – 'the most important person, me. The bride. On her special day.'

Siobhan looks at me for a moment. Her eyes narrow slightly as she computes these new facts and their ramifications. You can practically see the cogs turning. On the one hand, possibly for the first time since about 1978, she has not got her way. On the other hand, Allegra will still have a role that requires her, Siobhan, to be sitting up front and centre in a position commensurate with her importance in her own if nobody else's mind. But then again, I have effectively collaborated against her with her own daughter and that surely demands retribution.

But, pulsing beneath all this is the undeniable, the unassailable, the irrefutable fundamental fact that I. Am. The. Bride. Who knows what uncharacteristic inner strength this might unleash within me? Know thy enemy is the first rule of warfare, and she can no longer be sure she does. I can see her wavering. That's right, I think, drawing myself imperceptibly up to my full matrimonial height, which is at least six inches taller than my normal, day-to-day height. Feel the power of the bride! Believe in the power of the bride! I shall not be cowed! Bend, bend to my will!

I meet her eye. She feels the power. Her mouth curves into a mirthless smile. 'Well, that sounds wonderful,' she says. 'Of course, Allegra has always been terribly sensitive. I try to coax her out of it, but sometimes you just have to give in to it for their sakes, don't you?'

'Yes, yes, you do.'

'We should probably get going,' she says, standing up and heading back into the hall.

'I'll get her for you,' I say and shout up the stairs for Christopher to bring Allegra down.

'Hello, Siobhan,' he says as they descend. 'Sorry we didn't hear you come in. We were upstairs saying goodbye to Henry and Patrick. We were all much distressed at the thought of parting for ever, so I've told Allegra that she should come round at least once a month to check that standards of feline comfort are being maintained. Will you drop her off or should I come and collect her, do you think?'

Wrong-footed twice in twenty minutes, Siobhan is now so unbalanced that she agrees to deliver Allegra to our door every third Thursday of the month on her way to yogalates class.

'That sounds painful,' says Christopher courteously as he opens the door and ushers them out. 'I hope it clears up soon.'

He closes the door, turns to me and we quietly high-five each other.

'A perfectly executed pincer movement,' he says. 'Do you think she'll cause you any trouble when she's had time to think about it?'

'Nope. I think together we got her beat.'

'Hooray for having a husband!' says Christopher, punching the air in triumph. 'Can I have chips for dinner?'

'Yes.'

'Hooray for having a wife! Hooray!'

CHAPTER FOURTEEN

Dad is standing by the front door waiting for me when I arrive. It is mid-August, the height of summer, and he has his coat and scarf on. Well, you can't be too careful. He has his travelcard – bought yesterday for today because, no, really, you can't be too careful – in one hand and a bag in the other that I suspect contains an emergency ration of jam sandwiches and bottle of Vimto.

'Big day today, eh, Dad?' I say by way of greeting.

'Aye,' he says. 'Aye.'

To the casual observer, he would undoubtedly be indistinguishable from a man only recently woken from a deep coma. To close family members, however, it is clear that my father is fibrillating with excitement at the prospect before him. For today he makes his Personal Contribution to the Wedding. He is coming into town to help me choose the booze for the big day.

My dad knows about wine. We don't know how or when he started accruing this knowledge. It wasn't during his youth – only bitter was drunk in Lancashire until 1982 – or student days, when by all accounts an interest in the intricate complexities of the grape would have done nothing to enhance your standing with peers who would happily stick a straw in a petrol tank and drain it dry if there were nothing else within crawling distance. Nor, says Mum, has he ever shown any interest in it during his adult life. And she keeps a close eye.

Nevertheless, we found him one day at a party at Annie's house, deep in conversation with a wine buff, throwing about words like 'full-bodied Barolo', 'bouquet of a much younger wine', and generally demonstrating that to a list of hobbies that already included watching football, searching for purveyors of Uncle Joe's Mint Balls and annually retelling his joke about Dolly Parton's greatest hits, he had unexpectedly added oenophilia.

Add to this the fact that ever since I was hit in the face at the age of twelve by a speeding netball I have had no sense of smell and therefore all wine tastes like vinegar to me. So, it was inevitable that when the subject of wedding wine and booze came up last time I was home, Mum pulled me aside and hissed, 'This is it! This is your chance to get your father involved! In case he feels left out!'

'Don't you mean, "In case he's aware I'm getting married"? Or perhaps "In case there's any infinitesimally small part of him that gives a monkey's uncle about what occurs on the day?"'

'Either way. Ask him to go with you.'

'All right, all right. Dad, will you come with me and help me find a hundred bottles of wine and champagne that are as palatable as possible for the money allotted?'

'What are you buying a hundred bottles of booze for? Is your Auntie Eileen coming to stay?'

'No, it's for the wedding. My wedding.'

'Well, that makes more sense. She likes meths anyway.'

Thus we are on our way to a wine seller's in Farringdon. He settles himself in a corner of the train, with his paper. I open up my book and divide my time between reading and gazing out of the window. We occasionally catch each other's eye as we turn a page and smile gently. It is very restful. I might take an off-peak train journey with my father every week. It would be better than a massage.

When we reach the wine seller's, the manager, Simon, greets us and leads us downstairs and into a cavernous, wood-lined vault, with bottles racked floor to arching ceiling. A happy, happy look steals across Dad's face. Again, a casual observer couldn't tell, but to me the fractionally raised eyebrows and the almost invisible lift to the corners of his mouth are as a blazing beacon.

'Welcome to the Pleasure Dome, Dad.'

'Aye,' he says. 'Aye.'

I spoke to Simon about the kind of thing I would be needing so he has brought along a few bottles for us to try. He pours a measure of the first into each of three glasses. I taste mine. Tastes like vinegar. Vinegar with a hint of – no, wait, just vinegar.

'Mmm,' I say neutrally, signalling wildly with my eyes at Dad to leap in and save me from having to proffer an opinion.

'Are you all right, pet?' he says with concern.

'I'm fine. What do you think of the wine?'

'It's very nice,' he says. 'But I'd prefer summat a bit more complex. I've had more nuanced gobstoppers.'

At this Simon brightens visibly. Soon the vault is full of the sound of wine-lovers at play. 'Take a mouthful of the La Grille . . . '

'Herbaceous . . . '

'Isn't it? I've got a fuller-bodied Dashwood Sauvignon if you'd rather . . . '

'Gooseberries an' all . . . '

'Oh, here's the Chardonnay! Reputation ruined by Bridget Jones, but one of my favourites . . . '

'Who's Bridget Jones? . . . '

Occasionally I leap like a dolphin out of the sea of incomprehension and snatch at a brief morsel of under-standing. Like when Simon points at a case and says, 'That works out at £6.39 per bottle.'

'We'll take it!' I cry, but the chat flows ceaselessly on as they turn to the champagnes. Or cavas. Or prosecco. Whatever we're getting. I don't know.

'Little bit of yeastiness to that,' says Simon as he puts a bottle down. I know this is a good thing in bread and a bad thing in vaginas, but I have no idea what it means for wine. I am about to ask when he picks up another and says, 'This is the one I bought for my friend's wedding toast.'

'We'll take it!' I shout, louder this time, and mark its name down on my scrap of paper. Dad and Simon concur. The talk closes briefly over my head once more while they do the reds and then we go upstairs to fill in the paperwork and hand over my credit card.

'What happens about it getting to and from the reception?' I say, as my poor, battered card takes yet another solid beating.

'What time's the wedding?' says Simon.

'Three o'clock,' I say.

'And how far is the church from the reception?' he says.

'Five minutes.'

'Right,' he says. 'We'll deliver it, chilled, by half three and provide all the ice and holders you need to keep it cool all evening. We'll pick up the bins, empties and any leftovers at nine on Monday morning. We'll count them up and refund you on the Tuesday. Is that all right?'

I am so grateful for the advent of such certainty and competence into my life that by the time he reaches the end of his speech, to my eyes he seems bathed in a beatific glow.

'That would be – just wonderful,' I breathe like a love-struck teenager.

'And you'll need glasses too,' he reminds me.

'Yes,' I say, by this time all but dissolved in a little puddle of gratitude at his feet. 'How many?'

'Two hundred and fifty,' he says. 'Because people put them down all the time and forget where they've left them.'

'Whatever you say, Simon.'

'We'll deliver them at the same time and your caterer

can just put them – dirty – back in the packing cases and we'll pick them up on the Monday. Any breakages, we'll deduct £2 from the deposit.'

'That's fine,' I say, handing my card back with nary a tremor. 'Whatever, whatever you say, Simon.'

As we walk out of the shop, I feel that a huge weight has been lifted. We have the church. We have the reception venue. And now we have booze. Even if everything else – dress, orders of service, food, weather – turns to shit and hits a giant fan, a wedding can still take place. Not a good wedding. Not a happy wedding. But a wedding nevertheless.

'Right, Dad,' I say. 'Shall we go home?'

'Nay, lass,' he says. 'Let's go for a happy cakey.'

So we do.

Today we have our final class with William, which is devoted to sorting out the service itself. I always supposed this would be the simplest bit. You know, apart from the cupcakes. I thought you would just have to choose from a simple list: 'Do you want: (a) old-fashioned "do you take this woman to be your lawful wedded wife" words; (b) modern version "X, are you happy to marry Y or should we all just go down the pub"; or (c) hippy-dippy-make-up-your-own-vows-about-drowning-in-the-fathomless-pools-of-each-other's-souls-forever-shit?'

And we would say, 'We would like the old-fashioned "do you take this woman" stuff, please,' and then I would have time to meet a friend for lunch.

But once again nothing is simple. First of all, because William and Christopher like to mull over the historical background of every change made to the Book of Common Prayer since its first draft, we end up having to choose between thirty-nine different versions of the old-fashioned vows.

Unfortunately, the one thing they all have in common is that they require the bride to 'obey'.

'How would you feel about that?' asks William warily.

'People will laugh,' I say. 'It'll be a comedy line. I'm up for that if you are.'

'The vast majority of brides these days don't say it,' acknowledges William, despite an expression on Christopher's face that we both know by now means he is spoiling for a fight over the issue. 'Let's just cross it out, shall we? Now, is Christopher going to "cherish" you?'

'If she's not obeying me, I'm not going to cherish her,' he says.

'I'll cherish you if you obey me,' I offer. 'Can we do it that way round?'

'Ah – no,' says William faintly.

Oh well. It was worth a try.

Next, we have to choose hymns, all of whose verses are again pondered over by William and Christopher, examined for historical appropriateness and complementariness to the various pieces of music my fiancé has handed over to be played elsewhere in the service. Then we pick our readings – which is actually quite quick, because the Bible is apparently the one book Christopher cannot quote entirely from memory, so we just gladly nod our heads at William's suggestions. William says he will collate everything we have chosen, slot it into his order of service template and forward it to us for proof-reading, so that we can check it and send it off to the printers.

Then all that is left is to find a mutually agreeable date for the wedding rehearsal, which turns out to be forty-eight hours before the day itself ('Not long enough to forget everything,' says William reassuringly), and two hours after we arrive he finally waves us off towards something called the Diocesan Registry in the London Deanery to get our Bishop's Special Licence. This is needed, for various archaic, obscure reasons that may have eluded me amidst all the intriguing gossip about the origins of 'Guide Me O Thou Great Redeemer', to enable us to get married in his particular church.

'Well,' I say as we walk down the road clutching the forms William has given us, 'do you feel prepared for marriage now?'

'I feel prepared for marriage to William,' says Christopher thoughtfully.

'Close enough,' I reckon. Close enough.

Like Dr Johnson's House, the Deanery is in a tiny, hidden pocket of side streets in which you can forget that the periwig ever went out of fashion or that the internal combustion engine was ever invented. We ring the heavy brass doorbell and a lady welcomes us in with a wordless smile. She gestures for us to take a seat and somehow – still without speaking – gives us to understand that the person we need to see will be with us in a moment. She glides back to her seat. It is as if the place has been going about its singular business for so long that speech is unnecessary. The ancient tasks with which it is concerned seeped into the building so long ago that it is possible that the receptionist herself is a ghost, simply the essence of the very first receptionist who ever worked here clothed in newer fashions in order not to spook us, the need for a flesh and blood entity to ensure the smooth running of the system having long since passed.

The arrival of the man we need to see does nothing to dispel this beguiling notion. His soft tread barely disturbs the pile of the immaculate carpet and he too simply smiles and gestures to us to follow him, which we do. A series of oak doors swing open silently before him as he takes us further into the bowels of the Time Machine.

Finally, he brings us into a room lined with leatherbound volumes of law books, forms, precedents, encyclopaedias and, for all I know, the original volumes of the Domesday Book and Shakespeare's first folio. We sit down at a polished mahogany table and he asks us, in a voice just above a whisper, whether we have brought all the necessary documents. I nod eagerly and draw – with as little rustling as possible – the passports, certificates and everything else I have painstakingly amassed to prove that Christopher and I are who we say we are, live where we say we do and are altogether fine, upstanding citizens who should, prithee, sirrah, be allowed to marry.

'Marvellous,' he whispers, taking them from me. 'Thank you.'

He looks carefully though them all and eventually slides across the table towards us a fountain pen (if he had just gone the whole hog and sharpened a quill in front of us, I think I would have expired of happiness on the spot) and a piece of thick, embossed cream paper.

'Please read this and sign at the bottom,' he says. I reach for the pen.

'Ah,' he coughs politely. 'I'm afraid it is just the gentleman who signs.'

I blink. Christopher grins. Uncapping the pen with a flourish, he signs. 'Get used to this,' he says with satisfaction. He thinks he's so funny.

'I do apologise,' says our host. 'It just that ecclesiastical rules don't seem to change as quickly as the world.'

'It's quite all right,' I assure him.

And it is. Here – and only here, I will specify at length to Christopher when we leave the House That Time Forgot – I don't think I'd have it any other way.

As we head rapidly towards September, the day in the Deanery becomes my last memory of peace. The days start to whip past at a frightening speed. I am called upon to make frightening final decisions about menus, to chase down a million overlooked details that must now – now! Right now! – be sorted out and am unstoppably driven by my own internal anxiety engine to check and recheck other people's tasks.

Have the cupcake people translated my email accurately (yes), can Jo do a few more sausages just in case (yes, of course), do we know where all the family guests are sleeping the night before (I don't, Mum does, what am I playing at, questioning her?) What about the night after? Who's going to swallow David's keys when he wants to drive home backwards after a skinful?

I squeeze in a couple of mini-fittings with Jean, who has constructed the bodice in the proper material and is now working, unseen, on the skirt. At the weekend my sister arrives and we – and our mother, of course – will go round to see the finished article for the first time. And at seven o'clock every evening I change into my tennis kit and head on autopilot over to the park for what have become my daily matches with Rosie.

'Two weeks to go,' she shouts as she lobs the ball over the net. 'Run!'

'Have you remembered that you are going into town to pick up the orders of service this afternoon?' I say to Christopher, as I run my eye down the tattered scrap of paper that is doing duty as today's list.

'I have,' says Christopher, picking up his jacket from the hall table. 'And that is where I go right now, like the superhusbandhero I am.' He leaves. He comes back.

'Forgot my phone.' He leaves again. He comes back again. 'Forgot my wallet.' He leaves yet again. He comes back yet again. 'Forgot my book.' He leaves. I wait. He does not come back.

I decide to take advantage of these few hours of blessed silence by sinking into a hot bath which, in a moment of wild extravagance, I fill with bubbles right to the rim. I also have a stack of trashy paperbacks on the side as well as Ducky, my yellow plastic duck from childhood whose presence still fills me with an entirely disproportionate amount of good cheer and who will join me in the water as soon as I have lowered myself in and exhausted the initial pleasure of watching my skin turn lobster pink in the lovely heat. Just as I am about to invite him in, my mobile rings. I pick it up. It's Christopher. I contemplate dropping it in the water but am worried about electrocution. I don't know if phones count as electric, but then I don't know why electricity doesn't leak out of the skirting-board sockets and kill us every time we step on to the carpet, so I probably shouldn't take the risk.

I reluctantly press the green button. 'Hello?'

'They've given us soft covers,' he says immediately.

'I'm sorry?'

'They were supposed to give us stiff covers and they've given us soft covers. The wrong covers. Covers that are not right. Covers that show no respect for marriage. Or for the fact that they cost £3.25 a pop. Shall I go back and smash someone's head in?'

'No. Just bring the bloody things back here and we'll take a look at them. Maybe they won't be so bad.'

'All right,' he says, sounding slightly calmer. 'I'll be home in an hour.'

I slip beneath the bubbles again, but my mood is ruined. I spend the next hour trying to keep my rational side and my ancient Ducky afloat. Flimsy orders of service are not going to ruin the wedding, I tell myself sternly. Although it is, of course, typical that the one thing I leave solely in the hands of Christopher is the one thing that goes wrong. No, wait. Bad path to go down. I wrest my thoughts back and send them down a more constructive highway. Why are weddings only ever 'ruined' anyway? Why can't they ever be 'damaged' or 'slightly dented'? 'That is a very good point, you know,' I say to Ducky. Ducky, alas, has sprung a leak since we last bathed together and is listing further and further to the left. Soon he is lying on his side in the water, gazing at me with one baleful eye. I give up and get out. There is no point in subjecting yourself to the pity of a plastic duck.

By the time I have dried and dressed, Christopher has returned, bearing his box of non-delights. He takes the lid off and I lift out one of the little cream booklets.

'Oh, these aren't too bad at all!' I exclaim, turning it over in my hands and flicking the covers back and forth. 'It's just like very, very thin cardboard – I wasn't expecting it to be much thicker than this anyway! This will do fi—'

I stop. I stare at the front cover.

'What's wrong?' says Christopher.

'We're getting married "at 3.00 p.m.",' I say.

'We are, aren't we?' says Christopher, confusedly. 'That's what it said on the invitations, anyway. That's what time people are going to be turning up, that's for sure.'

'Yes, that's the right time but "3.00 p.m." is wrong. It should be three o'clock or 3 p.m. It shouldn't be 3.00 unless you're a military commander giving orders to troops and "3.00 p.m." is just wrong.'

'No, it's not.'

Oh great. One of those arguments.

'Yes. Yes, it is.'

'How do you know?'

'What do you mean, "how do I know"? I know. I know through being taught, through reading, through – God, umm, let me see now – *having a brain*?'

'Is it really wrong or is it a snobby, fish-knives-type thing?'

It goes on like this for some time. Eventually I convince him of the truth of my contention and he gets on the phone to the printers who agree to do another batch – I hover at Christopher's elbow until I hear him say 'Numeral three-space-oh-apostrophe-clock on cardboard covers please' – for cost price. A fragile peace descends.

'Ah well,' he says. 'At least come Sunday, we'll be away from all this, in the tranquil pastoral bosom of Hay-on-Wye.'

'You mean Monday,' I say.

'No,' he replies, 'I mean Sunday.'

The fragile peace shatters into something well north of a million tiny pieces and a record-breaking third screaming row in under an hour immediately gets under way.

He has, it emerges, booked our train for first thing on Sunday. He denies all knowledge of my desire to leave on Monday so that I can have time to oversee the return of cakestands, go to the family Sunday lunch, catch up with my cousins properly, and generally bathe in the afterglow of a successful wedding. Or, just as vitally, be supported in the aftermath of a total fucking disaster. I wanted that day. I needed that day. That day was my breathing space. To go straight from wedding to honeymoon is too much. It means packing for a holiday instead of just the wedding night, it means having to get the house ready for our housesitter before I leave on the wedding morning instead of at my leisure the day after. It means, in short, that a day has just been cut out of a timetable already so overburdened that even the time this row is taking is threatening to cause it to burst its bounds.

'Well, we can't rebook it,' he says stubbornly. 'It would cost a fortune at such short notice – and we've just slightly overspent on our orders of service.'

Referring flippantly to his first major cock-up of the day is a mistake. Every major and minor frustration rushes to the fore and I start to rage and sob incoherently and uncontrollably, until Christopher becomes so concerned that he tries to backtrack.

'Look – we'll rebook. It's only money.'

'We. Can't. Afford. It.'

'Yes, we can. We'll take in a lodger. I'll whittle figurines to take to market. Sell my hair.'

Eventually I sob myself to exhaustion and Christopher disappears to the kitchen to make one of his famous pots of tea. They take – God knows how but somehow – forty minutes to make but I have to admit they yield a succession of the finest cups of Twinings Breakfast you may ever hope to taste.

By the time I have finished a second cup, I am rational once more. We will not rebook. I will do all the important jobs – like cleaning the bathroom and stocking the fridge and meeting my work deadlines, and as many of the others as I can – with Christopher's swift and very, very, utterly, utterly unquestioning help, and if by the end of it we still have to prevail upon Rosie's good nature by leaving her to change the bed before she sleeps there or wash the cats' bowls before she feeds them, we will just have to beg her to forgive us. And by us, I mean Christopher, as it is all his fault. He nods. I forgive, though I'll never forget.

CHAPTER FIFTEEN

It is now ten days before the wedding. I eye the phone nervously. There is no getting away from it. I have changed my mind about not wanting a hen night. When my sister first offered to organise one, I declined graciously yet firmly. Not, as my sister assumed, because I have no friends, but because I am a woman well aware of my limitations and knew I would have neither time nor strength to spare to attend one. What, I thought, is the point of having a party just before a wedding, which is itself supposedly the party to end all parties?

I can see the point that a last all-female hurrah might have had in the past, when marriage meant the end of all freedom. If you knew the future held nothing but polite calls and afternoon teas whilst enduring the nightly horrors of the marital bed ('What is that big pointy thing heading towards me, Mr Carruthers? Is it perhaps a mobile towel rail, or a baton for conducting the delightful string quartet we have play in the drawing room for our guests every Sunday? It's what? It goes where? Thou must surely be kidding me, Mr Carruthers. I wish most devoutly to be elsewhere'), or hiding evidence of your husband's gambling/opium/

scullery-maid addiction from prying eyes before having to trail after him to India or America when he decided to up sticks and try to improve the family fortunes in foreign lands, you might well feel entitled to one last glass of fortified wine with the ladies.

But nowadays, surely, I thought, there's no need. I'm sure marriage does change things in some nebulous psychological way, but not practically. It's not going to make any difference to how often I see my friends. Children (other people's) have done that, certainly – you can't get a mother of an under-three out with a crowbar and after that, although they may be desperate to leave the house, they can never find a babysitter and/or their keys in time to join you in the planned revels – but not getting married. Marriage no longer truncates our social lives or circumscribes our options. We no longer have to give up work (chance would be a fine frigging thing) or squeeze out an infant a year. We enter into it freely, fairly certain that there will be no ghastly horrors lying in wait for us on the other side. I've seen my Carruthers naked and while I won't say I didn't scream in horror the first few times, I've got more or less used to it since. And if he ever tries to dislodge me from any of my physical or metaphorical comfort zones in order to further the family fortunes, I shall politely but firmly tell him to stick the idea up his bum.

The modern hen party is just a great excuse for a party. But, if you do not want a great excuse for a party, if you suspect that you would be better off conserving your energies as you rush around like a blue-arsed fly, trying to fit a hogshead of tasks left undone into a pint of time instead, if you know – as someone who hasn't been out twice in a week since she was nineteen – that the idea of another party, in addition to the bridal palaver that is filling your every waking hour and draining every particle of money from your purse, will fill you with dread, then don't have one. There is no need.

Except, I realise as the distance between me and The Big Day becomes measurable in weeks rather than months, there is. Yes, I am running round like a blue-arsed fly. Yes, I probably would be better off conserving my energies. However . . . however . . . a strange need to gather my friends around me, an unexpected need for some kind of rite of passage is beginning to stir and rise. When one of my aunts sends me an email that ends, 'Just think – next time we speak, you'll be a married woman!' I feel so dizzy I have to sit down and, for days afterwards, the phrase 'A married woman. *A married woman*!' keeps tumbling around in my head, setting off an avalanche of images wherever it lands.

A married woman.

A heavily aproned woman as wide as she is tall, with a child on her hip and three more at her feet. The photographs of ancestors a couple of generations back, looking at the camera with hard stares, not even of resignation because there hadn't been another option to resign from. Nora Batty without the comedy.

A married woman.

Graceful, elegant and glamorous, the wedding band contriving to add an alluring air of unattainability to her, adding to rather than detracting from her desirability. Do I think I am going to be French after I get married?

A married woman.

Bored. Boring. Miserable. Frustrated. Trapped, and drinking to forget.

A married woman.

Contented, mature, smug, happy. Nigella Lawsonish. Suddenly vouchsafed the ability to keep surfaces clean, bills paid, fridge stocked and house tidy.

None of these can be right. Or at least not wholly right. Nothing's clear any more. At least back in the days when you knew you were destined to become Nora Batty, there was the comfort of clarity. Doubtless this didn't totally offset the disadvantages of a pro-lapsed uterus and early death, but still, at this point it does occasionally seem more appealing than a leap into the unknown.

Looking down the guest list, I notice that within our congregation is going to be just about every possible variation on togetherness you could think of. We have unmarried heterosexual and married homosexual couples, and vice versa. We have blissfully happy third marriages and painfully unhappy firsts. We have marriages that have survived affairs and those you can be fairly certain won't survive the first dropped cup.

It's a bleedin' lottery, it seems to me. History is no guide either. I have friends whose parents have been married for forty years – one tells me that her mother's face still lights up when she gets the father's phone call, saying that he's on his way home from work, while he says that walking through the door back to her is still the best part of his day – but who have messed up their own relationships as badly as anyone else. The weight of the expectation can be enough to crush your chances of happiness, it seems. And I have friends who have grown up with miserable parents staring across a deepening chasm worn by the ebb and flow of a million festering resentments, but who have gone on to forge the happiest of marriages and partnerships. Although one of them tells me that this is not a result of glorious freedom from expectation, but of sitting down with a stiff drink when you reach your twenties and very carefully compiling a very thorough list of everything you have seen over the years, and then on the other side of the paper making a list of exactly the opposite, and taking the latter as your creed for life.

These, then, are the twin threads of fear that are snaking their way round my soul. First, that anyone who gets married is taking a gamble. You might have worked hard to minimise the dangers – living with someone, sampling his and others' goods, etc., not being dictated to by social law, church rulings or parental desires – but you are still, ultimately, flying blind. You need friends who have been through the experience and lived to tell the tale. To fight the feeling that you are leaping into a void with no idea where you will land.

And second, there is still, even now, in the third millennium, a fear of losing your identity. It's almost as if some kind of folk memory is at work in some tiny, buried oubliette in your mind, telling you that marriage will cause you to lose yourself, to be subsumed within your new status. After all, if the only thing I can see and hear when I gaze into the future is the label A Married Woman fluttering in the breeze, what's to stop others doing exactly the same? I laugh when I think of myself as Christopher's wife. Christopher laughs when he thinks of me being a wife, but other people, y'know, might take it seriously.

So perhaps that is what is, what has always truly been, behind the hen night. The urge to surround yourself with the friends who have known you best and longest. Who will be there on the other side, carrying their caches of memories like external hard drives to remind you who you were, and who you are, and who you will continue to be. And if they are wearing L-plates and sparkly deely-boppers when they send you off, so much the better. I need a hen night.

This conclusion, of course, means phoning my sister to tell her so, and enduring a long and heartfelt diatribe that will take in my many and varied character flaws, including but not limited to my thoughtlessness in changing my mind at the last minute, my selfishness in adding to her organisational burdens, my inability to think ahead, and my stupidity in thinking that she or anyone else will be able to attend at such short and inconvenient notice.

I knock back a bottle of whisky and dial her number.

'Hi, Em. How are you?'

'I'm grouting the bathroom. It's like Christmas come early.'

'I see. How's work?'

'What do you want?'

'Well, I was just thinking . . . And it really doesn't matter if not . . . But I was wondering if, you know, maybe it wouldn't be quite too late to say I'd quite like a hen party after all . . . '

She sighs a gusty sigh. Is it despair? Contempt? Is she about to slam the phone down or reach through the receiver and strangle me?

'Em? I'm sorry – forget I spoke.'

'What are you?'

'I'm – um – stupid?'

'Yes.'

'Thoughtless?'

'Yes.'

'Selfish?'

'Yes. Fortunately,' she adds, 'I am none of these things. I am a far-seeing, all-knowing, generous and loving genius and I have already organised your hen party.'

'Really?'

'Yes. I knew you'd do this. I consulted Christopher and we both agreed your dismissal of the idea was just another example of your limited imagination. So it's next Friday evening at The Mandeville Hotel near Oxford Street, which even you should be able to find.

A chic and sophisticated evening is planned, despite your presence. And Gillian's. There will be teeny-tiny sandwiches, posh cakes and champagne.'

'That's brilliant! That's perfect! That's just what I would have wanted if I'd given any thought to the matter at all.'

'I know. Like I said – genius.'

'You really are. Who's coming? Me, you, Mum, Gillian and Rosie-bum, obviously . . . '

'Obviously. And Helen, Anna, Charlotte, Liz, Donna, Big Claire, Little Claire, Katy and Salayha.'

'How did you know who to get? And how did you get in touch with them?'

'Christopher stole your phone while you were in the shower a few weeks ago and sat in front of your computer scrolling through it, the guest list, your Facebook account and your email address book, and anyone you'd invited and I'd heard you drivel on about or you'd emailed with any discernible degree of fondness recently, I got in touch with. We had the technology.'

'Well, you know, thank you very much.'

'You're almost welcome. I'm coming down on Friday afternoon, so – be round at Mum's, dressed up and ready to act grown-up by six o'clock and we'll all go into town together. Wear a skirt and an expression of delighted expectation. And bring a cheque to cover the afternoon's pay I'm forfeiting.'

'Will do.'

*

Because we are going into town with Mum, who worries so much about missing the train and being late that she always ends up building enough time into her travelling schedule to allow for the complete breakdown of the public transport system, a global flu pandemic and a rebuilding of society's entire infrastructure, we are, of course, the first to arrive.

'Never mind,' says Emily. 'I'm sure in some cultures it is the epitome of cool to arrive six days before the party starts.'

'Oh, stop it,' says Mum. 'We're only forty minutes early. And if I hadn't pulled that child out of the way of the train doors at Sydenham, we wouldn't be here at all.'

'It wasn't a child,' Emily points out. 'It was a thirty-five-year-old man who was moving slightly too slowly for your taste so you grabbed his collar and yanked him into the carriage. He threatened to sue. We had to pretend not to understand English.'

'Well, whatever. He was holding us all up, anyway.'

We order a pre-high-tea round of drinks. As we sip decorously, Emily asks if Christopher is having a stag night.

'Sort of,' I say. 'He's going to Cambridge for tea with his old history tutor.'

'I see,' says Emily. 'I guess you won't have to worry about him running off with a stripper then?'

'Not unless Simon Schama's learned to lapdance,' I say.

Fortunately my friends start to arrive just then and a

flurry of greetings, introductions and compliments fills the air and drives this unsettling image from our minds. When everyone is settled at our table and the first stand of tissue-thin sandwiches has been placed before us, Gillian arrives, panting and dishevelled.

'Sorry I'm late, Luce – hi, everyone – but there was a woman giving birth on the tube. Her waters broke right in front of me.'

'Oh my God!' says Helen. 'So you stopped to help?'

'No,' says Gillian. 'I slipped on the sodding stuff as I was getting off, hit my head on the platform and passed out. Only for a second or two, but when I woke up, some bastard was trying to take my bag and it's my favourite bag, so I pushed him and he fell on to the track.'

She stopped to take a swig of my champagne. 'Hey, this is nice, Luce – can I have one?'

'It's on its way,' I say, having seen the waitress note Gillian's arrival and return to the bar to fill another glass.

'Oh, great. So,' she continues, settling herself at a corner of the table, 'luckily by then, two of the Underground men had come over to help me, so they lifted him off the track and then he broke free of them and scarpered. So I gave them my address and every-thing and said to get in touch if they ever found him and needed me to testify – and then I felt a bit stupid because I thought maybe that only happens on television?' She looks around for elucidation.

'No, I think we have a criminal justice system in real life too,' offered Emily.

'Oh, OK, good. And then the younger one asked if he could give me a ring even if they didn't ever find him again, and I thought, Why not? So I said yes, so hopefully although I've ruined my shoes and got a massive bruise on my head – look, massive, see? – and on my bum – I won't show you that one – maybe I'll get a date out of it. But I'm sorry I'm late. I really did try to be on time.'

We all mutter faintly to the effect that it's OK and these things happen. Only to Gillian, but they happen.

'So, how are all the preparations going?' asks Helen, as we turn our attention more fully towards the little crustless marvels masquerading as sandwiches.

'Everything's under control, I think.'

'Got the dress?'

'Yes. Well, not quite. I've got my first fitting in the real thing tomorrow.'

Helen and Little Claire, who have overheard, look slightly shocked. 'You haven't seen the finished version yet?' Little Claire says.

'No. Why, when was yours done by?'

'Six weeks before my wedding,' she replies.

'Eight,' says Helen. Seeing my face she adds hurriedly, 'But I'm sure it will be fine. I mean, I didn't have to change anything about my dress once it was finished, so I could have had it two months later and there would still have been no problem.'

'Mine was a disaster,' says Little Claire. 'I hadn't realised my dressmaker was an alcoholic and she'd started drinking again just before she started working on it. We had to send it away and get it done by someone else as an emergency.'

'Anyway,' says Helen, booting Little Claire in the shins until she lapses, too late, into silence, 'tell us about everything else. Have you got the cake? The flowers? The music? Orders of service? What hotel are you staying at?'

I tell her and everyone else who has now turned to listen that I've ordered the cupcakes from a lovely website. No, I haven't seen or tasted a sample. Why? I explain my photographs vs. Google decision.

'Still,' says one of the assembled guests, 'I think I'd rather rely on my own taste buds than an algorithmic sorting system.'

Well, at least I've seen the flowers, I tell them. Two beautiful displays of calla lilies and other lovely white blooms flanking the altar, just as they did when I went to the church's Easter service.

'And your bouquet?' says Charlotte.

'I'm not having a bouquet.' The table explodes in disbelief.

'Why not?' everyone roars in outrage.

'Because it'll make me feel stupid, carrying a stupid bunch of stupid flowers. I'll feel like a . . . like a – girl.'

'Well, that would never do,' says Gillian, nodding sagely. 'To look like a girl on one's wedding day – that really would be ridiculous. I don't know what you were all thinking, ladies.'

'You know what I mean,' I protest.

'No, no we really don't. I think I speak for all of us,

in fact, when I say – we think you're being a bit of a tit.'

Salayha, ever the peacemaker and even more gently spoken tonight as she is fasting for Ramadan and therefore steadily weakening with hunger and dehydration as the clock creeps closer to the magic hour of seven o'clock and feeding time, says that I'm not.

'You are,' says Anna firmly. 'You have to carry something because I'm telling you, *you need something to do with your hands.*'

There is a heartfelt chorus of agreement from all those who have been down the aisle before me. It occurs to me that the traditional hen party is monumentally mistimed. You need to get your girlfriends together right at the beginning and squeeze every last drop of information and insight from them before you embark on the road to bridal perdition. Why didn't I think of that? Next time, I promise myself, next time.

'Can't I just take up smoking?' I ask.

'Send your florist a sample of your dress material and ask her to do you a bunch of pale flowers to go with it,' says Emily. To reassure the crowd more than me, she takes a notebook out of her bag. 'I'll add it to my list of Jobs for Her to Do,' she says and a general air of relief descends.

Someone asks about the music. 'Yes,' I say confidently. 'We've got some of that. And Katy here –' I say, gesturing towards my friend, 'is going to be singing solo while we're off signing the register. She's great. She sounds just like a CD. What are you going to be singing, Katy?'

'Purcell's—'

'There you go,' I say triumphantly. 'Whatever that is, I'm sure it's lovely.'

'And which hymns?'

'Can't remember.'

'Entrance music? Exit music?'

'No idea – Christopher's dealing with all the twiddly stuff.'

'How did the rehearsal go?' Katy asks. I think back to that brief, blurry event two, three, four – who the heck knows any more? – days ago.

'Fine,' I say. 'Except I can't remember anything I'm supposed to do.'

By the time the sandwiches have disappeared, we have also established that I still cannot walk in my shoes ('But I'm wearing them for an hour a day and I think they're about to give in any time now'), that I'm going to get ready in a Travelodge and am returning home after the wedding to try and sort the house out before leaving on the stupidly early train the next day rather than staying in a hotel for the night.

'So,' says Anna after a moment's silence, 'on the day, you'll be turning up without having ever set eyes or ears on the cake, music, flowers—'

'Or food,' I add, suddenly realising that I've never tasted any of Jo's produce either, though she does come recommended by someone I have no reason to believe wishes me harm.

'—or food,' she continues. 'From a Travelodge, and in a dress that we can only hope embodies all that you requested when you see it properly for the first time on Saturday. And you will then be turned loose in the Church with no greater idea of your duties than a vague sense that you should propel yourself forward?'

'That's one way of looking at it. Yes.'

A slight pall descends. Fortunately, the cakes and the next round of champagne cocktails arrive, and just as the clock strikes seven Salayha grabs a glass and holds it aloft.

'Everybody relax and just enjoy yourselves!' she cries. 'It's all going to be wonderful! We're going to see you get married,' she says, turning to me as her eyes fill with the easy tears of the romantic with low blood sugar. 'And I don't care what anyone says, I love Christopher! And he loves you – so much! It's beautiful! Someone get me a cake because if I drink this without eating something, I'm going to fall over. Cheers!'

We all drink, and we carry on drinking – not madly, but steadily and with dedication to the art, until Emily decides it's time to play the one hen night game she has had time to prepare.

'It's a version of *Mr & Mrs*,' she says, flourishing a handful of index cards. 'I made a list of questions that, according to the crack team of skilled psychologists and neuroscientists working in the field of glossy women's magazine quiz compilation, will reveal to us whether a couple is destined for a lifetime of happiness'

– she pauses as we all cheer – 'or doomed to misery and despair.' We cheer again. It's possible our drinking has not been as restrained as previously thought.

'So, how well does Christopher know his beloved? We – by which I mean I – asked him the following questions. You – Mangan – have to guess what he replied. Are you ready? Are you set? Let's go. Question one: What was Lucy wearing when you first met?'

'Oh, he'll remember that,' I said confidently. 'He always remembers what I wore. It's one of the many reasons I thought for the first six months of our relationship that he was gay.'

'So what were you wearing?'

'Can't remember. It was years ago.'

'Christopher said: "A black skirt, a very pale pink shirt, knee-high black leather boots and a caramel-coloured leather jacket. Her hair was wet because it was raining and she was wearing her glasses on top of her head. I thought she must be finding the food by smell, as she went straight for the canapés, but our subsequent years together revealed that not only is she essentially blind, she also has no olfactory capacity. If I had known she was quite so physically deficient, I might have thought twice about falling in love and planning to continue my hitherto robust family line with her."'

'He does go on, doesn't he?' comments Anna.

'Honey,' I say, shaking my head, 'you have no idea.'

'He says he would also like to mention here that from that day to this you have not once worn heels again, and he will be seeking to remedy this oversight via some specially written marriage vows. Question two: What is Lucy's favourite television programme? Christopher said . . . .?'

'Oh God, there's too many . . . Anything American. He can't tell them apart.'

'Christopher said: "*Desperate CSI Will & Friends in the City*. Or that one with the shaven-headed men doing implausible things in confined conditions – is it *Prison Break*? But I don't like to think about her watching that. And I especially don't like her to think about what she's thinking about when she watches that."'

'Question three: What annoys you most about Lucy?'

'That I won't let him eat Scotch eggs for breakfast.'

'Wrong, I'm afraid. It's your unwillingness to walk further than six feet in any given direction beyond your front door.'

'And he wants me to wear heels as well! I spy some irreconcilable differences coming up in the not-too-distant future.'

'Question four: What annoys Lucy most about you?'

'We have not world enough or time for me even to begin to draw up the shortlist.'

'He says, "My insistence on getting into bed with her every evening."'

'Oh, yes – that would be right up there. He's correct. Another point for the almost-partnership, please.'

'Question five: What is Lucy's greatest fear?'

Christopher gets this one right as well. He's put, 'Hippies. Nuclear war. Living with someone.'

Question six – 'What do you wish you knew about Lucy?' – defeats me.

'I've no idea. What does he wish he knew about me?'

'What you're doing when you're supposed to be listening to him. And how you got into university.'

'Fair enough.'

'And finally – there are only seven questions because I got bored typing them out – what time of day is Lucy at her best?'

'Well, he'll definitely say it's not mornings.'

'"She really doesn't like mornings –" a champagne-fuelled cheer goes up round the table – "and she loathes anyone talking to her after about ten o'clock because that's when she starts catching up on the reading that her reading earlier in the day hasn't given her the time for, and ideally she wouldn't see anyone or anything who didn't have pages, DVD extras or pink icing between noon and then, so it's difficult to say. But I'm still certain that Lucy is just the bestest all the time anyway. Goodbye, ladies, and enjoy your evening."'

'Oh, he loves you so much!' says Salayha, still starving and tearful.

'And he doesn't mind saying so,' says Big Claire. 'I have to present Al with newborn twins before I can get him to express affection for me.'

I am secretly pleased with how well Christopher has

done and how much he has impressed my friends. Even my mother looks slightly better disposed towards him than usual, though I suspect the cocktails are helping.

'Your final score is six out of seven,' announces Emily.

'Well, whaddya know?' I say, reaching for another titchy éclair. 'There may be something in this "opposites attracting" business after all.'

A bit later I excuse myself to go to the loo. When I come back, there is a giggly but slightly furtive atmosphere. I look round the table. Helen is slipping her BlackBerry back into her bag. Emily quickly flips shut her notebook. A number of people are helping themselves with ostentatious unconcern to cake. And Gillian is looking innocent – the surest sign possible that something is amiss.

'What's going on?' I say suspiciously as I slip back into my seat.

'We were just talking,' says Helen.

'About what?'

'Oh,' she says vaguely, 'you know. This and that. Mostly . . . um . . . that.'

Helen is a barrister. It says on her chambers' website that she has one of the brightest legal minds of her generation. I wish they could see her now.

'Come on! Something's up – tell me! Oh God – you haven't ordered a stripper or something, have you?'

'No, of course not!' says Helen.

'A friend of mine,' says Gillian, 'went to a strip show and the bloke threw his jockstrap at her and it landed on her head, so she wore it there till the end of the show. A week later she discovered she had crabs, in her hair.'

We all make loud noises of disgust and disbelief.

'It's true,' she says, sanguine. 'Remotely contracted crabs, that's what she had. Just goes to show, you can't be too careful.'

This prompts everyone to pile in with their most grotesque stories. Big Claire, a GP, wins with the tale of a male patient who came to see her with a suppurating sore on his penis of a sort she had never seen before. She got down her STD textbooks from the shelf and started looking through them to see if she could find anything similar in the photographs of the rarer diseases and symptoms. Eventually she gave up and, closing the books, looked at him apologetically and said she didn't have a clue what it was. At which point, he said with a thoughtful frown, 'I've been shagging my friend's dog. Do you think I might have caught something from her?'

This led – and I don't want to think too closely about how – on to a game of 'I Have Never, Never', during which we learn that my mother has never, never escaped her Catholic upbringing, Gillian should never, never be allowed to play this game, and that I really should have got out more while I had the chance.

'So,' I say, because I am a woman rarely distracted from her original goal, no matter how many lice-infested jockstraps you throw at me, 'what *were* you lot up to?'

'Such a nasty, suspicious mind,' sighs Charlotte.

'I know,' says Anna. 'So sad to find such cynicism in one so young.'

Just then, Helen's BlackBerry rings. 'Hello?' she says. We wait while the voice on the other end chatters. 'That's great,' she says. 'Can I call you back in five minutes with the details? Thanks.'

She turns back to everyone and says, 'We've got it!' and everyone exclaims in relief.

'Got what?' I say, helplessly. I do feel like a hen now, bobbing round the farmyard, scratching for hints and picking up tiny scraps of information.

Emily glances at everyone and they all give nods of tacit approval for her to explain. Apparently, my friends collectively deemed the daytime rental of a Travelodge room a place for suicide, not bridal preparations. Thereafter, as a brief straw poll revealed that most of them had not yet bought a wedding present, they decided to club together to pay for a day and a night at the Rookery Hotel, a five-minute taxi ride from the church. 'And if it's not,' concludes Emily, 'blame Helen because it's both her knowledge of London's boutique hotels and Googling skills we've all relied on while you were in the loo. That was them on the phone, just confirming that you could sign in early and that the penthouse suite is indeed big enough to house you, Gillian, me, Mum, Auntie Eileen and Silvana. We are all of the opinion that you will, after the event, come to appreciate this much more than the five-eighths of a dinner service that were otherwise coming your way.'

'Oh my God,' I say, looking round all the grinning faces. 'Thank you – thank you so much!' I mean for the room, of course, but I mean for more than that too. I mean for taking a decision out of my hands, for giving me something much better than my own, idiot plan, for – just like my sister in organising this night despite instructions not to – knowing me better than I know myself. For adding yet one more example to the list of the hundred thousand million ways they have, between them, helped and made my life and me happier over the years.

'That's what friends are for!' says Salayha. They are indeed.

The next day my sister and I are remarkably hangover-free. 'I think from now on I will eat cucumber finger sandwiches every time I go out drinking,' Emily says. 'They clearly have remarkable protective qualities.'

'Maybe that's why you never see the Queen puking her guts up after a night on the razz,' I say.

After lunch, Mum, Emily and I set off for Jean's. This is the first time we will see the dress in its full glory and I am suddenly terrified and tearful. The closer this sodding wedding gets, I think furiously to myself as I slouch down in the back of the car so that the other two can't see my eyes filling with tears, the more unstable I become. It is going to be a miracle if I can get down the aisle at all next Saturday without collapsing in hysterics. Perhaps Gillian was right and I should do it all on rollerskates. Dad can just give me a great push through the church doors and I'll be at the altar before I've time to blink, never mind anything more embarrassing.

By the time we knock on Jean's door, I have added waves of nausea to my list of symptoms. She ushers us into her downstairs room, the one with the Giant Mirror of Truth covering the main wall, and Mum and Emily hustle me through. The dress is waiting on the mannequin in the centre of the room. I am actually too scared to look, so I fix my eyes on the box (containing my Tiny Shoes of Crippling Pain) I am carrying.

'Oh my God!' says Emily. 'It's beautiful!'

I raise my eyes. Everyone is smiling – Jean with satisfaction, Emily with happiness and my mother with relief. The dress looks amazing – the pale gold of the material shimmering, the train just long enough to form a little pool at my feet . . . It looks like a gorgeous glass of champagne rendered in silk.

'Try it on, try it on!' says my sister, hopping from foot to foot. I step out of my clothes and into the dress. Jean lifts it round me, I slip my arms in and she laces it up at the back.

'Now the real test,' she says. 'Turn around.'

It is then that I see the point of the Giant Mirror of Truth. Arbiter, impassive judge, faithful recorder of the bad stuff, you must also accept its verdict on the other matters too. And what the giant mirror tells me is that I look bloody marvellous. I'm sorry, there are no two ways about this – this dress is a freaking miracle. For the first time in my life I am wearing something that is so fantastic that it actually has the power to improve me, rather than let me overpower it with my talent for ruination. I look slim. I look elegant. The collar hides my upper arms and broadens my shoulders just like it's supposed to. The corset nips in my waist. The padding looks like a real bust. The train looks just fantastic. It's so strange to be wearing something so different. I still feel like me, but a better me. Or a me with better legs. I don't care which. All that was lumpy is now smooth and streamlined. All that is hideous is concealed from the world.

I stammer out every word of praise and gratitude that I can muster, but Jean brushes them aside. 'Didn't I tell you everything would be all right?' she says with a grin. 'Now, take it off again so I can teach your mum and sister how to sort you out on the day.'

I don't want to take it off – I intend to wear it every day after my wedding, for ever – but I realise that I have very little say in the matter. With this dress, other people have all the power. If anyone decides to unlace it, there's very little I can do about it.

'Right,' Mum says once I'm again standing naked save my knickers. 'Put on your Spanx pants and your tights and shoes and let's do this properly.'

I stand there while my relatives receive their instructions. 'Pull it up gently to here,' says Jean. 'And then, if you can't get the corset on smoothly because she's too hot and sweaty, just put some talcum powder on your hands and spread it over her midriff.'

I catch sight of Emily's face in the mirror. And pray for a cold day.

'And then every time you pull on the corset, just smooth out each side of her spine, so you don't get a groove there,' says Jean.

'All that tennis,' sighs Emily. 'And you've still got a fat back. Excellent.'

'And then round the front,' Jean says to me, 'you'll need to move your boobies –'

'Boobettes, we call them,' interjects Emily.

' – into position, and then let them finish lacing and zip it all up at the back. Then you can adjust the collar material like this – and like this – to exactly the right width, so it stands just above your shoulders like this – and comes down over the chest here so you've got another layer to add to your little bosom –'

'I bought myself a new, 36E bra for this wedding,' whispers Emily in my ear. 'When I'm done with it, I'm going to fit it with doors and rent it out as a holiday home.'

' – and then just pull it down over your upper arms, if you're still not feeling happy with them –'

'I'm not,' I assure her. Three months of racket-wielding has done so little to tone or diminish my sausage limbs that I am thinking of offering myself to medical science as a living study.

'And then finally you arrange the train – later you can hook it up with this loop to this button here, you see, to make it into a bustle so you can walk around and greet your guests – but until then, just spread it out like this . . . And there you are.'

We all stand for a moment in silent awe at the transformation Jean – and the half-stone I have lost – has rendered. I feel as if I am suffocating with corsetry and happiness.

'I honestly can't believe it's you,' says Emily, circling me in disbelief.

'I know,' I say. 'I'm finally living the dream.'

'You look like a tiny adult!' says Mum. 'With everything in proportion at last!'

'I hereby rename Jean, Jeanius,' says Emily and we all bow down low before her.

'Oh, get away with you!' she says, laughing.

'No, but seriously, Jean,' I say, dragging my eyes away from the strange and splendid vision in the mirror. 'Thank you so, so much.'

'It's my pleasure, darling,' she says, hugging me carefully. 'And you have a wonderful day.'

'Looking like this?' I say, turning back to the mirror, which is now my new best friend. 'No problem.'

CHAPTER SIXTEEN

MONDAY

I cannot believe what a difference it makes, knowing that I am going to look OK coming down the aisle. I all but skip around the house, and catch myself humming on more than one occasion. Is this how beautiful people feel all the time, I wonder? What a life that must be.

Oscar Wilde once said that he was finding it harder and harder to live up to his blue china, the most beautiful thing he owned while he was at college. My dress is having a similar effect on me. Ever since I put it on and saw myself in the mirror, the vision has been dancing before my eyes and I have been seized by mad notions of self-improvement.

Today, for example, I booked myself in for a more extensive body waxing than I have ever hitherto contemplated. On top of that, when the salon receptionist heard it was to prepare for my wedding, she suggested having a massage, manicure and pedicure too and I agreed to the lot. Christopher was delighted when he heard.

'I knew, if I just kept on at you long enough, you would eventually agree to feminise yourself!' he said.

I didn't have the heart to tell him it was nothing to do with him. I just don't want to let my dress down.

'Jesus effing Christ!'

It's not as if getting anything waxed is ever an experience easily mistaken for being licked by marshmallow kittens, but this is something else. With every strip torn off hitherto unvisited territory, I swear a little louder and jerk a little higher off the table. By the time the woman is fumbling around in places I have never seen and would be quite happy to pretend never existed, I am turning the air blue.

'Is this place soundproofed?' I ask through gritted teeth.

'No,' she says. 'Most people take a couple of painkillers before they come.'

If I were planning on there ever being a next time, I promise, I would do the same. I lie back under the fluorescent strip light and wonder whether it would be any different in a luxurious spa. Part of me states firmly that as the fundamentals of the act remain unchanged – woman locates five most sensitive parts of your anatomy and proceeds to tear out whatever she finds there by the roots – externalities mean little. Another, slightly larger part of me – possibly the part that is whimpering – doggedly insists that soft lighting, a little soothing music and a therapist who doesn't look as if she is just filling in time before her next shift at the abattoir might at least help take the edge off.

I should have got out after the mani-pedi, while I

still had the chance. For the manicure, Ariadne – for that is my captor's name – grabbed my hand under her arm, sawed at each nail with a piece of sandpaper wrapped round a stick and pushed back my cuticles with a chisel and didn't stop till they reached my elbows. She attacked my toes with equal vigour but I can comfort myself with the thought that if they drop off by next Saturday, I will at least be able to fit into my shoes.

By the time she has finished stripping me bare, I am actually shaking with shock. 'Hmm,' she says, looking down at my battered and outraged flesh. 'D'you not get waxed very often?'

'No,' I quaver. 'Why? How can you tell?'

'You're having a bit of a reaction to the procedure,' she says.

I look down. From waist to knees I am bright red and puffy. I look as if I am wearing quilted cycling shorts. Quilted cycling shorts, I am interested to note, dotted with little crimson spots of blood.

'Don't worry about the blood,' she says. 'That's the normal bit.'

Fortunately my endorphin rush kicks in at this point and I start to laugh. Ariadne soon puts a stop to that by beginning my massage.

I am astonished at the amount of physical pain involved in Ariadne's ministrations. I attempt to list the possible reasons for this to try to keep myself from crying out as she pummels my flesh with her smashing, hamlike fists:

1. She has mistaken me for someone who did her a great personal wrong in early life.
2. She has mistaken me for a taffy pull.
3. She has mistaken me for someone who is going to pay her no matter how bruised I become.

At a particularly heavy-handed moment, during which there is every indication that she is going to break one of my ribs, I – in a slightly strangulated voice because her elbow is in my throat – ask her if she couldn't go a bit easier on me.

'Oh, it isn't supposed to be about pleasure,' she explains sunnily. 'It's about draining the lymph system' – she thumps me in the solar plexus and then the kidneys as I double over – 'unlocking your chakras' – she drives her thumbs into my soles and calves as if wanting to make personal acquaintance with my shinbones – 'and releasing your vertebrae.' As she sits me up and presses her full weight down on the top of my head, I have visions of my spine coming apart and little chunks of bright white bone skittering all over the floor like dropped dice.

At last, it is over, and a feeling of deep, sweet peace comes over me. I think the word 'pleasure', when used in relation to a massage, must loosely translate as 'lovely when it stops'.

As I stagger home, my mobile phone rings. It is my cousin Nicola, ringing to wish me good luck. She can't come to the wedding because she lives in Wiltshire, is pregnant with triplets and since July has been unable to stand up without falling over. She offered to roll here, but the doctor advised against it. I haven't seen her since her own wedding a year ago and we end up talking for forty minutes, during which she gives me one piece of advice.

'On the day,' she says sternly, 'do not get involved in any problems. Delegate. Delegate, delegate, delegate. Someone comes up to you crying that the booze hasn't arrived, hand them off to the best man. Someone's been sick, call your sister. Someone's getting too drunk, call anyone less drunk. Do not get involved.'

'Right,' I say, clutching the phone so hard to stop myself scratching the single giant itch masquerading as my nether regions that my knuckles go white.

'Oh,' she adds, 'and don't get all your waxings and everything done too near the day. You'll be too tense and it'll just be horrible. I ended up shaking and covered in a rash after mine.'

'Thanks,' I say as I walk, crabwise, through my front door and collapse on the sofa. 'I'll bear that in mind.'

TUESDAY

After I've sat in a cold bath for an hour, the puffiness has gone and I look human again. For the rest of the morning I concentrate on work, trying to meet a month's worth of deadlines early so that I can enjoy my day and my honeymoon unencumbered by the know-ledge that there will be tasks piled up on my desk to greet me when I come home.

When I next look up, it is lunchtime. As I sit with my dismal cottage cheese lunch (this isn't dieting, by the way, this is disorganisation. What with one thing and another, I haven't been to the supermarket for ten days. We eat randomly defrosted things or takeaways in the evening and whatever is at the back of the fridge and hasn't developed an independent pulse or the power of locomotion. I suspect by Friday we'll be snuffling for grubs in the garden. Delicious and nutritious – at least compared to cottage cheese. How anything that so closely resembles a yeast infection has maintained its reputation as a viable foodstuff for so long, I'll never know) I panic that our guests on Saturday are going to starve. I call the caterer and order 10 per cent more canapés. I call Crumbs and Doilies and order 10 per cent more cupcakes. I call Wine Simon and order 10 per cent more champagne. I call God and order 10 per cent more money. He tells me to get back to work.

WEDNESDAY

My mother comes round to check on 'the final details'.

Are there enough chairs for everyone over sixty to be able to sit down at the reception?

Yes.

Do I have an address for returning the cakestand?

Yes. Here it is.

Who is returning the cakestand?

She is.

Don't I think it would have been nice to let her know about this before now?

Yes, it would. The cakestand slipped my mind. I am very sorry.

That is OK. How will Dad get his buttonhole if the flowers are arriving at the church in the morning and he is going straight from the feeding of the five thousand at his house to my hotel in the afternoon?

Christopher or an usher will bring it – along with my bouquet – from the church to the hotel.

Will he know the way?

In either case, he will be a thirty-five-year-old man who is familiar with London, maps, walking and/or the hailing of taxis. There is every chance that he will navigate the 567 yards between the two locations successfully.

Have I broken in my wedding shoes yet?

I can walk for about seven yards now before collapsing in pain and am hoping that adrenalin will get me through the final three on the day. It is possible that my shoes will have filled with blood by the time I have stood, kneeled and come back down the aisle, and will have to be cut off me with secateurs, but by then none of us will care.

Should she bring some secateurs?

No. We'll manage.

How will she get home in the evening the bag she is taking to the hotel in the morning, as she does not want to take it to the church?

Emily is coming to pick up all bags that are not ours the next morning. If we have had to leave – thanks to

Christopher's honeymoon-booking debacle over which we will choose not to linger now – before she arrives, we will leave them in reception, where the staff appear to have looked after bags for absent guests before and have promised not to pour paraffin over them and set them aflame before you get there.

Will I be wearing my glasses as I walk down the aisle?

No. I think it will be less frightening not to be able to pick out individual faces but to see a general, smiling – hopefully – blur as I go past.

Where will my glasses be, then, because I'll need them for the reception, won't I?

Yes I will, and for this reason they will be in Dad's breast pocket as he escorts his essentially blind and crippled daughter to her destination. He will at the altar hand my glasses over to me and me over to Christopher in a terrifically unsettling underlining of my new status as chattel but, on the upside, enabling me to read the order of service and join in whatever hymns William and Christopher picked out.

Did she ask about the cakestand?

Yes. The address is in her hand.

Oh yes, she remembers now.

Four hours later, we have examined every branch of the question tree, crawled to the end of every twig, prodded every knothole, turned over every leaf, picked off every insect, climbed carefully down, brushed ourselves off and pronounced ourselves satisfied. We are both very happy.

THURSDAY

Work, work, work, work – I am a machine. Deadlines! Hah! I meet and crush them in my mighty mechanical jaws. I chew them up and spit them out. By the time Rosie turns up to drive us to the park, I am done.

We set off a little mournfully. Tomorrow, my sister will be arriving from Bristol and I will be staying at my parents' overnight as a nod to ancient proprieties, so this will be our last game of tennis.

We play later than we have ever played on this, our last night. There is a definite fin-de-siècle/end-of-an-era air about it and we reluctantly stop only when bats start emerging from the derelict outbuildings behind us and the sole part of my opponent I can still discern is a pale oval of face that, thanks to the blue fleece and trousers camouflaging her in the darkness, seems to be floating unanchored across the court.

'Let's go,' I say at last.

We pack up our rackets and balls and climb into the car. We wend our weary way to the park gates, to discover that they are locked.

'We'll have to leave the car here, walk out of the side entrance and come back for it in the morning,' says Rosie.

We get to the side entrance. It is looped with metal chains and festooned with padlocks. After a moment's heartfelt swearing, we prepare to climb the railings. It will be the first time I have done such a thing while sober. Rosie goes first. She flings her racket over, scrambles in mid-air for a moment in a way I find highly amusing and drops down neatly on the other side.

I complete the first two phases of this manoeuvre successfully but then catch my foot as I drop and end up crashing heavily down on to the pavement. A yell of pain rends the night air, closely followed by Rosie's panicked cry of 'Jesus Christ – how long's your dress!' as I tip sideways into the gutter and reveal a pair of torn and bleeding knees.

'Long enough,' I groan, touched by her concern but slightly woozy. It is, after all, a good quarter-century since I last did damage to any part of my body other than my liver. It is quite a shock. After a few minutes, Rosie drags me to my feet and we stagger homewards, arms wrapped round each other's shoulders.

'Perhaps this means you won't trip when you're going down the aisle,' says Rosie hopefully. 'Perhaps you've got it all out of your system now.'

I don't answer. Because there are no words.

FRIDAY

I have bandaged my knees, which have turned various vibrant shades of red and purple (at last I have a colour scheme for my wedding. Perhaps I should call back the florist and cake suppliers and ask if they could adjust my order. 'I want the whole lot redone. The new theme is Contusion and Swelling. Ta!'), and am tidying the house as best I can with my new unbending gait.

Christopher watches with interest as I make my ungainly way.

'It's going to feel as if I'm getting married to Douglas Bader,' he says happily. 'And that's secretly always been the dream.'

'Why don't you stop watching your poor crippled fiancée and help me instead?' I snarl.

I reel off a list of twenty jobs. 'Consider them done,' he says. 'Badly, and inefficiently, but done.'

By the time he is due to drive me over to my parents' house, ours looks habitable. Rosie can, I reckon, stay here for two weeks without catching anything or getting killed by a falling pile of paperwork, laundry or unsorted recycling. The milkman's order, the boiler's timer and the wine rack have been adjusted to meet her needs. The fridge and freezer and cat food cupboard have been fully stocked. The cats themselves have been wormed, inspected for fleas and passed fit by Christopher – 'Though I have still been able to do nothing about Henry's personality,' he says, as he hands the yowling cloud of ginger fluff over to me to say goodbye. 'He seems set fair to sail through this life on looks alone.'

I bury my face in Henry's fur. 'Goodbye, Henners,' I sob. 'Goodbye.'

Christopher takes him from me. Henry's eyes are wide with outrage.

'Forgive her, awful cat,' says Christopher. 'She under-goes a wedding tomorrow, and then the horror of a honeymoon. This has rendered her temporarily insane. Thus she cries about leaving behind a pair of cats who no more care whether she lives or dies than they do about the outcome of the Ashes as long as someone is around to feed them Butcher's Classics twice a day. Now you, Patrick.'

I hug Patrick and cry into his fur until he too is gently removed and I am ushered into the car and taken to my parents' house. I have calmed down by the time we get there, mainly because if my mother catches me crying over a cat then, wedding or no wedding, she would beat me to a bloody pulp.

'They're here!' my mother sings out as we pull up. 'Come in, come in!'

We go in and have a cup of tea. When he has finished, Christopher, who is sitting on the sofa between my mother and my sister, puts down his cup and stretches an arm round each of them. 'Just think,' he says. 'Today – strangers. Tomorrow – family!'

It's quite the most frightening thought I've had yet.

Twenty minutes later – after Mum has unpacked my bags and made sure I haven't forgotten anything ('Have you got your left ring finger with you?' 'Yes, it's on my hand') – it is time for Christopher to go.

We walk to the car. 'Well,' says Christopher. 'Feeling ready for tomorrow?'

'Not in the least,' I say.

'No, seriously,' he says.

'Oh, seriously? Seriously – no, not in the least.'

He thinks I'm joking, but I wonder if I am. Yes, I'm ready in all the practical ways – everything's arranged, everything and everyone are where they are supposed to be and all the rest of it. But how can you really be ready to get married? You might as well say, 'Yes, I am completely prepared for whatever life may throw at me for the next forty years. I have considered and planned for every possible personal, professional, practical, emotional and spiritual eventuality. I am good to go.'

'Well,' he says, hugging me close, 'let me put it this way. You'd better be there tomorrow, with a smile on your face and a song in your heart, or I will dedicate the rest of my life to hunting you down in order to knock your tiny block off.'

'I love you,' I say.

'I love you too.'

'Seriously?'

'Seriously.'

He kisses me, gets into the car and drives away. And that, I suddenly realise as I watch the car disappear round the corner, is the last I will see of him until I am standing at the altar tomorrow afternoon. Although if Dad doesn't remember to put my glasses in his pocket before we leave, possibly not.

I walk slowly back towards the house. When I think of my wedding day I have always felt as though I am viewing it down a long, slightly unfocused lens. Now, suddenly, everything feels as if it is rushing towards me and I can see it all in detail. I really will be walking down the aisle. I really will be in a big(gish) dress. I really will be standing in front of an altar and a priest and making promises I intend to keep for a lifetime. I shiver. Whether this is with pleasure, anticipation, stark fear or an interesting combination of the three, I cannot decide.

At that moment, another car screeches round the corner, breaking my reverie/potential freak-out. It is the first of the fourteen uncles and aunts who are arriving this evening.

''Ow do!' shouts my uncle as he parks up, with a fine disregard for the conventions of physics and spatial reasoning.

'We've just brought a few bits and pieces to help tide us over!' cries my aunt as she opens the boot and removes half the local butcher's shop. 'Just give us a hand with this, will you?'

'What's in here?' I say, staggering under the weight of the greaseproofed bundle she passes to me.

'Pig's head,' she says, nonchalantly.

'What?'

'Pig's head!' my uncle roars, as if deafness rather than the fact that I am carrying a *fucking pig's head* in my arms is the problem. 'It's a present for your dad. We know you can't get them in London, so we had our Thomas fetch one back from his girlfriend's.'

'His girlfriend kills pigs for a living?'

'No, she's a butcher. You'll meet her tomorrow. Lovely lass.'

I envisage her standing in a pew in a blood-spattered apron and a cleaver in her hand. Still, she looks jolly and she'll be handy if any fights break out.

'Can't wait,' I say as I lug my parcel into the house.

I'll say one thing for family, they don't half take your mind off things.

By the time we sit down to eat, everyone has arrived except my uncle Alan. His arrivals are always difficult to time because he is the one who switches his car engine off whenever he's going downhill to save petrol. Of course, then he has to use the brake so heavily in order to keep control that it slows him down considerably, so his journey time depends on how many slopes there are en route and, alas, the AA book has yet to cater for this particular need and mark them on its maps in sufficient detail to allow for accurate calculation.

As Dad serves up the first course – potted shrimp, and very nice it looks too in the little brown dishes Grandma won in the 1947 Offal Fettling Championships when she beat Tommy Ollerenshaw in the race to whittle a pair of clogs out of a beef heart, I believe – Emily raises her glass in a toast. 'To this –' she says in sepulchral tones, gesturing along the length of the table, 'The Last Supper.'

I burst into tears. 'Oh my goodness,' says Mum, jumping out of her seat and burying my head in her bosom. 'It's going to be one of those nights, is it, you daft thing?'

'Why is she crying?' says Dad, bemused.

'Because tomorrow's her wedding and she's just a bit took,' says my auntie Maudlin, helping everybody to bread.

'Tomorrow? Is it?' says Dad. 'By 'eck. Good job I

made a nice tea then. Come on, Boogaloo. Cheer up, there's a good lass.'

I sniff, gulp and apologise, in roughly that order, and settle down to the meal. I perk up even more when I see that Dad has made my favourite for the main course – roast chicken with extra bacon rolls and bread sauce. Emily lets me get the first forkful of delicious morsels to my lips and then, shaking her head regretfully, says, 'Funny to think that after tomorrow I'll be an only child.'

This makes me laugh and cry together until gravy shoots out of my nose. While my aunts are mopping my face with the fifteen scrunched-up hankies simultaneously withdrawn from fifteen cardigan sleeves, Alan arrives. Once the detailed analysis of his journey time and petrol consumption has been shared (quicker than his hitherto record-breaking 1999 visit, apparently, but he still cannot break the efficiency barrier set in the summer of 2002, but then he thinks that will be possible only in a period of equally hot weather), the evening becomes one of ancient reminiscence and nostalgia. For Alan, in addition to being a demented spendthrift, is also the oldest of Mum's brothers and sisters and therefore the unofficial keeper of family lore and legend. Once he arrives, the memories, the myths and the increasingly impenetrable family sayings always start to flow, but never thicker or faster than they do tonight.

At one point it turns into a kind of family Mastermind, with me in the hot seat.

'Where did "Nice under a coat" come from?'

'It was 1957. Dolly Mansfield had bought a red pleated dress that made her look like the back end of a bus. She asked Grandma for her opinion and it was all she could think of to say. They haven't spoken since.'

'Correct. Who said, "This is delicious, Agnes. Do you mind if I leave it?"'

'Great-Auntie Rae at her sister-in-law's boarding house in Bridlington, 1806.'

'Correct. And why?'

'The reasons were threefold. One – Great-Auntie Rae's bosom was so big it put a strain on her brain and made her slightly simple, two – the dish in question was boiled tongue; and three – they were in company so she felt she had to be polite and this was the closest she could manage.'

And on it went, into the night, everyone adding their stories to my mental dowry, me reaffirming my membership of this loving, benighted, daft-as-a-brush, suffocating, indispensable, clamorous, life-draining, life-affirming clan before I headed off the next day to affiliate myself with another. Eventually we had to get up from the table and go to bed. The family rules against physical affection were tacitly laid aside on this special night, and everyone hugged me before they went upstairs to fight over the bathroom.

'Goodnight, chuckabutty.'

'Nernight, kid . . . '

'Sleep tight, don't let t'bugs bite . . . '

Until finally it is just me and Emily left. We watch the last of our relatives thunder up the stairs ('Gerrout of

346

the way, y'daft gowk, I'm coming up!') and listen until the shouting from those already there ('Does anyone else want a wee? There's room for one more down here, I reckon!') has faded to a murmur.

'Still,' says Em, turning to me with a bright smile. 'At least going straight from hotel to honeymoon doesn't seem quite so bad now, does it?'

'No,' I acknowledge. 'No, I can't say that it does.'

We mount the stairs together in silence. We clean our teeth. We stand on the landing for a moment, trying to remember where we're supposed to be sleeping.

'I think I'm on the floor in here with the cousins,' says Emily, nodding towards our old room.

'I'm in the spare room with Auntie Maudlin,' I say.

'OK then,' she says, making no move to go in. We stand there for a moment longer.

'Weird, eh?' says Emily.

'Weird,' I agree.

'Oh well,' she says, grabbing me and hugging me hard. 'You'll probably still feel like family even afterwards.'

'I hope so.'

'See you –' she drops her voice to the funereal tones she used for the toast, '*tomorrow.*'

'Sleep well,' I say as we head off to our separate rooms.

'Fat chance,' she says. 'Thomas farts like an Aberdeen Angus. I sleep, I die.'

Yes, I think, as I creep into bed without waking Auntie M. I'm going to miss all this.

CHAPTER SEVENTEEN

The alarm is set to go off at eight but my aunt falls out of bed at seven. It doesn't wake her, but it wakes me. I lie there for a few minutes but have to admit that even I, champion sleeper though I customarily am, am not going to drift off again at this point.

So I creep out of bed, round the snoring heap on the floor, pull on my dressing gown and go downstairs. Dad, the perennial early riser, is already in the kitchen, making preparations for the first shift of cooked breakfast he will be called upon to begin making in an hour's time.

To my blurred and heavy-lidded vision, the kettle is nothing more than a glint in the early morning sun, but it is enough. I head towards it.

''Ow do, Dad,' I say, as I pass him at the breadboard.

''Ow do, love,' he says, turning to look at me. 'By 'eck, you look grand.'

'I'm not ready yet, Dad. Pink terry towelling would be an odd choice for a wedding gown.'

'Oh good,' he says with relief, turning back to his slicing and buttering. 'I did wonder. But then I thought – what do I know?'

I switch the kettle on and measure out my last coffee spoonful as a single woman. It is far more momentous than it sounds.

'What can I make you for breakfast?' says Dad.

'Can I have some toast, please?'

'Coming up. And perhaps a little bit of bacon? I've just put mine on, I can add some more.'

'Go on then, as it's a special occasion.'

'I'll say,' says Dad. 'You've not been up this early since you were teething.'

We share out the sections of the morning paper – sport for him, magazine for me – and eat in companionable silence until the telltale sounds of lavatorial trumpeting and enormous bras being snapped round enormous bosoms inform us that the rest of the family is preparing to join us.

Dad folds the paper up and pushes his chair back with a sigh. 'Ah well,' he says. 'It's always nice while it lasts.'

He takes up his post at the grill and sets to work. Mum dashes into the kitchen.

'Where is she?' she asks.

'Who?' I say.

'You,' she says.

'Me? I'm here.'

'It's true,' says Dad, nodding. 'I can see her too.'

'When you weren't in bed, I didn't know where you could be. I thought you might have fallen asleep on the toilet, but Alan was in there and he said you weren't.'

'No. I was here. Eating crustless toast and reading the paper.'

'How are you feeling?'

'Full.'

'No, I mean about today!'

'What's today?'

'Oh, you! Are you nervous? Are you excited? I am!'

'I can tell. You've relaid the table eight times while you've been talking.'

'So – how do you feel?'

I ponder. I am not used to being asked how I feel, except by doctors, and it takes me a moment to decide.

'I feel calm.'

'That's because you are dead inside,' says Emily, suddenly appearing in the kitchen doorway. 'Is there any bacon ready yet?'

'I thought you just lowered rashers into your mouth raw?' I say. 'Who's been teaching you the refinements to be practised upon uncooked pig?'

'You're in my seat,' points out Emily.

'It's my special day,' I point out in return.

'Move.'

I move. She sits. I sigh.

'Go up and have a wash,' advises Mum. 'If your uncle Alan's got stuck in there, just call your auntie Eileen. She used to grease pigs for the Garstang County Fair in her younger days. She'll sort him out.'

Fortunately, the bathroom is fat-uncle free and I am able to perform my ablutions without incurring major psychical traumas beforehand. As I get out of the shower, Emily comes in holding my mobile phone.

'You keep getting texts,' she says. 'I hope nothing's wrong.'

'Read them out while I dry myself,' I say. She plops down on the stool and starts scrolling through. They are all from Christopher.

'8 a.m. I am up.'

'8.15 Cats fed and booted out. Henry objects wildly. Patrick's mien one of weary resignation. I imagine that over at your parents' you are looking much the same. Xxx.'

'9.15 I have showered, shaved and morning-dressed. I look exceedingly handsome. I am very glad I am getting married today. Are you?'

'9.17 I have left the house and am on my way to meet Richard at the church to collect the flowers. He wants to know if you have come to your senses yet and have called the whole thing off. I laughed like a – no, wait, I didn't.'

'9.20 We have lucked out with the weather. It is beautiful day, cloudless sky and very warm. Do not wear a coat to your wedding. Xxx.'

'Well, that all sounds good,' I say from under the towel as I dry my hair. 'Under control.'

'Yes,' says Emily snapping the phone shut. She peers under the towel. 'And are you really feeling as calm as you look?'

I hesitate. I am not feeling as calm as I look. I am not panicking, although I am apprehensive. But I don't want to tell anyone this as it will just make it worse. So –

'Yes, I am,' I say.

'I see,' says Emily, sagely. 'You don't want to make it worse. OK. I'll tell Mum to keep a lid on herself.'

'Thanks,' I say.

'No problem,' says Em. 'Now, I need to clean my teeth, so get out of my way. Honestly, you do nothing but get under my feet.'

'Sorry,' I say, and scurry off to the bedroom to get dressed.

'Come on, come on, hurry up!' cries Mum from the hallway. 'It's time to go!'

We are, of course, today running on *über*-Mum time, which is to say we are quadrupling instead of merely doubling the amount of time a normal person would allow for each stage of our journey. Thus the five-minute drive to the station has been allocated twenty minutes, the fifteen-minute train ride to Charing Cross has been given an hour, and a ten-minute cab ride to the hotel has been given thirty minutes, plus an extra ten because you can't be too careful with London traffic. By rights, we should have left a week before Christopher proposed.

'Get in, get in!' cries Mum, holding the wedding dress aloft as Emily, Eileen and I come down the garden path. When we are safely ensconced in the back seat, she lays the dress reverently across our collective lap. 'OK,' she says to Dad who is sitting patiently behind the wheel awaiting instructions. 'We can go.'

He turns left instead of right out of the road, just to see what she will do. She just about puts her head through the roof but it does give the rest of us a laugh.

Gillian is supposed to be meeting us at the station. And – wonder of wonders – she is there when we turn up.

'Holy moly,' I say when I see her. 'Is it really you?'

'It really is,' she says proudly.

'How did you manage to get here so early? Did you sleep on the platform last night?'

'No,' she says. 'When I got in from my usual, fun-filled, Friday-night extravaganza I took eight handfuls of ProPlus, washed down with three black coffees, had a shower, got changed and came straight here.'

'So you haven't actually been to bed yet?'

'No,' she said. 'I'm due to crash at about twelve, so I need to start drinking at about eleven. But we'll all be ready for a glass of something by then, won't we?'

'We've brought some champagne – well, not champagne, but something fizzy. Carbonated meths, possibly – for brunch.' Brunch, in my family, being the meal you eat between rather than instead of breakfast and lunch.

'Brilliant,' says Gillian. 'Couldn't have worked out better, you see?'

The journey into town passes uneventfully, save for the cries of 'Mind the dress!' that pierce the air every time the train stops, starts or judders in between. Still, at least it keeps Gillian awake.

We are bowling along relatively peacefully in the cab, pointing out places of historical and personal interest to Eileen as we pass them.

'That's the pub where Charles Dickens drank,' I say. 'That's the church I'm getting married in later today.'

'That's the law firm where I used to work, and that's the bookshop I used to hide in and cry every lunch-time.'

'That's the first place I was ever sick in London,' says Gillian, pointing to a shop doorway. 'What a proud day that was.'

Just as I open my mouth to tell them where I was first sick in London (the bin next to the carriage doors of the 11.37 from Catford Bridge), Emily grabs me by the neck and pushes me violently to the floor.

'Is this a gesture of affection that I am misinterpret-ing?' I ask, my voice muffled by the proximity of a luggage-strewn floor. 'Have you been overcome by a sudden wave of emotion and have chosen to express it via the medium of broken bones?'

'No,' says Emily maintaining her vicelike grip as she, along with everyone else, stares out of the window. 'We've just seen Christopher. He's walking along the pavement about a hundred yards in front of us. And it's bad luck for you to see each other so I've made sure you don't.'

'I think it's still quite bad luck to break the neck of the bride,' I say. Her grip loosens a fraction, enabling me to sit up slightly and take some sweet, sweet oxygen back into my lungs.

'He's with someone,' says Gillian, craning her neck out of the window. It's like watching ET scan the horizon for spaceships.

'Is it another woman?' I ask. 'Are they kissing? Can we all go home?'

'No, it's – it's a blond man. Quite tall. Red cheeks. Strange face. And he's carrying flowers.'

'It must be his lover,' I say. 'Well, that's almost as good. Driver, turn around, please.'

'Ignore her,' says Emily. 'Who is it really?'

'It's his best man, Richard. They must be bringing Dad's buttonhole and my bouquet to the hotel.'

A minute later we overtake them. Emily gets the driver to beep his horn and Mum, Emily, Gillian and Eileen all wave at the boys as we go past. I'm waving too, but beneath window height. When Emily deems the peril to have receded sufficiently, I am allowed up.

'Here we are,' says the driver as he pulls up. 'The Rookery Hotel.'

Eileen and Gillian grab the keys from the rather handsome man at the reception desk and rush me up the stairs to our room so that I am out of the way when Christopher turns up. We unlock the door and go in.

'Oh, wow!' says Gillian, gazing round.

'Oh. Wow!' I agree wholeheartedly.

It is not a room. It is a suite. A suite spread over two floors, with the upper laid out round a central circle, looking down on to the enormous bed and almost equally enormous Victorian bath that dominates the lower. Gillian darts round, as usual, inspecting everything.

'Look, Luce – there's a whole living room up here! Sofa, television, coffee table – Ooh, I love this rug, I wonder where it's from?'

Most people would turn back the corner, if indeed most people were that interested in a rug's origins in the first place. Gillian dives head first under it.

'Ow!' she says. 'What did I hit?'

'Your head on the leg of the coffee table that is standing on the rug,' I say.

She emerges, rubbing her head and looking rueful. 'You would think,' she says thoughtfully, 'that I would have learned by now.'

You would. Meanwhile, my aunt is roaming around downstairs, admiring the other luxurious furnishings and stroking the layers of throws and covers that adorn the bed in the way only hotels and Sunday supplement magazines ever manage to make look right.

'Ee, it's a proper do, this, isn't it?' she says admiringly.

'It is that,' I agree.

A few minutes later, Emily and Mum come in with the bags. Another round of exclamations – Mum is particularly taken with the opulence of the curtains ('Right down to the floor!') and the wisdom of having a modern bathroom off the bedroom to back up the beautiful but in her eyes untrustworthy Victorian showpiece on the dais – and then it's down to business.

We hang my dress carefully in the wardrobe. We unpack and distribute hairdryers, shampoos, unguents, shoes, tights and cosmetics to their rightful owners. We put in the minibar fridge the couple of bottles of fizz we have brought to fuel our endeavours. We have a ten-minute panic about where my headband has got to before Mum remembers that for particular safe keeping she put it in her bag. Not that bag, the other bag. No, the other other bag.

As we accomplish all this, Mum and Emily tell me that they did see Christopher and Richard, who arrived as they were signing us all in. 'Richard seems lovely,' says Mum. 'It's a pity you couldn't be marrying him, really.'

There's not a lot I can say to that, so I don't.

'And Christopher tried to get us to tell him what you would be wearing, but we wouldn't say anything,' says Em. 'I think he is quite genuinely worried that you're planning to get married in a jogging suit and trainers.'

'I suppose there's no point asking how he looked, is there?' I say.

'Not really. Just furious, as usual. Maybe happy furious. Maybe nervous furious. But without the proper training, it's impossible to tell. He was a good colour, if that's any help.'

'Who's having the first shower?' shouts Mum from the upper deck. 'Gillian?'

'What? What?' says Gillian, who has apparently fallen momentarily asleep standing up. We must be coming up for eleven o'clock. That's four hours to go before I get married. My stomach, and possibly a couple of adjacent organs, turn over.

'Do you want to have a shower now?' I say to her.

'Oh. Oh yes, good idea. If I'm not out in twenty minutes, come and get me. Sometimes when I'm like this I think the bathmat is my bed.'

'It would be great if you could try not to crawl under any more rugs today,' I say.

'Roger, wilco and out,' says Gillian, saluting and disappearing into the little bathroom.

'Emily, you could have one at the same time,' says Mum.

Emily looks mildly disturbed. 'I'm very fond of Gillian and everything, Mum, but I think that's crossing a line that—'

'I meant in the old-fashioned shower and you know it,' says Mum, leaning out over the balcony to try to belt her, but failing because – well, because they are on separate floors.

'Oh, OK,' Emily says obligingly, and hops in.

Because I have to get ready last, the better to maintain my pristine bridal aspect for the day's main event, I have nothing to do. I sit on the bed and listen to Mum and Eileen squawking and flapping overhead. It sounds like a couple of drunken emus trying to nest. This reminds me of the bottles in the minibar and I try to decide whether a glass or two would settle my stomach or do quite the reverse. There is only one way to find out.

'Who wants a drink?' I say, popping one of the corks.

There is a chorus of requests, though notably not from Gillian. I bang on the door to check she is still alive and merely deafened by the running water. So it proves, so I leave a glass of booze just outside the shower, warn her not to step on it, and back out.

We sip relatively politely from our glasses while Emily and Gillian dry their hair, get into their finery and put their make-up on. Mum and Eileen had their showers at home, so Eileen has got dressed and put her face on too. Mum is still in her travelling clothes because she is having her make-up done by Silvana, who is due to arrive any minute.

'Well, isn't this nice?' says Eileen.

'I wonder how Christopher's getting on?' says Mum.

'He'll be working his way through an eight-course fried breakfast with Richard by now,' I say. 'He'll probably have a heart attack before we get to the "I do's". Which would in many ways be a relief.'

'Oh, give over,' says Mum.

But I mean it. Not because I don't love him. I just hate change. And walking down aisles in posh frockery.

Silvana arrives, filling the air with perfume and warm flutters.

'How is everyone?' she says solicitously. Seeing me, she smiles understandingly. 'Eet ees strange time, yes?' That's it exactly. Suddenly, I feel better.

'You should probably work your magic upstairs,' I say, showing her to the upper floor. 'More windows, more light, fewer people having showers.'

She sets out her potions, lotions and powders, sits Mum in a chair and starts work.

I have my shower and then my sister starts work on my hair. Gillian sits on the bed and watches us.

'How many practice runs at this have you done?' she says conversationally.

'None.'

'None?'

'None.'

'We ran out of time,' I explain. 'Suddenly there just wasn't another opportunity for me to go up there or her to come down here, so . . . '

'So,' says Emily, taking over as she forces my head upside down between my knees so she can rub something else glutinous into my hair, 'I just took a bit of advice from my hairdresser – who's cut Lucy's before when she's been at mine, and still remembers her stupid thin hair and rugby-ball head – about what to do and, you know, I'm sure it'll be fine.'

'And if not,' says Gillian, walking over to the bedside window and fingering the muslin curtain, 'I bet I could make a veil out of this for her if the man downstairs could just lend me a stapler.'

'Stop touching it, Gill,' I beg, having been restored to the perpendicular by my sister and able to take in a view of something other than my own crotch once again. 'You'll only end up bringing the lot down.'

'Good point,' says Gillian, letting the folds drop back down and returning to the bed. 'Are you nearly done, Em?'

'Nearly,' she replies. I really hope so. She appears to be sawing at my hair with a sharp implement and I don't know if I can stand much more.

'It's backcombing,' says Gillian, seeing the fear and confusion in my eyes.

I give a strangulated cry about not wanting to look like Diana Ross nor either one of the Supremes.

'Not like that,' says Emily, sighing. 'Just a bit at the back here, because the hairdresser said – and I can see what she means now – that you need a bit of height . . . shush, shush, just a little, tiny, almost unnoticeable bit of height – behind the headband, otherwise it looks . . . well, just wrong.'

I say nothing. There's still time to wash my hair again if need be.

'OK,' she says five minutes later and giving my hair one final spray with one final – glossing? fixative? volumising? colourising? disinfecting? – liquid. 'Now I've finished – ta-dah!'

She spins me round to face the mirror. From all the spritzing, spraying, tugging and pummelling my throbbing scalp has received I am expecting to see a bouffant helmet of horror that is seconds away from developing an independent heartbeat, but instead I see a lovely, smooth, shiny bob that looks exactly like my normal hair but ten times better. She really is quite clever, my sister.

'You really are quite clever, sister,' I tell her.

'I know,' she says. 'I could probably go into business with this. Personal grooming lessons for shut-ins.'

'That's not a bad idea,' says Gillian. 'My friend Jane is a social worker and she once went round to an old lady's house who hadn't gone out or had a wash for years. She had this great, piled-up, unwashed mass of hair and Jane finally persuaded her to come into the bathroom and let her wash it. When she unpinned it and took it all down, she found a nest of mice in there.'

There is a moment's silence.

'Yours looks great, though, Luce. Really great.'

Silvana calls down that she has finished with Mum. We head upstairs to admire her handiwork. Mum has changed into her wedding outfit so we get the full effect. She too looks really great – tall, slim and glowing with excitement and happiness. I hope by the time I leave here I am managing at least one of those.

'Sit down,' says Silvana. 'Everybody else to downstairs, pliss.'

'We'll order lunch,' says Mum, waving the room service menu. 'What do you want, petal?'

'Nothing, thanks.'

'Nothing? Really nothing?'

'Really nothing.' I am feeling better, but there is no way I can eat.

'All right. Silvana, you wanted the smoked salmon, didn't you?'

'Yes, pliss.'

'Right. Come on, the rest of you, let's go down and give them a ring.'

They all go downstairs and, upstairs, peace descends.

Silvana massages, dabs, smoothes and paints with the same delicate expertise as before and I find it just as soothing. I almost drift off into a doze, staying only awake enough to follow her whispered instructions to open my mouth slightly, look down, look up, tilt back. I reluctantly come to when she announces that she has finished.

'Now you put on your dress and shoes and headband,' she says. 'Then I do last touches and you are ready to be married!'

I go downstairs. While I change into my giant support knickers, Mum and Emily take the dress off its hanger and lower it to the floor, ready for me to step in.

As she bends over, Em looks up and fixes me with a gimlet eye. 'Don't even think,' she says, 'of sweating.'

I wouldn't dare.

I step in and they lift the thing up around me just as Jean instructed and pull the laces in. And then in a bit more.

'Your back fat's really gone down, kid,' my sister says admiringly. They tug the corset in a bit more.

'Can you still breathe enough?'

'Just about.'

'You won't be walking very fast, after all,' Gillian says. 'Not with those shoes.'

I sigh. The breaking-in of my shoes has been only a partial success. There is no doubt that they are going to cripple me, possibly permanently, before the day is out. I slip them on and try a few steps. The pain, added to that of my still empurpled knees, makes me grimace wildly.

'This is ridiculous,' decides Gillian. 'Luce, you're never going to wear these things after today are you? Realistically?'

'No,' I say.

I really cannot think of any outfit I might possibly wear in the future for which white and gold brocade would be the ideal finishing touch. I suppose I might one day play Elizabeth I in an am-dram production of *Shakespeare in Love*, but even then it would probably require slippers rather than heels. Amateurs are sticklers for historical accuracy.

'Right,' she says and disappears out the door.

'Should we follow her?' says Emily doubtfully.

'No,' I say. 'Her handbag and Berocca's still here. She'll be back.'

Ten minutes later, she is, with a Stanley knife.

'Sorry about the wait,' she pants. 'The man on reception didn't want to give it to me – health and safety, all that rubbish. I had to explain that your shoes were about to ruin the biggest day of your life and that I had to have something that could cut the toes off and make slits down the side.'

'You explained that you had to have something that would cut the what off and slit the who now?'

'Look,' says Gillian in tones of utter reasonableness. 'You know how much misery rotten shoes cause. No one can see these shoes as you're walking down the aisle, and if you have to hitch your skirt up to manage stairs at the reception or something afterwards, nobody's going to care. So let's just cut a few bits off them, put vents in the sides so your feet can flob out a bit and you can be comfortable all day.'

We all look at each other. Eventually we nod. Gillian smiles delightedly and dives for my feet.

'Wait, wait, you idiot!' I scream. 'Let me take the bloody shoes off first!'

'Oh, yes!' grins Gillian from the floor. 'That's a good idea. Otherwise you might be even worse off than before.'

'Yes, you know, I might.'

She accomplishes the task successfully and without – miracle of miracles – slicing off any of her fingers in the process. Meanwhile, Emily arranges my headband and my hair, Mum smoothes out my dress and Silvana puts the finishing touches to my make-up. Then everyone steps back, looks at me and breathes a sigh of relief.

'You know, Luce, you don't look half bad,' says Gillian.

'What are you talking about?' says Eileen. 'She scrubs up lovely!'

'It's a job well done, certainly,' says Emily with satisfaction.

'You look grand, pet,' says Mum. 'If I had my time again I'd let that doctor give you the growth hormone when we had the chance, but still – all in all, you'll do very nicely.'

'Bloody hell,' says Eileen. 'Look at the time. Your

father will be here in a minute. We'd best get off to the church.'

One by one, they all kiss me, careful of my dress and make-up, and head off to the church. Eventually it is just me and Gillian left.

'Well,' she says. 'Fucking hell, eh, Luce!'

'You can say that again,' I say.

And suddenly we are laughing. Laughing so hard that I fear for my make-up, my corset and – given the amount of time it takes me to get these blinking support pants off – my bladder. We have no idea why. In fact, at one point, Gillian stretches out her long, gangling arms and gives a massive shrug of incomprehension, which only makes us laugh harder.

'All right,' she says. 'We've got to get a grip. I've got to go.'

'OK.'

We stare at each other for a second and then hug, hard. It wouldn't take much to turn our hysterical laughter to hysterical tears, so it is fortunate that my dad picks that moment to knock on the door.

Gillian kisses me and goes, as he comes in.

'Hi, Dad.'

'Hello, love.'

Silence.

'How was it all at the church, Dad?'

'Oh, fine, you know. Lot of people. And a vicar.'

'Good. Good.'

Silence again.

'Do you think I look nice, Dad?'

He looks slightly startled and then looks closely at me.

'Aye. Aye. Because you normally wear jeans, don't you?'

'Yes.'

'Made a bit of an effort today, then?'

'Yes.'

'Grand.'

The phone rings. Our taxi is here. We make our perilous way down the stairs ('You'll have to let me hold your arm, Dad. No, the other one. The one nearest me') and out on to the street.

The traffic is solid between us and the church.

'They closed the main road at noon,' explains the cab driver. 'So everything's a bit fu—' He stops, in deference to the dress. 'A bit fouled up.'

The minutes tick by and we crawl along – in silence – at an almost imperceptible speed. Now I'm sweating. I am going to be so late. I am suddenly grateful that it is Dad in the car. I couldn't cope with anyone who was given to overt displays of stress. It's all I can do to keep down my own choking panic. I tell myself that it doesn't matter how late I am. It's not as if anyone's going to die if the ceremony doesn't start on time. It doesn't matter how creased my dress gets from being sat and sweated on for so long in the car. It doesn't help. Not in the least. This must be how Mum feels all the time. I must try to remember to be nicer to her in the future, for this is no way to live.

Just as I am about to give full vent to my second ever

fit of the screaming abdabs (as my first was occasioned by Christopher moving in, at least it will be a nice way to bookend the relationship), a gap in the traffic opens up. Our driver is off, ducking down side streets, mowing down cyclists, pedestrians and pigeons, and draws up outside the church bang on time. Mum is there, waiting, with the vicar. Dad pays the cab driver while Mum helps me and my dress out.

'Is it crushed to buggery?' I whisper.

'No,' she says, pulling and straightening. 'It's fine. I'm quite glad we didn't go for the cheap stuff now.'

The vicar steps forward, smiling. 'Are you ready?' he says.

'As I'll ever be,' I say.

Mum kisses me and disappears into the church. Dad and I are left alone in the entrance of the church while William goes to get the verger.

Two middle-aged women stop in the street and smile at us. I smile and they each raise a hand, not quite in a wave, not quite in a blessing, but somewhere between the two.

I take my glasses off and give them back to Dad, who tucks them into his inside pocket.

The verger arrives.

'Ready?' he says.

I am.

The doors open, the music starts, and off we go. As we enter the church everyone stands and turns towards us, smiling. Blimey. A girl could get used to this. I wonder if I could make my friends do this every time

I come into a room? Wouldn't it make every day go with a swing? Just as I am thinking this, I trip over the carpet that starts at the first pew, but only the back three rows can really see.

Walking down the aisle takes both for ever and no time at all. I have vague memories of friends at the hen night advocating a stately head turn from side to side to acknowledge everyone's presence, but I am so happy to see everyone and so excited when I manage to identify anyone from their blurry outline that I rapidly descend into nodding-dog mode, which I am sure looks extremely sophisticated.

Years and nanoseconds later, the serried ranks of smiling faces finally fall away and there in front of me stands the altar ('Stop when you see steps!' – another vital piece of advice comes rushing back to me) and Christopher, his scrubbed face frowning sweetly above a decidedly unscrubbed morning-coat ensemble. I make a mental note to restrain myself from brushing him down when I go and stand up there.

Dad holds my glasses out to me. I put out my hand to take them and he catches it and kisses it before giving me my specs and shuffling back to his place in the front pew beside Mum. She rolls her eyes at this wholly unwarranted display of affection between a father and his daughter on her wedding day. Gillian is crossing hers to try to make me laugh and my sister is covertly miming being sick. Suddenly the prospect of losing my identity in another's doesn't seem quite the worry it once did. In fact, it seems quite attractive.

Fortunately, the presence of the vicar looming over us from the altar step is enough to keep front-row shenanigans to a minimum thereafter. I hand my bouquet to Allegra, who looks up at me with pleasure as she exchanges it for my order of service.

'Don't we,' she says, stroking her shiny dress, 'look nice?'

'We really do,' I agree.

I join Christopher at the altar and he leans forward to tell me I look beautiful. 'Did it take long?' he murmurs, amusingly.

'You could have built a boat quicker,' I mutter back.

William smiles down at us and we all give the slightest of nods. The service begins.

'Dearly beloved, we are gathered together in the sight of God and in the face of this congregation, to join together this Man and this Woman in holy matrimony . . . '

And that's when I start to believe we are really getting married.

'We are gathered here today to witness . . . '

It's a very strange feeling to hear these words suddenly directed at you. How many times have they been said over the centuries in this church alone, and yet suddenly when they are said to you it is as if you are hearing them for the first time? They bind you to the past as they bind you to each other. So public, up there on the altar, but so intimate as you stand there promising to love each other and only each other for the rest of your time on earth.

'Christopher David Nicholas, will thou have this woman to be thy lawful wedded wife, to live together after God's ordinance in the holy estate of matrimony?'

He will. That's a relief.

'Lucy Katherine, will thou have this man to be thy lawful wedded husband, to live together after God's ordinance in the holy estate of matrimony?'

I fight a terrible urge to reply, 'Do you know, when you put it like that . . . ' The fact that my godmother has promised me sixpence if I don't misbehave during the ceremony keeps me focused.

'I will.'

We make our vows and Richard steps forward to give him the wedding ring. Christopher slips it on to my finger and before I know it –

'I now pronounce you man and wife. Whom God has joined together – ' this is always my favourite part at any wedding and it still is at my own, this touch of blood-and-thunder at the end – 'let no man put asunder.'

We kneel – I squeak only faintly in agony – for the blessing and then we stand and Christopher may kiss the bride. It is the first time he has ever done so smiling. We turn and face the congregation and everyone stands and sings 'All People that on Earth do Dwell'.

Then we – no, wait, let's do this thing properly – my husband and I make our way to the vestry, along with various family members and Gillian, to sign the register as the choir sings something very nice and completely unknown to me. It sounds as if my input was banned from all the right things.

As the vestry door closes behind us, we all breathe a sigh of relief and the room fills with a great babble of chatter and laughter. I sign and Gillian witnesses ('Look at that,' she says proudly. 'They almost look like grown-ups' signatures'), Christopher signs and Richard witnesses.

'You're a fool,' he says to me. 'He's a terrible man, you know.'

'I know,' I say. 'But it's too late now.'

'Indeed it is!' says William smiling as he gathers up the papers and stows them safely away in a desk. 'Now, let's go out and the happy couple can walk back down the aisle together!'

We assemble again by the altar, and have to face the congregation once more as the choir finishes making its joyful noise unto the Lord. I take my glasses off. I don't know how people who can't go semi-blind at will get through these things. As the singing comes to an end, the organ kicks in with something new (no, still clue-less – 's nice though) and we head together down the aisle and out on to the church steps into the sun.

'Ee,' says my auntie Eileen. 'That were grand.'

There is a general chorus of agreement and then after a few quick photos under the arched entrance to the church, we all have to hotfoot it to the reception to get there before the guests.

Twenty minutes later, everyone is there and the party can begin. Champagne flows, canapés are plentiful and

I am almost mesmerised by the beauty of the cupcake tower. The weather is great and people are milling about outside and inside, finding old friends and maybe even, who knows, making a few new ones. The last anxieties roll from my shoulders as I can finally believe that everything has come together. Everyone comes up to kiss and congratulate us and it is all wonderful, wonderful, wonderful.

After everyone's had long enough to take the edge off their hunger and thirst, we all gather in the courtyard for the speeches. My dad gets up first.

'She's been no trouble, really, has she, love?' he says to my mother and the assembled guests. 'Always liked reading. Never went out. Did her exams. Went to university. Came home. Went to work. It's not been much of a life for her, but at least it never caused us any upset. I hope she brings Christopher as much happiness – or at least as little unhappiness – as she's brought us over the years.'

He raises his glass and everybody claps and cheers and drinks. Christopher gets up next and tells a few jokes based on the history of Dr Johnson's House and Georgian literary tropes and all his guests laugh. He tells a few jokes about the sausage canapés and all my guests laugh. He tells everyone what an idiot I am for marrying him and then the best man gets up and does likewise. Then I stand up and agree with both of them.

'But,' I add, 'they have both overlooked one tiny point, which is that I love him. Although – as I'm sure

...is friends and family will understand when I say – I don't know why.' They all nod vigorous understanding. 'It's not the endless fuming at the shortcomings of the modern world.' There is another murmur of agreement. 'It's not the rigid opinions or the inflexible will or the ability to regurgitate yards of political history at the drop of the hat. It's certainly not his clothes or benchmarks for personal hygiene.'

I pause for a couple of 'Hear, hears!'

'I think,' I conclude, 'it might be his hair. But whatever it is, I felt it from the day we met and I want it with me till the day I die – or at least until the day I kill him for all the other things, whichever comes first. Cheers!'

People cheer and clap again and the last vestiges of duty and responsibility flee my mind at last.

The steady circulation of drink, food and chatter is swiftly resumed and the rest of the evening passes happily. My family appear sated and my cousin tells me that it is the least poncy Southern wedding he has ever been to. My uncle Joseph nearly embarks on his repertoire of limericks, but my sister hits him on the head with a tyre iron and drags the body to safe concealment in the shrubbery. I give Allegra the first cake from the tower and fill a box for her to take some home. Siobhan thanks me warily. Clearly the power is still strong in me. Excellent. I grab a couple of cakes for myself. I haven't been able to eat anything all evening, but I know this will change as soon as I get to the hotel.

At around eight o'clock it is announced that the

newly-weds are ready to depart and everyone gathers in the courtyard to send us off. My mother kisses me and tells me Emily will be along to collect the bags from the hotel in the morning, so we have to be up and washed by ten. Christopher hugs her and then me.

'To think,' he says, standing between us with his arms around our waists and tears glistening in his eyes, 'I have a whole lifetime of this to look forward to!'

Richard hails a taxi and we get in. We wave until everyone is out of sight. A few minutes later, the driver pulls up at the hotel. Christopher tries to pay him but he won't take the fare.

'It's on me,' he grins.

'Oh, thank you!' I say when I have finally got all of my dress out of the car. 'Here, then, please have a cupcake. And a napkin.' I pass them through the window to him.

'Thanks very much!' he says. 'And congratulations!'

He drives off and we walk up the tiny road, too small for cars, to the hotel entrance. We pass a big restaurant window and everyone inside catches sight of us, smiles and waves and we wave happily back. It is lovely.

When we get to our room, there is a bottle of champagne on ice waiting for us from the hotel.

'Shall we?' says Christopher.

'I can't drink any more!' I cry, raising an exhausted hand to my brow and collapsing on to the couch.

'Nor me, really,' says Christopher, putting the bottle back in its bucket. 'Let's save it for a special occasion.'

we laugh, mostly through sheer relief that it has all gone so well, that we have – somehow – managed to have exactly the kind of day we wanted, without bank-rupting ourselves, or alienating this half of the family or that, or – hopefully – cutting into our friends' lives too much.

'We really did it,' I say.

'We did,' he says.

There is silence. We sit there, just the two of us. My husband and I.

'I love you,' I say.

'How much?'

'Nine hundred.'

'That's amazing. That's how much I love you too. This is clearly meant to be.'

That's good. I think so too.